ATLANTIC

The Well Beloved Engine

Brighton Atlantic: *LB&SCR No.424, class H2 superbly presented at London Victoria, its Doncastrian origins very evident but with Brighton refinements – bogie brakes, Hasler speed recorder (receiving attention) and 'raspberry' monogram on splashers; as BR No.32424* Beachy Head, *the last Atlantic to run in normal service in Britain, 1958.* Photo: Lens of Sutton.

A n engaging feature of the history of the Atlantic is that it is not short of surprises and paradoxes. For example, a major centre of British Atlantic expertise – in the design, building, maintenance, running and general mystery of Atlantics was Brighton, far from the industrial North as it then was, and in Sussex by the sea. In the same county some enthusiasts are to be found in the early twenty-first century assembling a fully-fledged mainline Atlantic. The record of the Sussex Atlantic school is a noble one. Suitable, therefore, for the dedication of this book – to my grand-daughter Livia, born in Brighton a hundred years after the dawn of the Atlantic era.

Cover Illustrations: *Centrepiece, LNER Class C7 No.2163, formerly NER Class Z. same number, Darlington, 1914 (courtesy Stephenson Locomotive Society). Clockwise from top right: PLM No.2290 of Class 2971, Cail 1907; Class 110, Robert Stephenson 1910 (courtesy Mr & Mrs D. Carswell); Ravensglass & Eskdale Railway Synolda (courtesy R&ER); Wheeling & Lake Erie Class E-1, No.2306 (formerly Wabash-Pittsburgh Terminal No.2006); Alco, 1905 (courtesy Howard W. Ameling); Milwaukee Road Class A No.1 Hiawatha, Alco 1935 (courtesy J.R.Quinn).*

ATLANTIC

The Well Beloved Engine

R.A.S. Hennessey

TEMPUS

First published 2002

PUBLISHED IN THE UNITED KINGDOM BY:

Tempus Publishing Ltd
The Mill, Brimscombe Port
Stroud, Gloucestershire GL5 2QG
www.tempus-publishing.com

PUBLISHED IN THE UNITED STATES OF AMERICA BY:

Arcadia Publishing Inc.
A division of Tempus Publishing Inc.
2 Cumberland Street
Charleston, SC 29401
(Tel: 1-888-313-2665)
www.arcadiapublishing.com

Tempus books are available in France, Germany and Belgium
from the following addresses:

Tempus Publishing Group	Tempus Publishing Group
21 Avenue de la République	Gustav-Adolf-Straße 3
37300 Joué-lès-Tours	99084 Erfurt
FRANCE	GERMANY

British Library Cataloguing in Publication Data.
A catalogue record for this book is available from the British Library.

ISBN 0 7524 2143 3

Typesetting and origination by Tempus Publishing.
PRINTED AND BOUND IN GREAT BRITAIN.

Contents

Introduction

This brief history of the 'Atlantic' form of steam locomotive is partly an attempt to place a straightforward chronicle in context, to present the Atlantic in its place and time as part of not only of the history of technology, but also as a component of social and cultural history. The Atlantics were popular with their operators, for a time at least, and more enduringly with the public in general and railway enthusiasts in particular. And they have remained so; why is this?

The Atlantic was erratically brilliant in performance. Its sudden rise to high fashion, its equally sudden fall from it, and the long twilight when it often worked in the backwaters of scenes of its former glory add poignancy to its story. It was more often than not an elegant machine; described by a wide range of commentators from engineers to its own firemen as the 'Queen' of locomotives. It was also a mettlesome machine in its day and continues to present historians with problems arising from its unpredictability and refusal to be defined and described within neat taxonomies or records; these individualistic qualities probably add to its appeal.

Any work which seeks to extend the boundaries of locomotive history necessarily depends immensely on the work of others. My heartfelt acknowledgements, therefore to the following people, and equally sincere apologies for any omissions: Howard W. Ameling, Robin Barnes, Kurt Bell, Wes Berris, Donald Binns, S.V. Blencowe, Seth Bramson, Richard P. Campbell, Terry Case, Paul Catchpole, Juan Celorio, Alan Clothier, Paul Copeland, Ian G.T. Duncan, Robert K. Durham, Bert Dyke, William A. Franckney, Tim Harris, Robert Herpai, Hal Hughes, Raymond Jorgensen, Lance King, Ed King, Stephen A. Lee, Steve Llanso, Ken McHugh, Terry McMahon, Rainer Mertens, Hiroshi Naito, Ole Nørregard Pedersen, Stig Nyberg, Ashley Peter, J.R. Quinn, Eric Rawlings, D. M. Rhind, J.T. van Riemsdijk, Philippa Rogers, Rabbi Walter Rothschild, K.J. Rowcroft, James Scott, Ralph D. Sharp, Jonathan Smith, Mike Smith, Bournemouth Railway Circle (BRC), Frank Stamford, Rolf Sten, Steve Suhs, Thomas T. Taber, John Tigges, Harold K. Vollrath, Christopher Walker, Graham Warburton, Steve Waterfield, Rev Harold H. Weber; the staffs of the Bodleian Library, Oxford; the Danmarks Jernbanemuseum, the DB Museum, the Library of the Institution of Mechanical Engineers; the Mitchell Library, Glasgow, the National Railway Museum, York, the Sveriges Järnvägsmuseum Gävle, the Railroad Museum of Pennsylvania, and the Ravenglass & Eskdale Railway Co. Where the source of an illustration is not acknowledged, they are from the author's collection, ultimate origin unknown. I also owe a great debt of gratitude, as ever, to my wife Jenny for her painstaking editing and commentary.

Chiaroscuro: Photographer J. Maynard Tomlinson catches the moment as LNER class C7 No.733 (NER class Z1, also No. 733, NBL, 1911) 3-cylinder Atlantic enters the murk of Bramhope tunnel.

Usages

Anyone with even a slight acquaintance with locomotive history will know that sources can differ amongst and even within themselves, a tendency not helped in the case of technical data by imperial-metric conversion problems. I have chosen what seemed to be on examination the most reliable sources and data, mindful of the fact that there is no universally acknowledged 'correct' source against which to measure one's choices. I have concentrated on a few crucial sets of comparative dimensions; grate areas in particular are an important part of the Atlantic saga, but generally the text confines itself to the minimum dimensions necessary to support its arguments. Few, if any, individual technical details are absolutely crucial to its general contentions. That said, one is mindful of an unvarying law of railway history – that someone else always knows better, or at least otherwise.

The titles of railways are given in their familiar forms; initials and acronyms are therefore employed frequently and can all be interpreted by reference to the Glossary and Index. On the grounds that pedantic precision can result in problems of readability, I have also and generally used the colloquial forms of railway titles, for example 'Prussian State Railways' rather than KPEV, still less (for English-speaking readers) Königlich Preußische Eisenbahn Verwaltung, but initials and titles are explained in text and index. The Glossary gives full titles, initials and cross references of these items.

Chapter 1
The Essential Atlantic

Definitions

What is, or was, an Atlantic? Frederick A. Talbot writing in *Railway Wonders of the World* (about 1910), just as the Atlantic era had passed its peak, waxed enthusiastic about the fast expresses then being operated in the USA:

> *The speed was so high and maintained so consistently day after day...that interest became centred in the engine. This was of a new class...it was of the 4-4-2 type, there being a leading four-wheeled bogie, four coupled driving wheels, and a trailing bogie* (sic) *under the fire-box.*

Nearly correct! But Talbot committed one error: the generous-sized firebox of the Atlantic – the essence of this type of the locomotive – rested on a single trailing axle, not a bogie. A better definition came from Frederick Westing, *Apex of the Atlantics* (1963):

> *What, essentially, was an Atlantic? It was a wheel arrangement composed of a four-wheel leading truck that gave good guiding qualities; four coupled drivers which could be (and usually were) of large diameter and were capable of handling enough adhesive weight for pulling trains over moderately graded profiles; and a trailing truck with two comparatively small wheels, a truck which could be either rigid or arranged for radial motion.*

There many are other, similar definitions. In the monograph *SJ ånglok litt A* (1971) devoted to the unusual Atlantics operated by the Swedish State Railways (SJ) Ulf Diehl sets the scene with his definition:

> *Atlantic denotes the axle-sequence 2'B1, i.e. two front running axles, two driving wheels, and one rear running axle.*

Diehl employs the 2'B1 notation favoured in Northern and Eastern Europe, rather than the 4-4-2 of the Whyte system used in the English-speaking world and Commonwealth, or the 221 notation used in France and Spain. All these notations refer unambiguously to an Atlantic steam locomotive.

True and Untrue Atlantics

Occasionally the phrase 'true Atlantic' has been employed, implying that there might be an untrue or false Atlantic of some kind. In *Atlantic Era: The British Atlantic Locomotive* (1961) Martin Evans wrote of the 4-4-2s of the Lancashire & Yorkshire Railway:

> *...a tender locomotive of the 4-4-2 wheel arrangement with inside cylinders cannot strictly be called an Atlantic.*

Evans evidently held this view fairly strongly for he continued:

> *in view of the importance of the Lancashire and Yorkshire engines of this wheel arrangement, the author has decided to include them in this short survey.*

Similarly, C. Hamilton Ellis, generally a broad-minded railway historian said in his *Some Classic Locomotives* (1949):

> *Let us consider carefully what an Atlantic is. It has outside cylinders... It is therefore incorrect so to describe the Lancashire and Yorkshire 4-4-2s...*

It may be significant that Diehl employed a definition of 'Atlantic' which makes no mention of cylinder location – the Swedish Atlantics he described were among the small minority of the type which were driven by *inside* cylinders.

The main defining feature of an Atlantic was a firebox placed behind (and occasionally partly over) the driving wheels, supported by a rear axle – it had nothing to do with cylinders being inside or outside the frames. The 'outside cylinder school' of definition made the fundamental error of confusing what is normal, orthodox, or typical (i.e. what the majority is or does) with what is essential. Certainly the majority of Atlantics had outside cylinders, but the inside-cylindered minority were no less Atlantics.

There was a good definition of the Atlantic in the 'great eleventh' edition of *Encyclopaedia Britannica* (1911) in an article ascribed to Professor W.E. Dalby of the City & Guilds of London Institute. Dalby, a respected and knowledgeable academic was upbeat in his view of Atlantics and played down their faults, also the Atlantic was no longer 'rapidly increasing in favour' in the USA. Nevertheless he got much of the essence of the Atlantic into his defintion:

> *[A] 'Four coupled' type with a leading bogie truck and a trailing axle, 4-4-2. It is used to a limited extent both in England [sic, the Scots used them also] and on the continent of Europe, and is rapidly increasing in favour in the United States, where it originated and is known as the 'Atlantic' type. It has many advantages for heavy, high-speed service, namely, large and well-proportioned boiler, practically unlimited grate area, fire-box of favourable proportions for firing, fairly low centre of gravity, short coupling-rods, and... a combination of the safe and smooth riding qualities of the 4-4-0 with great steaming quality and moderate axle loads.*

There were 4-4-2s which were, however, not Atlantics. The 4-4-2 wheel arrangement antedated the Atlantics, but in the form of the 4-4-2 tank engine which was decidedly a 4-4-0T with an extended bunker requiring the support of a trailing axle. The 4-4-2T firebox was slung between the driving wheels, as on a 4-4-0.

Some handsome tank engines of this kind first appeared on the London, Tilbury & Southend in 1880, shortly followed by William Adams' elegant 4-4-2Ts for the London & South Western (1882). Although neither class was in any sense an Atlantic they both partook of the elegant proportions of the 4-4-2 configuration, enhanced by the use of outside cylinders which sat well with this wheel arrangement.[1]

The well-known GWR 4-4-2T locomotives were referred to as 'County Tanks' – a reference to a class of contemporary GWR 4-4-0 tender locomotives bearing the names of counties; they were not referred to as 'Atlantic tanks'. The American *Railroad Age Gazette* described the new LB&SCR 4-4-2 tank engines as 'practically the equivalent in all important respects of the company's standard 4-4-0 express locomotives...' Even so, the term 'Atlantic tank' was used on occasion, for example in Belgium.[2]

Another non-Atlantic was the 2'B1 electric locomotive which had a 4-4-2 wheel configuration but which most emphatically had no firebox to be placed above or behind its driving wheels or anywhere else and which is has to be excluded from our investigation – interesting although it was in its time.[3]

There were three types of *hybrid* Atlantic. They have been included in this text partly because they have enough attributes to lie, if only just, within the boundary, and partly because their singularity puts the orthodox Atlantics into sharp relief. They are the 4-4-2+2-4-4 Beyer Garratt 'double Atlantics' used in Tasmania and Argentina; their fireboxes were placed behind their driving wheels, so some Atlantic logic was there; and the few 4-4-0 conversions to 4-4-2 (Western Australia; New York, Providence & Boston). The unique *Robbie Burns* (Borsig, 1907), preserved in Australia, is now a 4-4-2T, it but started life as a genuine Atlantic with a tender and it retains its Atlantic configuration.

Definitions are social constructions and people can take their pick. For working purposes an 'Atlantic' employed in this text is any 4-4-2 steam locomotive with a tender. Merely to have a 4-4-2 wheel arrangement is not enough, as the Greeks have it: *if the beard was all, the goat would be a priest.*

It is significant that the Atlantic has occasionally been used to define the locomotive. A standard and classic text for locomotive engineers, Forney's *Catechism of the Locomotive*[4] used the Atlantic as the basic locomotive form in its pull-out diagrams of the archetypal locomotive. The chosen example for this purpose was a Chicago & North Western 4-4-2. In 1999, the *Guide to North American Steam Locomotives*, compiled by George H. Drury still demonstrated the 'naming of the parts' of a basic steam locomotive by reference to a fine diagram of a Pennsylvania Class E6s Atlantic.

The Atlantic lends itself well to this task; it has the desiderata of an ideal locomotive: leading, driving and trailing wheels; a large firebox and generally, an excellent, comprehensible layout and good proportions. Because of the energetic use of the Atlantic by the railway publicity machines of its day the Atlantic also became the typical 'locomotive icon' for many people: advertisement designers, cartoonists, book illustrators. It was still being so employed in 2000, nearly a century after its golden age.

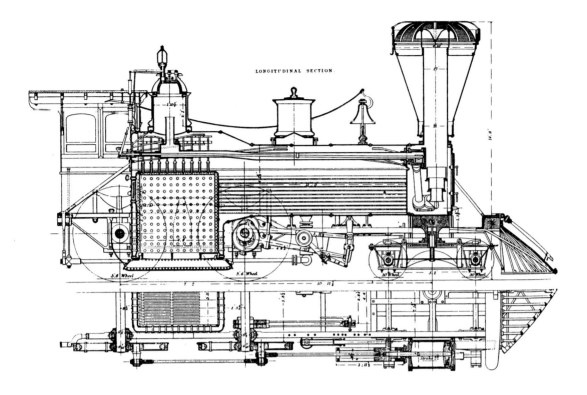

LONGITUDINAL SECTION.

The Firebox Question: above, *the firebox on a classic American 4-4-0, fitting between the driving wheels (Delaware, Lackawanna & Western No.57* Southport, *Danforth, Cooke 1857) with a grate area of 18.8 sq.ft, but* below *from Forney's* Catechism of the Locomotive, *1911 edition, a Chicago & North Western class D Atlantic of 1900, much larger (grate area nearly 50sq.ft), resting on a trailing axle: the Atlantic solution, and the way ahead for locomotive engineering.*

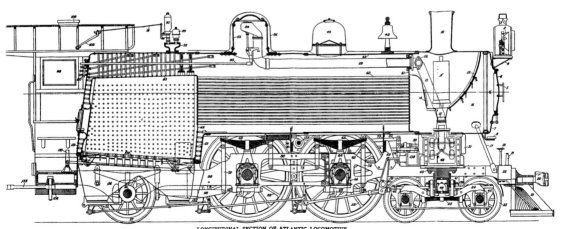

LONGITUDINAL SECTION OF ATLANTIC LOCOMOTIVE.

Atlantic Coast Line: *one of the original ACL 4-4-2s (class I-1) from which the type derived its name; No.153 assigned to the Wilmington & Weldon (Baldwin, 1894) its specification required an ability to move ten cars up a 0.6% grade at 40mph; a true Henszey Atlantic with short wheelbase, inside Stephenson valve gear and fairly modest grate area: 25.9sq.ft.*
Photo: Harold K. Vollrath.

Why 'Atlantic'?

Long before the Whyte[5] or other notations were employed to describe the wheel configurations of locomotives, vernacular terms were used in a few cases. What came to be a 2-6-0 was a 'Mogul', a 4-10-0, or 0-10-0, a 'Mastodon', and so on. After the adoption of Frederic A. Whyte's system in 1900 the familiar names stuck and new ones were added – they are easier on the memory and the tongue than mathematical abbreviations. The term 'Atlantic' is one of those that predated the Whyte notation, and it has endured.

Although the 4-4-2 type of locomotive existed prior to the adoption of its famous name, it was a batch of 4-4-2s delivered by the Baldwin Locomotive Works to the Atlantic Coast Line[6] in the USA (1894) that established the connection. The name was suggested by J.R. Kenly, General Manager of the ACL. As it happened the ACL did not adopt its eponymous locomotive to any great extent; it was an early convert to the 4-6-0 or 'ten-wheeler' type.

William P. Henszey, the designer of these early 4-4-2s took out a patent for the type but it was hard to enforce beyond the basic Baldwin form represented in the ACL machines. Rivals were quickly off the mark with variations, particularly the Brooks and Rogers locomotive manufacturing firms. Brooks distanced themselves from the Henszey Atlantic by calling their 4-4-2 variant the '*Chautauqua*' (see Chapter 2) but the name 'Atlantic' stuck, as also did a counter-legend regarding its origin.

Frederick Talbot, in his enthusiastically-phrased chapter on Atlantic-hauled expresses[7] in the early twentieth century wrote:

> *The performances of this class of engine [the 4-4-2] becoming appreciated, it has been adopted practically throughout the world in modified form, but is universally known as the 'Atlantic' from its first appearance in connection with the Atlantic City flyer.*

This error, an understandable one given the renown of the rival 4-4-2-hauled Atlantic City expresses of the Philadelphia & Reading and the Pennsylvania, entered railway mythology like an information virus which surfaces every so often. Martin Evans stated in his *Atlantic Era:*

> *...the 4-4-2 type won fame on the high-speed services of the Philadelphia & Reading Railroad, between Camden and Atlantic City, from which the nickname 'Atlantic' originated.*

Even the erudite John Jahn, author of a classic study of locomotive development[8] ascribed the term 'Atlantic' to the Atlantic City source.

Chautauqua in the Snow: *an elegant 4-4-2 by Brooks which it called a 'Chautauqua', not 'Atlantic', at Dunkirk, NY. Brand new in 1901, Chicago, Rock Island & Pacific No.1301 of class A-24 with inboard piston valves, slotted equalising beam beneath round-topped firebox, and three-toned whistle.* Photo: Alco Historic Photos.

The exciting express races to and from Atlantic City will also have been the first occasion that many people heard of the Atlantic type of locomotive. Although the Atlantic City expresses may have been better known than the enterprise of the ACL, it remains a matter of record that as a practical mainline proposition, the earliest 4-4-2s included a batch of pioneers on the Atlantic Coast Line from which they took their name; it was in Dixieland that they first took their stand.

The term 'Atlantic' perpetuates the claim that the Atlantic was essentially an American invention. American engineers did produce the original 4-4-2s, but the very first of these Ur-Atlantics were odd confections which failed to inspire much of a following. The first Atlantics to establish the 4-4-2 on the world stage certainly included the ACL engines but, contemporaneously 4-4-2s appeared in Austria, on the KFNB (*Kaiser Ferdinands Nordbahn*).

Over a decade before this, a putative 4-4-2 had been sketched out by Karl Gölsdorf, later to become Austria's leading designer of locomotives and one of the dozen or so world-class names in locomotive engineering. The KFNB Atlantics were designed by W. Rayl, although they bore a close resemblance to Gölsdorf's earlier essay. Like the ACL variety, they were only just Atlantics – the use of the trailing axle for firebox-support was fairly minimal, but it was nevertheless present.

The honours for designing the first practical Atlantics can, therefore, be fairly divided between Austria and the USA; the latter not only produced the first 4-4-2, but it also produced more Atlantics than any other country, nearly two-thirds of the total. It also developed the design to a greater degree than any other school.

Although the Atlantic has received much attention for its style and class, and for its erratic brilliance in performance, it was nevertheless an important rung in the ladder of technological evolution, in its own right. It was one of a series of more-or-less coeval engines that introduced the concept of the big firebox, supported by a trailing axle, able to 'crowd on steam' and sustain high horsepower: the Pacific 4-6-2 and the Mikado 2-8-2 were of the same kind. It broke speed records and gave the travelling public its first taste of high-speed travel in quantity, almost of a routine kind. Some of its family were in themselves important pioneers: the Great Western Atlantics, short lived but crucial components in the planning and evaluation exercises by which G.J. Churchward changed the face of British locomotive engineering, quickly on the GWR, more slowly elsewhere. The authors of *Steam in Africa* noted of the Cape Government 4-4-2s (of 1897) 'the engines which had a most profound effect on locomotive development in South Africa.'[9]

Taxonomies and Categories

The Atlantic had its own taxonomy of sub-species; choice from which depends upon context:

First, *historical*: the Atlantic had its own evolutionary history:

  a. The *early* Atlantics (the '*Palaeo-Atlantics*') from *c.*1882-1900;

b. The middle or *classic* Atlantic period, *c.*1901-1912, the 'Atlantic era' in which most Atlantics were built and during which the type had the status of being a fashionable machine;

c. Finally, the *later* Atlantics, *c.*1912-1970s which started with the building of some transitional locomotives embodying the lessons of earlier phases and prepared the way for the last phase, a brief renaissance in the 1930s. This was the time when some surviving Atlantics were redesigned or rebuilt; most of the species went to the scrapyards or, in a few cases, to museums. The last conventional Atlantics in steam ran in Mozambique, 1978.

Secondly, *geographical*: Atlantics, like most other locomotive types, were different in appearance and detail in different countries, even in different regions or on different railways of the same country. This 'geography of locomotion' is a well-known, although little-explored, phenomenon resulting from differences in physical geography, economics (for example the relative costs of capital and labour), and culture – educational standards; aesthetic norms. E.S.Cox, a widely-travelled locomotive engineer who attained high rank in the UK, summarised this phenomenon in his *World Steam in the Twentieth Century* (1969). He detected five major schools of design: American; British; French; German, and Middle European (more accurately, East European). There were also some other schools: Belgium; Netherlands; Italy; Russia; Scandinavia; and Spain. Cox's taxonomy is borne out by Atlantic design, although neither Italy nor Spain ran Atlantics, and the small handful in Russia were not typically Russian.

Thirdly, *technological*: not a discrete category since it manifests itself through the other two. For example, Reuter and Bock[10] listed half-a-dozen distinct types of Atlantic in the USA alone, a range which arose partly from the evolution of the 4-4-2 and partly from having a multiplicity of designers and builders with their own favoured technical features. But, if an enquirer after Atlantics were to be *primarily* interested in engineering design he or she might note: large and small Atlantics; some with bar frames, others with plate frames; and different forms of firebox supported by a variety of trailing trucks. Some Atlantics used saturated steam, others had superheaters; some were compounds, most were two-cylinder simples; a few had cylinders working the forward driving axle, the majority drove on the rear coupled axle and there were some inside cylinder Atlantics, as well as the outside cylinder 'great majority'. Atlantics ran on many gauges from 2ft 0in to 5ft 6in, most were designed for the standard gauge, and not a few for miniature railways, 15in gauge or less.

Because the Atlantic appeared when it did, not only was it a major innovation in its own right, it also embodied important developments when they became available including three-cylinder propulsion, feed-water heaters, roller bearings, boosters, and turbo-dynamo lighting generators. Each of these variations and accessories could supply the basis of a further categorisation. But any half-decent pedant can multiply categories indefinitely; the skill of the taxonomist is to know when to apply Occam's razor: *entities are not to be multiplied beyond necessity* ie beyond the minimum strictly necessary for the task in hand.

The Book of Records

The concept of an 'average Atlantic' would be misleading since the type evolved over time and any 'average' would be distorted by some unusual extremes. There were two definite attempts to produce a 'standard Atlantic' for a set of railway systems but most Atlantics were manufactured in batches or classes, each distinguished from its fellows, sometimes in minor ways only.

How many Atlantics were there in any case? Where were most to be found? Reuter and Bock estimated that a total of 3,544 Atlantics were built and that 60% of them existed in the USA and Canada. Since the Canadian total was six, it is a safe assertion that nearly two-thirds of Atlantics were to be found in the USA. World-wide, at one time or another there were some 250 classes of Atlantic and they ran on 117 railway systems. Reuter's totals ran thus:

World deployment of Atlantics

Country	Atlantics	proportion of total
USA and Canada	2,127	60%
Austria-Hungary	127	3.6%
Germany	424	12%
UK	310	8.7%
France	155	4.4%
Rest of Europe	102	2.9%
Rest of World	299	8.4%
Totals	3,544	100%

Putting these data in a wider context, the locomotive historian Philip Atkins[11] stated that the all-time grand total of steam locomotives manufactured was *c.*640,000; Atlantics were, therefore, about 0.55% of all steam locomotives ever made. Their influence on locomotive evolution, not to say the public imagination was, however, out of all proportion to this modest share. The 'Mikado' 2-8-2 was an exact contemporary of the Atlantic. Its design arose from the same kind of logic which produced the 4-4-2, although after a more sluggish start the Mikado established itself as possibly the most numerous type of locomotive on Earth, steaming on in great numbers long after the Atlantics had become history.

Atkins also states that the most intensive period of steam locomotive construction peaked around 1907; in respect of the Atlantic it was 1906. The financial panic of 1907 may have brought forward the tailing-off of Atlantic orders, although the main reasons were technical. The years in which the greatest stock of locomotives was held by the railways of the world coincide with the peak stocking of Atlantics: USA, 1924; UK, 1924; Germany, 1918; France, 1923. There were particular reasons for the peaking and demise of the Atlantic stock, some of which were peculiar to it as a locomotive form.

At the base of the Atlantic firebox lay the grate which supported its vital fire. 'It is evident that power output depends directly on the grate' wrote the twentieth century's leading locomotive theoretician, André Chapelon in his classic *La Locomotive à Vapeur*. The grate of the Stephensons' *Rocket* (1829) was nearly 6sq.ft ($0.56m^2$) By 1862 a Stockton & Darlington 4-4-0 had a grate of 12.8sq.ft ($1.2m^2$); by 1873 this had grown to 16 sq.ft ($1.5m^2$) on a Glasgow & South Western 4-4-0, and to 24.6 sq.ft ($2.3m^2$) on a Nord 4-4-0 of 1896. Then came the

Locomotive anatomy: *a diagram of 1901 by when the Atlantic was becoming an icon, the 'ideal locomotive'; closely based on the C&NW Schenectady model of wide-firebox 4-4-2.*

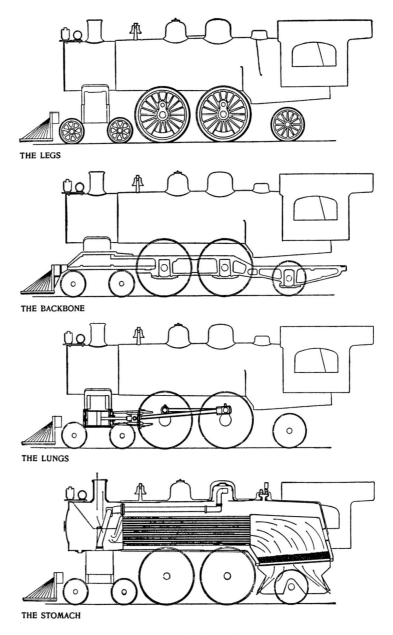

THE LEGS

THE BACKBONE

THE LUNGS

THE STOMACH

Anatomy of the locomotive 1901

Atlantics: the KFNB 4-4-2s of 1894 had grates of 31sq.ft ($2.9m^2$), as did the GNR large Atlantics in the UK. In the USA the full possibilities of the Atlantic were exploited more easily by a more generous loading gauge – the Cleveland, Cincinnati, Chicago & St Louis ('Big Four') Atlantics of 1904 had 50sq.ft ($4.2m^2$) grates, exceedingly large by European standards.

17

The great success of the Atlantics as steam-generators caused their large fireboxes and grates to be emulated widely on other locomotive forms. By the 'end of steam' in Europe, 50sq.ft grates (4.65m^2) grates were not uncommon. The largest attained were in the USA where grates designed to serve fires from low-quality coal reached 150sq.ft, or 14m^2. E.S. Cox remarked, 'this produced an inner firebox equal in volume to a good-sized living-room!'

After one or two false starts, the earliest Atlantics appeared in the mid-1890s. From the 1906 production peak of 423 engines, output declined to 10 in 1912. In the USA production fell to two in 1913, although it grew suddenly, albeit for one year only, to 80 in 1914 with the production of the magnificent Pennsylvania E6s Atlantics; the next year American output dropped to zero.

In the late 1930s, however, the Chicago, Milwaukee, St Paul & Pacific RR (the 'Milwaukee Road') turned out four huge Atlantics which were to skew Atlantic statistical analysis ever after. They were the largest Atlantics ever built, weighing 135.5 tons in working order. They were also the fastest of Atlantics, regularly exceeding 100mph in service and therefore amongst the fastest steam locomotives of all time. The smallest Atlantic was that constructed by Borsig (1907) for the Stannary Hills (later Irvinebank) Tramway in Australia, it weighed 14 tons.

To British railway observers the most familiar Atlantic is probably the GNR 'large Atlantic' weighing 69.5 tons, Some other world classics were: the Nord de Glehn Atlantics, weighing 69 tons; the Prussian S9, 74.5 tons, and the Gölsdorf 4-4-2s in Austria, 68.3 tons. The ACL 4-4-2s of 1894 weighed 58.8 tons. Many American Atlantics exceeded 100 tons in weight. The tallest European Atlantics were Gölsdorf's class 108 in Austria (boiler pitch 9ft 7in, 2,930mm); for many years the Shanghai-Nanking 4-4-2s held the world record (boiler pitch 9ft 9in, 2,972mm), but the Milwaukee Road *Hiawathas* of 1935 were to hold the all-time laurels, and not only for their lofty profiles. A restricted loading gauge kept Britain out of these stakes.

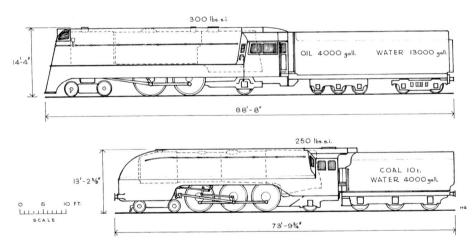

Getting in proportion: *a Milwaukee Road* Hiawatha *Atlantic of 1935 with an LMS streamlined* Coronation *class Pacific (1937) drawn to the same scale; John F. Clay noted drily that a* Hiawatha *was 'fairly small by American standards.' The larger American loading gauge meant that most American Atlantics outsized their European and particularly British contemporaries.* Diagram: courtesy, Stephenson Locomotive Society.

The Atlantic as Art: the 'Expression of an Age'

Physical data alone do not describe Atlantics 'in the round' and the strange, magical appeal that they exerted over so many people. Steam locomotives in general have their admirers, but the Atlantic was one of the few whose fans, pilgrims, acolytes, enthusiasts and whatever seemed to be disproportionately numerous.

Cecil J. Allen, whose dry and scrupulous prose recorded a good half-century of locomotive performance suddenly waxed forth: 'There is one legacy which the Atlantic left us... It is of having bequeathed some of the most lovely locomotive lines ever seen in Great Britain...'[12]. Reuter and Bock's standard work on the Atlantic was entitled *Eleganz auf Schienen*: 'Elegance on Rails'.

An important but elusive quality of the Atlantic was its generally elegant set of proportions. Given its origins and purposes, can a graceful steam locomotive be only a product of good design, or could it be perceived and accepted as high art? The futurists asserted that it could; why should a finely-wrought machine be less qualified as art any less than fine architecture or stained-glass windows? Arguments to the contrary sometimes emanate from minds which, like the Atlantic, run on rails.

The Atlantic has also been described as an 'expression of its age', unusually typical of the era that produced it. 'An Engine for the High Society' speeding 'crack trains' to the Riviera or 'the large Spas' was how Gustav Reder described the Atlantic in his monu-mental *The World of Steam Locomotives* (1975) in a chapter entitled 'The Belle Epoque'.

There was more to the Atlantic and its wide range of passenger clienteles than that, but Reder's proposition is a fair example of the 'contiguity of concepts' by which we tend to link, say, a locomotive, a car, a musical style, or a form of poetry with a particular epoch.

The roaring years of the 4-4-2s coincided with 'the last hurrah' of the railway builders; the era of magnificent terminal stations, and of the final mainlines, at least in Europe and America. Two of these grand but doomed gestures: the Great Central extension to London, the Wabash-Pittsburgh Terminal in the USA were, perhaps symbolically, Atlantic operators.

The classic Atlantic was an effective symbol of the Edwardian age: the times of Wilhelm II, Theodore Roosevelt, ragtime and tango, art nouveau, H.G. Wells, the *Ballets Russe*, and early Bolshevism − to take an eclectic rag-bag. What could be more typical of the Third Republic than a chocolate-brown de Glehn 4-4-2 compound spinning across Northern France? Or of Teddy Roosevelt's USA than a Pennsylvania E3 being thrashed good and hard at the head of a 'limited', its ecologically-innocent exhaust seen and heard for miles around?

There are other ever-elusive and practically unquantifiable Atlantic attributes and compara-tors: which was the greatest revenue-earner of the Atlantics ? Which was the least efficient − and by what criteria? The hardest-used? We have some clues regarding this last statistic, for example one of the pioneer ACL Atlantics ran up 1.4 million miles by 1923, but full, reliable sets of data for all Atlantics on this, as on many other aspects of performance, were not kept systematically for each and every locomotive, or have been lost or destroyed.

Some of the most important qualities and achievements of the Atlantic may well remain unknown, or the subjects of fruitless debate: who can pronounce with certainty on such crucial matters as the most satisying 4-4-2 to drive or the most awkward to repair and maintain? The most beautiful, most typical, even 'the best' of the Atlantics ? There lies some of the source of the Atlantic magic: ultimately, it remains an enigma.

Vestiges of dreams: Wheeling & Lake Erie No.2306, class E-1 (Alco, Brooks, 1905) originally one of six built for the Wabash-Pittsburgh Terminal, an audacious but ill-fated bid for Pittsburgh, rifled through mountains, sweeping over vertiginous viaducts and fine bridges, a fit highway for elegant Atlantics. Seen here at Brewster, Ohio, 1926 in connection with its role as pioneer roller-bearing loco-motive. Photo: Collection of Howard W. Ameling.

On a freight train at York, 1939 LNER No.5267, class C4 (Beyer, Peacock, 1904) originally built for the long vanished GCR London extension. Vivid comparison in Atlantic aesthetics, plate-framed UK version; bar-framed high stepper from USA. Photo: Stephenson Locomotive Society.

Notes to Chapter 1

1. See David R. Webb, 'British 4-4-2 Tank Locomotives' *Railway Magazine*, Vol 97, 599, March 1951, and Kenneth H. Leech, *Tilbury Tanks*, 'Loco Profile 27', 1972.

2. For example in *De Belgische treinen in beeld/Les trains belges en images* (1980) a picture of a 4-4-2T at Quiévrain is captioned 'Type 16 Atlantic T.'

3. The 2'B1 electric locomotive was an early development in electric traction; five were built for the pioneer Bitterfeld-Dessau line in Prussia; there were three classes on the KPEV: ES1 (1911-1927); ES2 (1911-1927); and ES3 (1911-1923), all operating on 16 2/3 Hz, 15 kV. See D. Bäzold and G. Fiebig, *Archiv elektrischer Lokomotiven, Die deutscher Einphasenwechelstrom-Lokomotiven* (1966). The PLM in France also ran some 4-4-2+2-4-4 articulated electric locomotives; but for the same reason, not Atlantics. See F.J.G. Haut: *History of the Electric Locomotive.*

4. Third Edition revised and enlarged by Geo L. Fowler, 1911.

5. Frederic A. Whyte (1865-1941), inventor of the wheel notation system; its European rivals base their notation on axles rather than wheels. Whyte had wide experience in locomotive design on various North American railways: LS&MS; B&O; Mexican Central, and NYC.

6. The name has given rise to confusion; the Atlantic Coast Line Company was a holding company. It did not become the ACL *Railroad* until April, 1900, six years after the Atlantics were delivered. Hence, Jove nods occasionally: O.S. Nock, *Railways at the Turn of the Century* (1969) – 'Atlantic Coast Lines, USA'; Similarly, Cecil J. Allen, *British Atlantic Locomotives* (1968), 'Atlantic Coast Railroad of the United States' – although both authors were generally well-informed and authoritative on locomotive matters, as was Gustav Reder (*The World of Steam Locomotives*, 1977) – 'the Atlantic Coastline.'

7. Frederick A. Talbot, *op cit*; the two expresses were the *Southern Belle* of the LB&SCR in the UK, and the *Atlantic City Flyer* (Philadelphia & Reading RR) in the USA, both Atlantic hauled. Poor Talbot! A great railway-populariser in his day, in the more politically-correct world of a century later he was charged with 'unreflective triumphalism...typical of the worst aspects of Western attitudes during the age of imperialism' (R Lee, 'Potential World Heritage Sites in Asia and the Pacific', on the web). For Atlantic City speedsters, see Richard M. Gladulich, *By Rail to the Broadwalk*, 1986.

8. J. Jahn: *Die Dampflokomotive in Entwicklungsgeschichtlicher Darstellung ihres Gesamtaufbaues* (1924) – the passage runs: 'Sie benutze sie für S-Zug New York (*sic*) – Atlantic City. Seitdem nennt man die bauart, Atlantic.'

9. A.E. Durrant, C.P. Lewis and A.A. Jorgensen, *Steam in Africa*, 1981.

10. W. Reuter and Claus Bock: *Eleganz auf Schienen, Die Enzyklopädie der Atlantic* (1982).

11. Philip Atkins, *Dropping the Fire, The Decline and Fall of the Steam Locomotive* (1999).

12. Cecil J. Allen, *British Atlantic Locomotives*, 1968.

Chapter 2
On the Eve

Preconditions of the Atlantic

The Atlantic had long antecedents, it was the 'child of invention and experiment'[1] developed logically from existing technology. It was also a good example of the principle of economic pressure, in particular of competition between railways, directing technological change. Railway managements, particularly in the USA vied to 'get there the fastest with the mostest' an imperative which pressed relentlessly on locomotive engineers. An eminent locomotive engineer put it thus: *Every locomotive engineer hopes that the product of his mental turmoil and anxiety will provide... a better locomotive than those presently in service... machines able to maintain higher average speeds with heavier loads than previously...*[2]

The main trunk of locomotive development accordingly spawned mutations, some of which caught on and determined the next line of advance; so locomotive morphology evolved from early 2-2-0s to the 2-2-2, 0-6-0, 2-4-2, 4-4-0, and so on. Sooner or later a 4-4-2 was likely to emerge.[3]

The Palaeo–Atlantics

The first unambiguous proposal for a genuine Atlantic, a 4-4-2 with a large firebox, some of which was abaft the driving wheels and resting on a trailing axle, was a sketch made by Karl Gölsdorf, March 1881. It was a modification for a 'Series 19' 4-4-0 of the Southern Railway of Austria, the *Südbahn*, where Karl was training under his father, Louis Gölsdorf, the locomotive chief (*Maschinendirektor*). In 1884 Gölsdorf, working for the Austrian State Railways[4] outlined a putative 4-4-2, but the proposal, essentially for an extended 4-4-0, did not bear fruit.

A genuine mutation appeared in the USA in 1887. It was designed by George S. Strong of Philadelphia, and constructed by the Hinkley Locomotive Co., Boston. The engine was a testbed for some of Strong's innovations. These included unorthodox valve-gears and, crucial to the Atlantic story, an unusual firebox, so large that Strong had to move onwards and upwards from the 4-4-0 notation which he had hitherto employed to the next stages: 4-6-2, in 1886, and the 4-4-2 next year. The Atlantic had arrived; it was called *A.G. Darwin*.

It was not the first 4-4-2, however. Also in 1887 a 4-4-0 of the New York, Providence & Boston Railroad which was found to have too great an axle load for the line's bridges had a trailing axle added to spread the load, making it a 4-4-2. The NY&P&B referred to

True Atlantic?: *the world's first 4-4-2 built by Rhode Island in 1887 for the New York, Providence & Boston, standing at Providence, RI, soon after completion. The 'bolt-on' trailing axle was clearly to ease the load on the other axles of what was essentially a 4-4-0.* Photo: Harold K. Vollrath.

it as an 'eight wheeler with trailer', however. The Cleveland, Cincinatti, Chicago & St Louis, the 'Big Four' converted two more 4-4-0s in this way in 1893–1894; 'hybrid Atlantics'.[5]

By 1890 the 4-4-2 was 'in the air'. The *A.G. Darwin* was followed shortly by a second and very similar Strong locomotive built by the Schenectady Locomotive Works for the Atchison, Topeka & Santa Fe Railway; it was completed in 1889, but converted to a conventional 4-4-0 in 1892.

The Third Atlantic: *second of George Strong's 4-4-2 engines with his patent twin-tube ('pair of pants') firebox and Camelback layout, virtually identical to the A.G. Darwin of 1887. Built by Schenectady in 1889 for the Santa Fe (No. 738) and soon afterwards converted to 4-4-0.*
Photo: Harold K. Vollrath.

Singles and *Columbias*

Another strand of American locomotive development encouraged the emergence of the 4-4-2. Hitherto, the standard locomotive of the USA was the all-purpose 'American' 4-4-0 which had served well for over fifty years. It was a reliable workhorse but the growing demand for higher speeds and haulage power encouraged designers to cast around for improvements. William P. Henszey of the Baldwin Locomotive Works thought that the 4-2-2 'single', a largely British development, might meet the requirements of his client, the Philadelphia & Reading Railroad which was anxious to beat the competition with some fast trains.

The Superintendent of Motive Power on the 'Reading' was J.E. Wootten[6], inventor of a broad, shallow firebox designed to burn anthracite culm (largely waste, composed of small pieces and dust). The 4-2-2 which emerged from Baldwin (1880) had this firebox, supported by a trailing axle. Baldwins guaranteed an average speed of 60mph and this was exceeded on the trial trip from Philadelphia to Jersey City (14 May 1880). However, the locomotive was not accepted because of the Reading's financial problems.[7] The idea of a racer 4-2-2 endured, however, and two more were built in 1895; Vauclain compounds with Wootten fireboxes (76sq.ft grate area) and 7ft driving wheels. They were little replicated, mainly because of their lack of adhesion and consequent inability to manage anything but short trains, also they were none too stable at high speeds. A few were tried out by other anthracite railroads like the Erie and the Lehigh Valley.

The concept of a very fast locomotive with a big firebox and large diameter driving wheels had arrived and was reinforced by the 2-4-2 locomotive, already well-known in Europe and now to enjoy a brief vogue in the USA. Baldwin built a small number of these 'Columbia' engines, 1893-1900. Alfred W. Bruce[8] thought the coal-burning 2-4-2, constructed for the Chicago, Burlington & Quincy Railroad (1895) 'immediately made obsolete all previous designs as had Stephenson's *Rocket* in 1829.' The Columbia had leading and trailing wheels and a deep and wide firebox behind the driving wheels, supported by the rear axle. The Baldwin Atlantic which derived directly from the 2-4-2 amplified its arrangements and proved to be a far more effective 'locomotive of the new type.' About 120 Columbias were constructed; like the 4-2-2 they lacked stability, but their role as an evolutionary link was crucial.

Plans for constructing the first 4-4-2 locomotives of orthodox design were drawn up in 1893 in Austria and the USA. In Austria, Rayl's Atlantic for the KFNB was essentially a 4-4-0 raised to a higher power by having a larger firebox than would be possible without a trailing axle. The Austrian case for priority in Atlantic design has merit because of Karl Gölsdorf's sketch of a putative 4-4-2 twelve years earlier. The precise moments when W. Rayl in Austria and William P. Henszey in the USA first drew up serious plans for Atlantics remain unclear. There was once folklore to the effect that an American Atlantic had been shown at the Chicago Exposition, 1893 – but this was in fact a 2-4-2.

In the USA the Atlantic Coast Line relied on 4-4-0s for passenger work, but required something speedier. The set of 4-4-2s requested by J.R. Kenly of the ACL were produced by lengthening the existing 2-4-2 Columbia design and the American Atlantic was the result. Thus both forms of 4-4-2, the stretched 4-4-0, and the stretched 2-4-2 emerged more or less simultaneously in 1894.

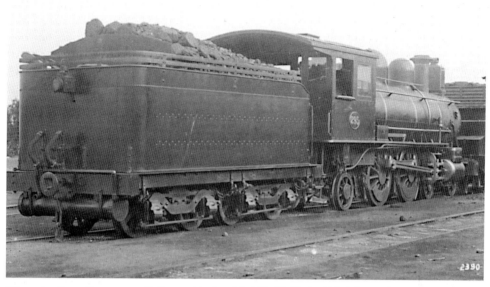

Hatrack: *Cape Government Railways 4th class No.295 (Baldwin 1896) from a design for the Nippon Tetsudo in Japan; a 3ft 6ins gauge soft-coal burner with a grate area of nearly 30sq.ft, greater than many a standard-gauge 4-4-2. Once a familiar sight around Kimberley; the nickname came from the disposition of bowler hat-like steam and sand domes. The American bar-frames impressed South African engineers and were widely adopted thereafter.*

They were quickly emulated: Baldwins produced similar narrow-firebox 4-4-2s for three more railroads in 1895.[9] In 1897 they exported a class of narrow-gauge (3ft 6in) Atlantics for the Nippon Tetsudo in Japan. The NT was not looking for a fast locomotive so much as one that could burn large quantities of inferior local coal. The new 4-4-2 idea was offered as a possible solution to the problem. At this time the British locomotive manufacturing industry was going through one of its periodic crises with full order books and unacceptably long delivery dates. An existing customer, the Cape Government Railways (also of 3ft 6in gauge and coping with coal of low calorific value) turned to Baldwins who supplied six NT-type Atlantics in sixty days flat. The Atlantic was now at work in Asia and Africa and the narrow-gauge 4-4-2 had been born.

Why did the Atlantic design catch on so quickly in different parts of the world? The exporting power of American industry was clearly one factor. But there were others; first, that since the Atlantic grew logically out of existing practice it emerged virtually simultaneously in Austria and the USA, shortly afterwards in France, the UK and Germany: the *structural hypothesis.* Secondly, an international 'guild' of engineers was in being by 1900, held together by journals, professional societies, conferences and informal meetings which shared ideas: the *diffusionist hypothesis.* One way or the other, the Atlantic was an idea whose time had come by 1895.

It received a boost when Baldwins designed a series of 4-4-2s with Wootten fireboxes for the anthracite-burning railroads of the Eastern USA; fast locomotives with high driving wheels which required supporting, trailing axles. Nine of these 'hard coal' 4-4-2s appeared in 1896; many more followed. Two of them were delivered to the Philadelphia & Reading for its subsidiary the Atlantic City Railroad which set them to work on its Camden-Atlantic City expresses with the results already described. The Atlantic's fame started to spread quickly, particularly after the Pennsylvania, stung by the P&R's successes, built three anthracite-burning Atlantics (class E1) to power its own Atlantic City expresses in the Summer season of 1899.

The Pennsylvania and ACR tracks to Atlantic City were often in sight of each other, and exciting train races could develop. The ability of 4-4-2s to generate high horsepower and great speed caught public imagination. Although some exaggerated and technically improbable records were claimed, the core of hard facts was unarguable: in July and August 1898 the famed ACR Atlantic No.1027 was never late, and on seventeen occasions ran at a start to stop speed of 70mph or more. This was astonishing and, for ordinary commercial service, probably unmatched at the time. A cautious British observer, Norman B. Macdonald recorded an average of 83mph for 35 miles. Something dramatic was going on and the first symptoms of Atlantic mania were becoming apparent.

Atlantics and Chautauquas

There was an unintended outcome of Henszey's attempt to patent the Atlantic. The patenting of a wheel arrangement, particularly when 4-4-2 tanks already existed in the UK, was fraught with difficulty. Henszey's patent covered the ACL type of Atlantic, with its inside-bearing, short wheelbase, slide-valve characteristics. Because Baldwin also held patents on the Vauclain type of compound (high and low-pressure cylinders mounted outside and above each other; pistons coupled to a common connecting-rod) some of the early Baldwin Atlantics were compounds of this type. Original, laterally-thinking minds were soon at work to circumvent these conditions.

The Schenectady Locomotive Works, a major Baldwin rival, was quick off the mark. It sent a new Atlantic to Saratoga Springs, NY, in the Summer of 1899 to impress the Master Mechanics Association which was holding its annual conference there. This locomotive had a wide firebox and piston valves, neither feature being a part of the Baldwin Atlantic ensemble. The show locomotive was destined for the Chicago & North Western, which eventually owned ninety similar models of this class D. Shortly afterwards Schenectady produced an Atlantic for the New York Central. It was similar to the C&NW model, but equipped with a 'traction increaser' which added to the weight bearing on the driving axles when the locomotive was getting under way. Starting a train was the most vulnerable moment for a 4-4-2 which, it was soon discovered, had a tendency to suffer wheel slip and lose traction. The traction increaser was brought into play by air cylinders which shifted the fulcrum points of equalising beams joining the rear driving and trailing axles. This could increase the weight available for adhesion from 42.41 tons to 46.7 tons, an ingenious idea but a potentially hazardous one which also ran against the grain of American operating philosophy: keep it simple.

Evolution of the classic
4-4-2: *from top, W Rayl's
Ur-Atlantic for the KFNB,
an extended 4-4-0 with
little advantage taken of a
trailing axle (Wiener
Neustadt, Sigl, 1894);
wide-firebox Palatinate
model (Krauss 1898) but
with boiler pitched conserva-
tively low; wide firebox
GNR Ivatt large Atlantic,
higher boiler (GNR
Doncaster 1902);
CCC&StL large Atlantic
as later displayed at the St
Louis World's Fair (Brooks,
1903) with high pitched
boiler, cavernous firebox and
conical boiler.
Diagrams from J. Jahn,
Die Dampflokomotive...*

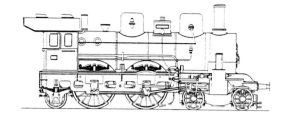

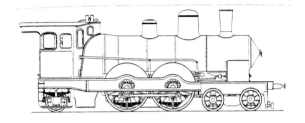

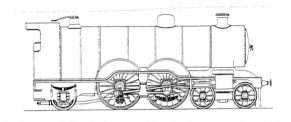

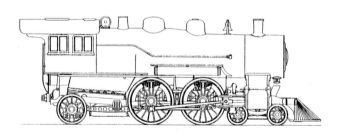

The Brooks Locomotive Works of Dunkirk, NY also developed its own Atlantic, even to
the point of giving it a new name, the *Chautauqua* locomotive. The name did not catch on
but it was occasionally used in professional literature. The name was well chosen: not only
was Dunkirk in Chautauqua County, but the shores of scenic Lake Chautauqua were the
location of a major centre of adult education, summer schools, correspondence courses and
related activities, well-known and respected throughout the USA. The Brooks 4-4-2s were
impressive-looking locomotives with piston valves, although not at first with the superheaters that encouraged the trend towards these devices. Their radial rear trucks were
controlled by centring springs which imparted a more steady and comfortable ride than was

generally the case with Atlantics. The early Baldwin models with trailing wheels in rigid pedestals were hard-riding, as were many early Atlantics. Brooks was also an enthusiastic user of cast steel components in its Atlantics which, with their spare elegance and general *hauteur*, demonstrated the wide range of aesthetic possibilities open to Atlantic designers.

Europe

In addition to Rayl's work on the KFNB, there were other early European designs for Atlantics. The French Atlantic, like its American cousin was derived from the 2-4-2 and the 4-4-0; a good case can be made for both sources. The Paris-Orleans Railway carried out some economic experiments by converting an existing 2-4-2 into a 4-4-2 in order to gain stability at speed, the first and least typical of the French Atlantics (1898). The production of two compound 4-4-2s for the Nord Railway in 1899 was a more important harbinger of things to come. These machines, essentially an extension and amplification of some successful Nord 4-4-0 compounds, were soon replicated by an entire class, the immortal 'de Glehn Atlantics'[10] whose sparkling performances on Paris-Calais expresses quickly became a talking-point amongst engineers and laity alike.

The P-O and Nord 4-4-2s had relatively narrow fireboxes; the next step in Atlantic evolution was taken in Germany, where in 1898 W. Staby, locomotive engineer of the Palatinate Railways, designed an inside-cylinder 4-4-2 with a wide firebox, not so wide as

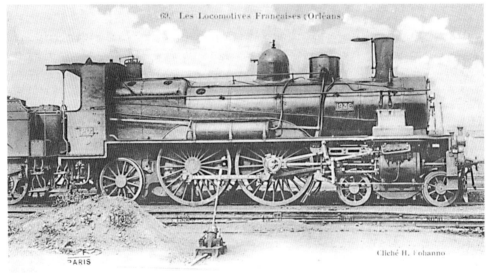

Machine nᵒ 193-C, à vapeur saturée, compound à 2 cylindres, tiroirs plans 2 essieux accouplés, bogie à l'avant et essieu porteur à l'arrière, pour trains de grande vitesse (Machines de la série 171 à 264, transformées en compound, en 1907-1910)

A much-converted engine: *Paris-Orleans No.193C, originally a 2-4-0 of 1869; rebuilt into a Fourquenot 2-4-2 by 1889; converted to 2-cylinder compound Atlantic in 1906; outside Gooch valve-gear, high-pressure Westinghouse brake.* Photo: H. Fohanno, F. Fleury.

with the American 'hard coal' Atlantics, but wide by European standards with a grate area of nearly 30sq.ft (2.8m^2). These 'Pfalz Atlantics' could draw 220-ton trains at 56mph and were soon adding fresh laurels to the growing reputation of the 4-4-2.

In the UK, the 'oldest firm in the business' of locomotive design and construction, the majority of locomotives were built by individual railway companies. This was an exception to the general rule of railways giving contracts to outside constructors like Schenectady, Baldwin or SACM to do their building for them. Some informed commentators knew all was not well with this arrangement; possibly the UK had too many design centres, too many mediocre locomotive designs and too many separate locomotive classes, many of them lack-lustre. Clement Stretton, British author of *The Development of the Locomotive...1803-1896*, had good knowledge of what went on in the USA and wrote:

> *How is it...that these American engines can do the work and convey the loads they do?...[their] successful working is due to the large fire-boxes, immense boilers, high pressure of steam...large valves, and consequently free exhaust.*

One major outcome of the British pattern, however, was the diversity of influences contributing to British Atlantic design. They included: an extended 4-4-0 (Lancashire & Yorkshire Railway); a double-single (GNR); an experiment to determine the optimum number and type of standard classes (GWR); and some straightforward emulation (LB&SCR).

Two centres of excellence, Horwich on the Lancashire & Yorkshire, and Doncaster on the Great Northern were quick off the mark. The Doncaster 'Plant' (always so termed on the GNR) managing, if only just, to produce the first British Atlantic, in 1898. It was designed by the new locomotive superintendent of the GNR, H.A. Ivatt who had been in office three years. Under his predecessor, James Stirling, the GNR had achieved fame with its swift and elegant 4-2-2 express locomotives, the 'Stirling singles.' The first GNR Atlantic, No.990 was a carefully-tested prototype which carried forward some of Stirling's ideas: outside cylinders and a generous firebox supported by a trailing axle. Batch production of its siblings started in 1900, the year in which Ivatt put the heart of the matter simply: 'The measure of the power of a locomotive is the boiler'[11]. He continued: 'Mr Sturrock [his predecessor-but-one] says the measure of a power of a locomotive is its capacity to boil water.' Sturrock's view (often attributed to Ivatt) hit the nail on the head and the Atlantic was its very embodiment.

The early GNR Atlantics, known as 'Klondykes' (*sic*) had their limitations, but they were popular with their crews since they steamed well. Whether or not Ivatt really perceived his original Atlantic (preserved in the UK's National Railway Museum at York) as an 'extended single' is open to debate. There was an attempt to present and perceive it in that way. Ivatt's tactful style of leadership emphasised continuity in an age of change – always a reassuring line to take – hence No.990's driving wheels were placed so close that one could barely place a penny, face on, between them, as near as a four-coupled locomotive might get to a 'single'. The resulting 'wheel bunch' was masked by some oddly-placed mounting steps.

Another line of argument (Colonel H.C.B. Rogers, *Express Locomotive Development in Great Britain and France*, 1990) was that the poor state of the GNR track caused Ivatt to space out axle loadings fairly evenly; the bogie bore 15 tons, the driving wheels 15 tons (front) and 16 tons (rear) and the trailing axle 12 tons.

Early English: *an Ivatt small Atlantic, No.983 (1900-1936) superheated in 1923; later fitted with outside-frame bogie, but here in its original, pristine condition.* Photo: Stephenson Locomotive Society.

The Lancashire & Yorkshire 4-4-2s of 1899 were more orthodox in their origins, designed as enlarged but conventional L&Y 4-4-0s. Their appearance and detailed design were less run–of–the–mill, however. With their inside cylinders, immense driving wheels (7ft 3ins diameter) and high pitched boilers they were the most gaunt of the Atlantic family, but they performed impressively, and eventually forty of them were constructed.

Meanwhile, in the *Railway Magazine* of January, 1899, Charles Rous-Marten, founder of the prestigious British school of accurately observing and recording locomotive performance, writing on 'Some New Great Northern Engines' took note of a portent, GNR No. 990 'the most novel and interesting type of all':

> *Leaving York with the so-called 'Flying Scotsman' express 2.25 minutes late, we had a load of no less than 293 tons behind the tender...Nevertheless No. 990 got away with it so readily that Naburn (4 miles 12.5chains) was passed in 6 min. 34 sec. from the start...this was admirable running with such a load...after passing Carlton Station the driver, finding that he would be at Newark before his booked time, promptly eased down to 50 miles an hour...No.990 acquitted herself with marked credit, and Mr Ivatt is to be congratulated on the high merit of her performances.*

Similar sentiments were being expressed in North America; later that year another journal, the *American Engineer and Railroad Journal* described a new Pennsylvania Atlantic with a massive grate area of 68sq.ft:

> *We do not know of a more worthy example of American practice and one containing so many evidences of thoughtful skill in design and thoroughly good workmanship in construction.*

The Atlantics were making their mark and their era had dawned.

Notes to Chapter 2

1. Robert Weatherburn, *Ajax Loquitur*, 1899, the passage continues: 'I was ushered into the world by a legion of mechanics and philosophers...'

2. The engineer was Oliver Bulleid, introduction of Cecil J. Allen and S.C. Townroe, *The Bulleid Pacifics of the Southern Region*, 1951. See also an advertisement of the Lima Locomotive Works (c.1925) headed 'Power!' which averred: *Railroading is elementary. All you have to do is increase your ton mileage and keep down your train mileage*, i.e. 'more with less', implying stronger engines. The Atlantic, pre-eminently a passenger engine had also to move fast. W. Schievelbusch, *The Railway Journey*, 1977; 'The railway's industrial product is transportation, a change of locality', a function carried out in quick measure by most Atlantics. The 'fastest with mostest' epigram was originally military, from Nathan Bedford Forrest, a largely self-taught strategist of genius and Confederate general in the American Civil War.

3. For the origins of the American 4-4-2 see Paul T. Warner, 'The Strong Locomotive', R&LHS *Bulletin* No.92; and the same author's 'Atlantic Type Locomotives', R&LHS *Bulletin* No.62.

4. The StEG, later kkStB; see Glossary.

5. W. Reuter and C. Bock, *op cit* introduced the concept and phrase 'hybrid Atlantic' for this small tribe of converted 4-4-0s; adopted and enlarged here (see Chapter 1).

6. Sometime general manager of the Philadelphia & Reading. The Wootten firebox usually implied a 'Camelback' layout, ie engineer's cab atop the boiler. A 'Wootten firebox' applied to anthracite-burning locomotives only; wide fireboxes on coal-burning engines were just that, wide fireboxes. Ironically, Wootten's successor on the P&R, S.M. Prince Jr, had doubts about Columbias and Atlantics; he preferred 4-4-0s; see his article: 'What is the ideal passenger engine?', *Railway Gazette*, 22 June 1900. Wisely, he hedged his bets and invested (or was required to invest) in Atlantics.

7. It had a strange history thereafter: it was purchased as a demonstration model by the Eames patent brake company, sent to the UK and suitably modified for the British loading gauge, but not entirely successfully; whilst on the Lancashire & Yorkshire Railway in 1882 its driver was tragically killed by leaning out of its generously-proportioned cab. During its brake-demonstration phase it was named *Lovett Eames*. See F.W. Brewer 'The Philadelphia and Reading Signals', *Railway Magazine* Vol LXXIX. No.472; Oct 1936.

8. Alfred W. Bruce, *The Steam Locomotive in America*, 1952.

9. Concord & Montreal; Georgia; Missouri-Kansas-Texas.

10. Strictly 'de Glehn-du Bousquet' Atlantics, see Chapter 3.

11. In response to a paper to the Institution of Mechanical Engineers on recent French practice, by E. Sauvage, 1900.

Chapter 3
The Gilded Age

The 'High Middle Ages' of the Atlantic

An important factor behind the spread of the Atlantic 1895-1907 was the heavy investment being made by railway administrations in improvements to track and rolling stock. In the USA, the Santa Fe under the leadership of E.J. Ripley (president, 1896-1918) spent nearly $300 million on improvements; just over $28 million in 1909 alone, a year in which it ordered a further twenty-seven Atlantics to run on its strengthened track and shortened routes. These were also the years in which E.H. Harriman controlled, *inter alia* the Southern Pacific and Union Pacific, for which he procured standardised locomotives including 'Harriman standard' 4-4-2s. Similar events took place elsewhere: 'In the first decade of the twentieth century... the Baltimore & Ohio purchased about fifty Atlantics, engines having 78 or 80in drivers and weighing from 75 to 100 tons.'[1]

An Atlantic in full cry: *Santa Fe No.520 of class 507 (Baldwin, 1904) a 4-cylinder balanced compound at 65mph on the* Santa Fe De Luxe *express (Chicago-Los Angeles, sixty-three hours); Atlantics at full-throttle were a fine sight, impacting on all five senses as they swept by; but ecologically sustainable transport they were not.*

Meet Me in St Louis

A good platform for Atlantic publicity was the Great Exhibition, or Exposition, a popular social phenomenon of the day. The first Atlantic to be displayed in this way was one of the ACL originals (Cotton States and International Exposition, Atlanta, 1895). The Paris Exposition of 1900 displayed Atlantics from France, a recent Nord Atlantic; Hungary (MÁV No. 701, awarded a *Grand Prix*); and Germany (a Palatinate P3^{II}, and a Saxon XV which also received an award). Atlantics also appeared at the St Louis Exposition, or 'World's Fair' (1904); the International Locomotive Show, Milan 1906 at which an elegant Gölsdorf Atlantic from Austria (108.22) was awarded the *Grand Prix*; Brussels in 1910 where a Danish 4-4-2 was a 'World Exhibition Engine', and the Buenos Aires Exposition in the same year, where a Buenos Ayres (*sic*) & Pacific 4-4-2 (NBL, Glasgow) graced the show. Even though the Atlantic was by then no longer at the technical cutting-edge it remained popular due to its prestige, elegance, and dash.

At the time of the *Louisiana Purchase Exposition* at St Louis in 1904 the Atlantic phenomenon was in full flight, still short of its zenith and enjoying the spirit of a glad, confident morn. Eleven superbly presented 4-4-2s were on show in the 'Palace of Transportation', out of a total of thirty-nine. The Atlantics included two compounds, one by Baldwin for the Santa Fe, and one by the newly-formed American Locomotive Company (Alco, 1901 embodying the Brooks and Schenectady works amongst others) – for the New York Central, a Cole 'balanced compound'. This was a locomotive with its high and low pressure cylinders in a horizontal plane, the hp cylinders ahead to drive the front axle, the lp cylinders placed outside and driving the rear coupled axle. The word 'balanced' was carefully chosen, an implicit criticism of the rival Vauclain compound from Baldwins which had cylinders in a vertical plane driving a common crosshead which, if not exactly 'unbalanced' certainly imparted hefty thrusts to side crankpins. The Santa Fe engine at St Louis, however, represented a step forward; the Vauclain arrangement had been turned 90° and was now horizontal; all cylinders drove the front axle, carefully balanced against each other.

Other St Louis Atlantics included a Baldwin Vauclain compound for the CB&Q, four fairly orthodox 4-4-2s for the Baltimore & Ohio, the Vandalia, the Illinois Central, and the Norfolk & Western. The first two were by Alco, the Illinois Central engine by Rogers (which was to join Alco in 1905), and the last by Baldwin. Locomotive engineering outwith the USA was represented by a de Glehn Nord-type Atlantic imported by the Pennsylvania from SACM in France, and a Prussian 4-cylinder von Borries compound Atlantic from Hannover, class S7, the only St Louis Atlantic to have a superheater.

There was also a handsome Atlantic by Alco (Schenectady) for the Cleveland, Cincinnati, Chicago & St Louis. It was placed on a slowly-revolving turntable, its wheels turned by electric motors and its electric headlight switched on, the beams sweeping the hall in which it stood. A Chicago & Alton 4-4-2 was a 'standard Atlantic' recently designed for Edward Harriman's 'Associated Lines', the most extensive railroad empire in the USA.

The Pennsylvania set up a temporary exhibition within Exposition grounds to demonstrate the latest contribution to the development of locomotive technology, a fully-fledged test plant. Here the Atlantics and other engines could be steamed and run up to speed whilst remaining stationary, gazed at by wondering multitudes. The duty fireman, Norman Suhrie amazed the crowds almost as much as the tethered, wheel-racing locomotives. He shovelled on relentlessly through the broiling Summer of 1904 apparently blessed with limitless stamina as he fed the

AMERICAN LOCOMOTIVE COMPANY,
NEW YORK.

Class 442–184   Road Number, 373

BUILT FOR THE C. C. C. & ST. L. RY.

GAUGE OF TRACK	CYLINDERS		DRIVING WHEEL DIAMETER	BOILER		FIRE BOX		TUBES		
	Diam.	Stroke		Diameter	Pressure	Length	Width	Number	Diameter	Length
4′-8½″	20½″	26″	79″	68″	200	97″	68″	362	2″	16′-¹⁄₁₆″

WHEEL BASE			WEIGHT IN WORKING ORDER—POUNDS.					
Driving	Engine	Engine & Tender	Leading	Driving	Trailing	Engine	Tender	
7′-6″	29′-10″	56′-7⅛″	42000	100000	42000	184000	140000	

FUEL	HEATING SURFACES, SQUARE FT.			GRATE AREA SQ. FT.	MAXIMUM TRACTIVE POWER	FACTOR OF ADHESION
Kind	Tubes	Fire Box	Total			
Soft Coal	3015	181	3196	44.8	23510	4.25

Tender, Type 8-Wheeled.   Capacity, Water 7500 Gals.   Fuel, 10 Tons

NEGATIVE No. B-245

State of the art: *the St Louis Exposition engine; Cleveland, Cincinnati, Chicago & St Louis No.373 of class I-62, (Alco, Brooks 1903). A large Atlantic with 200lb sq in boiler pressure, 6ft 7in driving wheels and grate area of 44.8sq.ft; tractive effort 23,510lbs. The Stephenson-link driven piston valves were a Brooks Atlantic trademark.* Photo: Alco Historic Photos.

capacious Atlantic fireboxes. He attributed his physical endurance to eating large quantities of chocolate bars whilst on duty. Because the St Louis Exposition occurred at the height of the controversy about the relative merits of compound and simple locomotives, eight compounds were put through their paces on the testing plant, half of them Atlantics. The results, *Locomotive Tests and Exhibits*, were published by the Pennsylvania in 1905. After the Exposition closed the plant was dismantled and re-erected at the Pennsylvania's locomotive works, Altoona, Pa, where it continued to play an important role in Atlantic development.

A less enduring feature of the St Louis Atlantic team was the excellently-crafted de Glehn compound (of the Paris-Orleans type) purchased by the Pennsylvania, in the same analytical spirit that had caused the UK's Great Western Railway to buy some of these near-legendary machines, to be described later. Although well capable of producing a steady 1,500ihp in its native France, coaxed carefully by the skilled *mecaniciens* of the P-O, it only touched 975ihp at St Louis and erratically at that. Afterwards, in spite or because of its sophistication it did not suit the rough-and-tumble of everyday Pennsylvania operations. It was 'the French Aristocrat' to the Pennsy hoggers, and it spent much of its short life out of use, an eloquent footnote to the 'geography of locomotion' hypothesis, and a warning not to read too much into certain tests, or to treat all tests as being of equal quality or rigour.

The Atlantic tests seemed to favour the NYC Cole balanced compound, although they were inconclusive in some respects (see Chapter 8). Nevertheless the 'Exhibition Atlantics' were seen

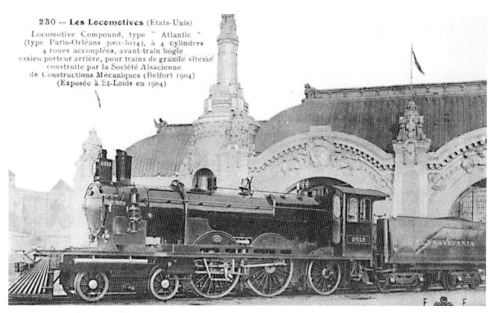

230 -- **Les Locomotives** (États-Unis)

Locomotive Compound, type " Atlantic " (type Paris-Orléans 3001-3014), à 4 cylindres 4 roues accouplées, avant-train bogie essieu porteur arrière, pour trains de grande vitesse construite par la Société Alsacienne de Constructions Mécaniques (Belfort 1904) (Exposée à St-Louis en 1904)

Meet me at the Fair: *the 'French Aristocrat', PRR No.2512 (SACM, 1903) a de Glehn 4-cylinder compound purchased for evaluation and displayed at the St Louis World's Fair, 1904; seen here outside the 'Palace of Transportation.' An excellently-crafted machine, but too exquisite for the Pennsy pragmatists.*

by vast numbers of people: 39 million had attended the Paris Exhibition; nearly 20 million came to St Louis. Even allowing for the many who failed to see the Atlantics, or saw them with unseeing eyes, the publicity potential of these events was enormous; 'bully pulpit' in one of the favoured phrases of President Theodore Roosevelt who visited the World's Fair, 26 November 1904.

The choice of a 'Big Four' Atlantic to impress St Louis Exposition visitors was symbolic: this locomotive was 'state of the art' for American express passenger engines and a pointer to the future: two-cylinder simples with big fireboxes over a trailing axle, a straightforward design able to generate plenty of horsepower. It was a favourite with postcard printers and book publishers. The Big Four Atlantics came towards the end of the first phase of classic Atlantic design, their firebox-supporting axles had inside bearings. It was already being found that the contents of a large ashpan under the grate could be blown, swept, or otherwise disturbed so as to get insidious fly-ash into axle bearings causing them to wear quickly or run hot. In the next phase of Atlantic design outside bearings were more generally adopted and some of the first-phase Atlantics had their inside bearings replaced by the outside variety: the L&Y locos were among the first to be so altered, shortly after the second batch of twenty were completed in 1902.

The Atlantics had other problems, in particular the rough riding of some classes and their limited adhesion which was apparent in the tendency for their driving wheels to slip on starting, particularly if weighty trains were set in motion with a heavy hand. The Atlantics were nevertheless popular with their drivers since they seemed to be immune from that which in their eyes was the cardinal locomotive sin, being 'shy of steam': their big fireboxes boiled water in large amounts, and quickly. It was soon celebrated as a good 'driver's engine'; the reactions of the firemen who had to feed the Atlantics were more mixed.

The Crampton Trap

The underlying reason for the initial success of the classic Atlantics was their ability to shift the growing weight of express trains reliably and quickly. In one important way the Atlantics sowed the seeds of their own destruction. On the GNR, the UK's leading user of Atlantics, one of the 'East Coast Joint Stock' six-wheel, first-class corridor carriages of 1893 weighed about 18 tons; by 1912 the GNR Atlantics were having to haul first-class bogie carriages of 34 tons. The 'deadweight hauled per passenger' on East Coast expresses rose in this period from 22.5cwt to 24.2cwt having already doubled 1880-1896. In Sweden the SJ was running ever-heavier expresses which now included 12-coach overnight sleeping car trains. These had either to be double-headed by class Cc 4-4-0s, or entrusted to plodding 2-cylinder compound 4-6-0s. The solution, inspired in part by American practice, was the stylish and potent Atlantic, class A of 1906.

Considerable investment was made in better track to support fast, heavy locomotives like Atlantics. When Ivatt took over at Doncaster in 1895 he was perturbed to find poor-quality main line track laid with light rails weighing 85lb per yard or less. By about 1910, 103lb per yard was becoming common on British main lines. Rous-Marten (*Railway Magazine*, August 1905) commented on ten years' change on the GNR:

> *The engines of that day [the mid-1890s] were designed for loads of 150 tons behind the tender...although they did unquestionably haul in very creditable style trains weighing 80 or even 100 tons more...they had to be 'pushed' to an undesirable extent, and...could not be depended upon for punctuality...Nowadays, however, when important expresses on the Great Northern Railway are largely composed of twelve-wheeled vehicles weighing 35 tons or more...an important express seldom fails to exceed 300 tons, and sometimes approaches 400.*

Rous-Marten then praised Ivatt for his foresight in designing an 'absolutely new type' of engine to cope with these growing loads, particularly No.990 the pioneer UK Atlantic. A recent journey behind one of its sisters, No.253 brought a 380 ton 'Scotch Express' from Doncaster to London in three hours and two minutes – two minutes early: 'the haulage power and the swiftness of the type were well demonstrated.'

The Atlantics were themselves part of this steady improvement, but then the new order soon found them wanting. Events on the Pennsylvania occurring shortly after Rous-Marten's panegyrics made this starkly clear. After two years of careful experiment, the Pennsylvania introduced all-steel carriages ('cars' in American usage) in 1907, promptly going in for them in a big way and ordering 500 to a standard design. The steel car, strong and heavy[2], had great safety appeal and therefore attracted custom; rivals had to follow suit. But whereas an E2 or E3 Atlantic could speed along comfortably with 300 tons of wooden cars on the *Pennsylvania Special*[3] it was soon found that they had to be double-headed, even triple-headed if schedules were to be kept, an expensive solution.

Two more blows were delivered to the Atlantic idea by the New York Central, both harbingers of things to come in that they arose from environmental and 'health and safety' considerations. The NYC, hitherto a dedicated operator of Atlantics (it ran up a total of

New York Central: *a typical NYC Atlantic, No.820 of class I-10h by Alco (Schenectady) 1906, being prepared for the road at Buffalo, NY, 1917. Their massive, stubby appearance masked 6ft 7in driving wheels; note shunting pole slots in buffer beam ends.* Photo: Harold K. Vollrath.

313, 1901-1907) was extending its tracks through tunnels to a prestigious new terminus, Grand Central Terminal, New York. The city authorities insisted that tunnel working should be by electric traction, and that passenger cars working through the tunnels should be constructed out of steel – deemed safer than wood in case of an underground accident.[4] At a stroke trains became much heavier, often beyond the comfortable limit of an Atlantic. The NYC turned to 4-6-0s, and increasingly to 4-6-2s, and larger. Its once-famed Atlantics were put to secondary duties, and then became candidates for the breaker's yard.

The phenomenon of developing locomotive technology to generate traffic only to find the new levels of business beyond the capacity of the innovation that had brought them about, was long-established. An early and dramatic example was the case of the Crampton locomotive, a form popular on mainland Europe, but largely ignored in the UK, Crampton's homeland.[5] The Crampton was a long, low engine with large driving wheels abaft the firebox; it had excellent steam distribution and ran freely. Like the Atlantic it was swift but unable to cope with the heavier, longer trains brought about by its very popularity. Like the Atlantics after them, the Cramptons were replaced by more powerful locomotives and relegated to lighter, secondary duties: the 'Crampton trap'.

As in the 1850s, so in the *Belle Epoque*. The Atlantics created traffic that eventually could only be hauled by more powerful engines. The Atlantic Coast Line soon abandoned its pioneering Atlantic experiment and reverted to 4-6-0s, one of the Atlantic's closest rivals and an older design. There was some irony here: the first 4-6-0s were delivered to the Philadelphia & Reading (1841-1847); the next was constructed by Hinkley of Boston; names that echoed in early Atlantic history fifty years later.

Exceptionelle pour l'epoque: **the Nord Atlantics**

The most dramatic waxing and waning of Atlantic status occurred in France. The Nord Atlantics of 1899-1904 were few in number, thirty-five, but colossal in their reputation and influence. They were generally referred to as 'de Glehn Atlantics' after the designer of the compound system which drove them. More correctly they were de Glehn-du Bousquet Atlantics, embodying the name of the Nord locomotive chief who combined the de Glehn system with refinements of his own, placing the whole into a 4-4-2 engine. Their performance was astonishing by the existing standards of 1900 and it took the technical world by storm.

Their greatest publicist, Rous-Marten[6] sang their praises in the *Railway Magazine*. Summing up five years of achievement (in 1905) he recalled some highspots which he had recorded such as working up Caffier bank, eight miles of 1 in 125 where a Nord Atlantic could maintain thirty seconds per kilometre 'mile after mile with curious and admirable evenness.' On another occasion an engine hauling 360 tons had covered 92.25 miles in 96.4 minutes, storming up 1 in 200 at 52.2mph, raising this to 57mph when the *mecanicien* admitted live steam into the low-pressure cylinders. It was all 'remarkable...I regret that I am unable to place beside them any parallel instances of equal work being done by British engines...' Because the Nord Atlantics were so swift on rising gradients it was not necessary as in Britain 'to run nearly so fast downhill.' This was music to French ears.

The Nord Atlantics were copied by other French railways and the PLM developed its own type of compound Atlantic, but only 155 French 4-4-2s were built for home use. In spite of their brilliant performance the French Atlantics were soon superseded by 4-6-0s and 4-6-2s. The 4-6-2 carried Atlantic logic one stage further with its large firebox, and six driving wheels to give better adhesion. The legacy of the Nord Atlantics endured, however, not only in their 4-6-2 cousins but also in the long and inconclusive debate about the virtues of compounding, in the move towards higher boiler pressures and, in the immediate future, the relative merits of the Atlantic vis-à-vis the ten wheeler and the Pacific.

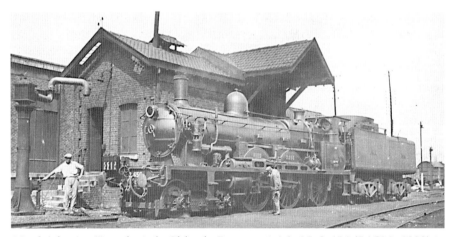

Nord Atlantics (I): *a classic de Glehn-du Bousquet 4-4-2, No.2.656 (SACM, 1902) in post-1911 superheated form, later SNCF 2.221.A.16; receiving attention, very possibly from the* mecanicien *and* chauffeur. Photo: H.J. Stretton-Ward.

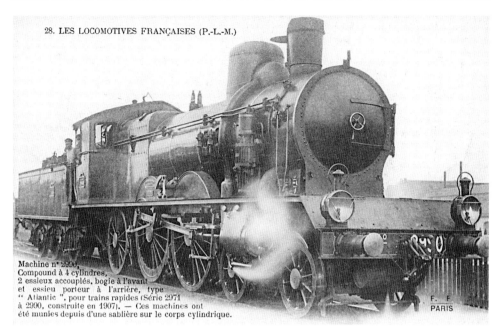

28. LES LOCOMOTIVES FRANÇAISES (P.-L.-M.)

Machine n° 2990,
Compound à 4 cylindres,
2 essieux accouplés, bogie à l'avant
et essieu porteur à l'arrière, type
" Atlantic ", pour trains rapides (Série 2971
à 2990, construite en 1907). — Ces machines ont
été munies depuis d'une sablière sur le corps cylindrique.

F. F
PARIS

PLM: *No.2990, an original PLM Atlantic of class 2971 (Cail, 1907) depicted on a Fleury carte-postale; 4-cylinder compounds with divided drive, later adorned with large smoke deflectors; steam pipe leading directly to hp cylinders.* Photo: F. Fleury.

A Down-side?

The introduction of high-speed trains as routine or commonplace, a development in which the Atlantic played a crucial role, exacted various prices – raising the danger stakes was one. From one standpoint, getting journeys over quickly was highly desirable, the whole point of rail travel. But as speeds grew so the near, and then the middle distance became blurred when viewed from train windows, virtually impossible to watch or study. Continuous observation of the far distance becomes tedious and fatiguing for the eyes. The Atlantic speed was an inadvertent preparation for eventual travel on motorways or airlines. The 'outside' became a series of distant and ephemeral impressions, good preparation, perhaps, for the era of a tele-visual, spectator-civilisation. This aspect of railway history has been little developed[7] and it is admittedly contentious, nevertheless the phenomenon of high speed is not so clear cut as traditional commentary seems to have assumed.

For all its fine performance the reign of the Atlantic was a short one, as the American and French experiences demonstrate in particular. Railway administrators became wary of adopting the 4-4-2, particularly as rival classes of locomotive with proven effectiveness were already available. Possibly the 'classic' Atlantic era was a span of about a dozen years; the heart of it but half that, say 1900-1906. But the Atlantic still had its strong supporters who were to take it a long way yet.

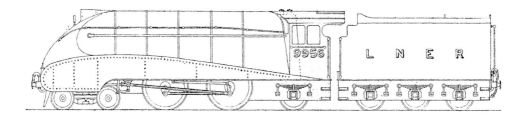

Design for 'O' gauge streamlined LNER Atlantic by F.J. Hearn, Model Railway News, *May 1947.*

Notes to Chapter 3

1. John F. Stover, *History of the Baltimore and Ohio Railroad* (1987); see also: Keith L. Bryant, Jr, *History of the Atchison, Topeka and Santa Fe Railway*, 1974, and Maury Klein, *The Life & Legend of E.H. Harriman*, 2000.

2. On the PRR, a 70ft steel coach (a 'dreadnaught', *sic*) weighed 50.4 tons and had 88 seats; its 53ft wooden equivalent had 62 seats and weighed only 40.6 tons – but a *higher* deadweight per passenger.

3. Introduced in 1905, offering an eighteen-hour schedule Jersey City-Chicago, at an average speed of 50.2mph (80.1km/h). On the initial run, E2 No.7002 was credited by some observers with touching 120mph (193km/h) – much disputed. The new steel stock of 1907 doubled the weight of the train.

4. Alas for the best-laid plans... three days after full electric working was started in 1907, an electrically-hauled express derailed, killing twenty-three people; no definite cause was identified, but the electric locos (1-Do-1, ie 2-8-2) were rebuilt with bogies shortly after.

5. T.R. Crampton, a native of Broadstairs, was a prolific inventor and versatile engineer. So popular was his patent locomotive in France that *prendre le Crampton* was acceptable *argot* for 'to take the train' until the 1940s; a high honour.

6. Rous-Marten (1844-1908) a New Zealander, did so considerable – and accurate – a 'PR job' for the French Atlantics, particularly those of the Nord that he was offered the *Legion d'Honneur*; he declined on the grounds that this might be thought to have influenced his favourable judgements. De Glehn was of Baltic-German ancestry, but born in Sydenham and therefore technically English; his brother-in-law had been Bishop of London.

7. See Wolfgang Schievelbusch, *op cit*; John Stilgoe, *Metropolitan Corridor, Railroads and the American Scene*, 1983.

Chapter 4
Atlantic Zenith – and After

The Flyer of the Flatlands

The Atlantics had their rivals but there remained niches where their particular qualities suited geographical or economic conditions very well, and here they endured. Whether the rising proportion of Atlantics constructed outwith the USA after 1907 represents some kind of cultural lag elsewhere, or brisk and ruthless American pragmatism with locomotive forms must remain open questions. The French, and the British GWR were similarly dismissive of the Atlantics once they had learned important lessons from them (see table in note 7 at end of this chapter).

In Prussia the State Railways (KPEV), which between 1902 and 1907 had been steadily building their class S7 Atlantics, embarked on their last phase of Atlantic building with the enlarged class S9 in 1908; nearly 100 of these were constructed by 1911. The Saxon State Railways also bought an improved Atlantic class, the superheated XH1 class from their local suppliers, Hartmann of Chemnitz – eighteen were taken on stock, 1909-1913. The classic

Survivor: *close-up of Danish class P No.919 (Hanomag 1909) with an American touch, a 4-cylinder Vauclain balanced compound with bar frames, but with many European influences also: conical smokebox door; windcutter cab and Otto Busse's own cast steel bogie frame. Long-lived and, apart from some frame-cracking problems, very adequate – No.919 lasted until 1962.*

Hungarian Atlantic, the State Railways (MÁV) class In, was constructed 1906-1908; twenty-four engines. Sweden (SJ) and Denmark (DSB) invested boldly in Atlantics in this later period: the Danes bought thirty-three from Germany, 1907-1910; the Swedish class A of twenty-six locomotives was built in Sweden 1906-1909. Far from being a failing species, the Danish Atlantics were extraordinarily long-lived and successful, eventually becoming Europe's last operational Atlantics. The SJ Atlantics were a less happy investment, but they had their moments – and few rivals for a striking appearance.

The UK had Europe's most varied Atlantic stock and here there was also a little late-flowering. The NER built a large class of 3-cylinder Atlantics 1911-1918 and the NBR built twenty-two, 1906-1922, the majority of them before 1912. Six GNR-type Atlantics were constructed by the LB&SCR at their Brighton works in 1911-1912 (Class H2), although the GNR ceased production of its standard 4-4-2s in 1908 by when it had a stock of ninety-one, in two classes.

Mainstream construction in France virtually dried up after 1906 except for a tail-end of the Midi class 1920 (1906-1908) and the prudent reconstruction of old 2-4-2s by the Paris-Orleans up to 1910. This abandonment of new 4-4-2 construction by the French was indicative of the unsentimental, rational attitude of the French school of design which had found Atlantics wanting in important respects.

There is no general cause-and-effect relationship which explains why one railway administration adopted or retained Atlantics and another did not, but there is a discernible pattern to the distribution of the Atlantics. They were popular locomotives for railways operating passenger trains on the plains, along river valleys, and on the flat, gentle littorals of the Baltic, the North Sea and the Bay of Bengal, as well as the Atlantic itself. Atlantics ran on the Florida East Coast whose summit was 16ft above sea level (West Palm Beach) and over the sea itself on level viaducts to Key West; in Mozambique they ran out over the Indian Ocean on a long pier.

The Atlantic was useful to the Magyars who ran trains across the level *puszta* of Hungary; to the Prussians of the North European plains, and the railway administrations of the Rhineland. In the UK the largest squadrons of Atlantics sped along the low-lying extension of the European plain that

Atlantics over the Atlantic: *the Florida East Coast extension, Miami-Key West (1912-1936) where FEC's score of Atlantics (Schenectady, 1904-1905) took passengers 'by train, out of sight of land.' Moving Westwards a 4-4-2 had the Gulf of Mexico on its starboard beam, the eponymous ocean to port.*

characterises Eastern Britain, the 'East Coast route' from London to Edinburgh and Aberdeen, the territory of the GNR, NER and NBR. In the USA the Atlantic was well-used on the Great Plains and in the lower-lying regions of the North East, such as the 'Water-Level Route' of the NYC. Atlantics were not strangers to upland regions; the North British 4-4-2s served the Border hills of Southern Scotland for a generation but the broad generalisation holds: Atlantics were lowlanders.

Atlantic-owning railways which operated in mixed terrain generally confined the 4-4-2s to the lowlands. In his history of the railways of Saxony (*Die Königlich Sächsischen Staatseisenbahnen*) K.E. Maedel notes that the two classes of Saxon Atlantic, XH1 and XV were *Für die Flachlandstrecken...* 'for the stretches [of railway] in the lowlands.'[1] Karl Gölsdorf had earlier expressed a similar sentiment: 'today [the Atlantic] is more restricted to the really *Flachlandstrecken*.'[2]

Similarly, in the USA the Norfolk & Western possessed a small class of Atlantics. Seven, built by Baldwin 1903-1904, and at the cutting edge of Atlantic technology with early electric headlights and piston valves; No.606 of this class was one of the select Atlantics exhibited at the St Louis World's Fair, 1904. But the N&W kept these engines well away from its lines in mountainous territory, operating them on the Norfolk division to the East of Crewe, Virginia, on trains operating partly over the ACL to Richmond.

Atlantic distribution also tended towards locations where trains had to be fast and reliable, and where incomes were relatively high. Although the use of the Atlantic, taking its history as a whole, was democratic, a noticeable proportion of its early work was on crack expresses, and luxury trains: the *Pennsylvania Limited*; the *Southern Belle*; the *Flying Scotsman*; the *Atlantic City Flyer*, and the Brighton 'Stockbrokers' Express'.

The 'Stockbrokers' Express' was an example of the way Atlantics contributed to the development of long-distance commuter traffic which, with the growth of middle-class affluence, was a feature of Edwardian times. The Lancashire & Yorkshire Atlantics were responsible for running the 5.10p.m. (the 'First Corridor') and the 5.55p.m. Manchester-Blackpool business commuter trains known as the *Club Trains*. The term came from the 'Club Carriages' attached to these flyers, entrance to which was restricted to members of an exclusive, by-invitation club. Club rules included an agreement to tolerate shut windows whilst the train was in motion. A century later air-conditioning might have mitigated this problem whilst the club committee would most likely be deliberating the rights and wrongs of mobile phone chatter; such is the faltering march of technology.

The 'club' was open only to first class ticket holders, and it exacted a hefty premium fee in addition. A similar rationing-by-price existed in the USA on the contemporaneous New York-Chicago Atlantic-hauled expresses. The *Pennsylvania Special* which rivalled the NYC *Twentieth Century Limited* consisted of three cars: (i) baggage, smoking, barber's shop, buffet, library; (ii) twelve-berth sleeper; and (iii) composite with six private state rooms, parlor and observation platform. The standard $20 fare was increased by an $8 supplement and Pullman fares all of which totalled $33. Like the *Twentieth Century Limited* it was mostly a train 'for business men rather than sightseers.'[3]

Ernest Protheroe's *Railways of the World, c.*1910, contained a coloured plate of an 'Egyptian *Train-de-Luxe*', the Cairo-Luxor Express of four cream carriages behind an elegant, orangey-brown de Glehn 4-4-2; clearly not a train for the many. 'It had a short reign as a luxury engine' thought Gustav Reder. In later years the Atlantics did plenty of good bread-and-butter work hauling commuters, early morning workmen's trains, fish expresses and local freights. Even in their golden era most of their work was on fast passenger trains as such, not necessarily trains for the *haut monde*, although the image of an engine for the trains of conspicuous consumers proved to be tenacious.

The Atlantic Empire

Political economy also determined Atlantic distribution. The great years of the 4-4-2s coincided with those of high imperialism. Because 'trade followed the flag' and imperial administrators often organised the procurement of locomotives, the fashionable Atlantics were to be found on some of the railways which came under imperial administration. Economic penetration also took other forms, for example some 'Harriman standard' Atlantics appeared in Mexico on SP subsidiaries and a small class of Glasgow-built 4-4-2s ran on the British-owned Buenos Ayres & Pacific in Argentina.

Although Egypt was ostensibly part of the Ottoman Empire, *de facto* it lay under European, particularly British, hegemony during the Atlantic era. The Egyptian purchase of ten de Glehn 4-4-2s from Cail in 1905 was much influenced by British administrators who later added further tranches of foreign-built Atlantics until the Egyptian State Railways had over ninety of them. At one period Egypt had, *pro rata*, the most 'Atlanticised' railway system of any. Similarly, the British-administered Sudan Government Railways had four neat 4-4-2s from Robert Stephenson of Darlington, 1910. Egypt and the Sudan were promising Atlantic country, without severe gradients, sandy (this could aid adhesion) and with reasonable timetables.

The British administrators of the railways in India ordered nearly 120 Atlantics for various systems. Atlantics were also to be found in small quantities on two British-influenced railways in China.

Egyptian elegance: *the classic lines of a well-conceived machine; R.G. Peckitt's Atlantic No.736 of class 735, later class 1 for the ESR (Berliner, Schwartzkopff 1913), similar to the numerous class 760, or 26. Well-proportioned, later enhanced with a restraint of additions (headlight, turbo-dynamo) although the clerestory cab roof was lost. A sensible engine for a level terrain with drifts of adhesion-enhancing sand.* Photo: ESR, collection of Alan Clothier.

The International Atlantic Trade

The USA was self-sufficient in Atlantics, as were Britain and Germany – but none of these net exporting Atlantic manufacturers was absolutely self-sufficient, if we take hard line criteria, since both the USA and the UK imported a tiny handful of de Glehn compounds from France by way of evaluating them. Germany, a self-sufficient net exporter of loco-motives (including Atlantics) imported two Vauclain compounds from Baldwin (1900) for Bavaria. France, birthplace of the de Glehns imported twenty 4-4-2s from the USA.

Sweden built most of its Atlantics but it also imported two from Germany; Denmark bought all of its Atlantics from Germany. The rest of the world imported its Atlantics from the USA, UK, Germany or France. This trade grew towards the latter part of the classic Atlantic era, for example with the heavy Egyptian purchases of the 1920s. It kept Atlantic-production going longer than would have been the case if usage of 4-4-2s had been restricted to the industrialised world.

Only Austria and Hungary were individually self-sufficient in Atlantics, and very excellent ones they were.

American in Paris: *a Baldwin 2-cylinder simple 4-4-2 delivered in March 1903 to the Etat Railway, No.2903* Montaigu *(later No.221.003); withdrawn 1928. Photo from a Fleury carte-postale for data-conscious collectors, axleloads duly inscribed in kilograms; available for adhesion (poids adherent) – 34,000 kg (34 tons; 17 tons per axle). Photo: F. Fleury.*

Anthracite burner: *Philadelphia & Reading Camelback Atlantic No.344 of class P-5sc (Reading shops, 1906) smoking hard at the Reading Terminal, Philadelphia, 1913. The extra-wide Wootten firebox bulks out over inside-bearing trailing wheels; unusually for the USA a 3-cylinder simple – middle piston valve discernible in centre of smokebox saddle; 4-4-0 No.400 (Reading shops, 1911) pours out further reek in the distance.* Photo: erstwhile Reading Co.

The Geography of Locomotion

Locomotive design in particular countries, even on different railways within them, responded to pressures of geography, economics and culture. Obvious examples would be the Wootten-firebox Camelback Atlantics in the USA, running on railroads with easy access to cheap anthracite culm, and the complex de Glehn Atlantics in France, where there were highly trained and well-educated drivers and where good coal was rare and expensive and needed to be eked out intelligently. The low axle loading of the Gölsdorf compound Atlantics was an answer to lightly-built railways in difficult terrain, the results of geomorphology, a shortage of capital and, as in France, generally poor-quality coal. None of these determinants is really more than a tendency, not a hard cause-and-effect relationship, for personal preferences came into the process also. The adoption of Atlantics in Egypt was in part an outcome of its lack of gradients, but owed more to the fiat of its administrators. F.H. Trevithick believed in the efficacy of the 4-4-0 and 4-6-0, but 'there was a change of plan' under his successor R.G. Peckitt. Drummond on the LSWR simply did not like 4-4-2s; Ivatt on the GNR did; boards of directors relied heavily on such advice. A.W. Gibbs had considerable ascendancy on the Pennsylvania; it is less likely that the E6s experiment would have taken place in his absence, or that the GWR would have carried out comparative experiments so long and carefully without Churchward.

Social and economic geography connected with the Atlantic saga in another way. The Atlantic era coincided with the period when the railways were at their zenith as general transportation systems. Most people in the industrial world lived within locations on, or framed around railway systems. This was especially so in the land of the Atlantics, the USA in the railway-framed *Metropolitan Corridor*, so named by John R. Stilgoe in his work on the subject. A new machine like the Atlantic, which dramatically accelerated traffic along the corridors, became quickly known. Publicity departments worked its potential hard; professionals and the laity were soon aware of the Atlantic and its achievements. It was amongst the few locomotives to achieve celebrity status with the informed public, even if its halo of prestige and repute masked some technical deficiencies.

The Big Users

Some railway systems invested heavily in Atlantics, usually railways of the plains and river-lands. In the USA, the Pennsylvania ran 561 Atlantics at one time or another, mainly on its easier-graded Lines East: AT&SF, 183; C&NW, ninety-one; CB&Q, fifty-seven; the NYC subsidiary, the 'Big Four', sixty-two; the NYC&HR, 213. In the UK the GNR operated express trains up and down the East Coast Route, with some of its 116 Atlantics; at York it handed these trains to the NER which had seventy-two Atlantics. To the East across the German Ocean, the Prussians owned 347 Atlantics and at one time or another the Egyptians operated ninety-four of them.

Miniature Atlantics

An interesting outcome of the reputation and popularity of the Atlantics was their replication on miniature and model railways. The early years of the private, steam-operated, miniature railway coincided with the Atlantic fashion; the Atlantic form was well-suited to small railways laid along level ground. Rising incomes, albeit modest by later standards made holidays a realistic proposition for larger numbers of people than ever before and encouraged miniature railways in seaside resorts, leisure parks and at exhibitions. Some wealthy people could afford their own railways on estates or in extensive private grounds. By 1914 miniature Atlantics were growing in popularity even if their 'twelve inches to the foot' prototype was starting to lose ground.

The more extensive growth of model and toy railways also gave 'Atlanticism' further scope, although very few of the resulting 4-4-2s were steam-powered since this was the realm of the clockwork, electric or push-Atlantic, not 'true' Atlantics by any means.

Atlantic critics: the 'Glorified Single'

By 1912 it was widely accepted that Atlantics had few rivals in hurrying along fast, but necessarily relatively light, trains. Their drivers liked their easy steaming, although keeping a hard-worked 4-4-2 going at speed was tough on the fireman and more than one class of Atlantic was nicknamed sardonically 'the mankillers'. The travelling public, and especially the railway connoisseurs, warmed to Atlantics. Nevertheless scepticism and opposition grew apace in some quarters.

Even at the height of the 'Atlantic mania' when some railways were starting to order inappropriate Atlantics, for example some of the one-off orders in the USA which might have been better met by 4-6-0s, Rous Marten was speculating in his wordy way (*Railway Magazine*, July 1906):

Why build an expensive Atlantic engine if a cheaper 4-4-0 will do what is wanted...? [Although] I regard the 4-4-2 as in most respects an ideal type of engine for fast and heavy express work...my sole doubt is whether this work could not be done as well by cheaper 4-4-0 engines...I simply desire to be satisfied that [Atlantics] are not purchased at too high a relative cost...Of course, if we could put 24 or 25 tons on each driving axle as they do with some American Atlantics, the case would be totally altered...As regards the six-coupled express type [4-6-0, 2-6-2] I reiterate my opinion that it is necessarily destined to be the heavy express engine of the future...

Neither do I doubt that the next important locomotive development which we shall see in this country – setting aside the general adoption of the compound principle, which I deem inevitable – will be in the introduction of the 4-6-2 or 'Pacific' design. Neither do I doubt that when it does come it will be a success.

A fair prophesy for all the hedging, although the 2-6-2 was to become the standard passenger locomotive only in Russia and compounding, with one or two notable exceptions, failed to penetrate cultural barriers in the UK. Rous-Marten's suggestion was nevertheless near the mark: for all their achievements, the Atlantics were to be supplanted by 4-6-0s and 4-6-2s, perhaps more quickly than he guessed.

The 'Atlantic mania' had been patchy and restricted in its effects. Even in the USA where the 4-4-2 flourished most, some major railroads resisted its charms: the Denver & Rio Grande operating in mountainous territory, and some other important lines: the Delaware & Hudson; Delaware, Lackawanna & Western; Louisville & Nashville; also, strangely given its ideal Atlantic running ground – the Seaboard Air Line. Many railroads experimented briefly with a few Atlantics and then dropped the idea: the Great Northern (10); Southern (10); New Haven(12); Georgia[2] and Northern Pacific[3]. A mere half-dozen Atlantics ran in the whole of Canada.

In the UK only seven of the 120 or so operating companies used Atlantics. Most French companies ran Atlantics (except the Ouest) but in small numbers when compared to the battalions of 4-6-0s. Spain and Italy had no Atlantics, the Russian Empire had but a handful confined to the Warsaw-Vienna Railway; there were few 4-4-2s in Asia and Africa; fewer still in Latin America.

The counter-Atlantic case was almost as old as the design itself. S.M. Prince of the Philadelphia & Reading thought that 'nothing has been accomplished by [these Atlantic] engines that can not be more satisfactorily accomplished by the 8-wheel American [4-4-0] and the ten-wheel type.'[4]

In Britain, the Scottish engineer Dugald Drummond, locomotive superintendent of the LSWR put the anti-Atlantic case succinctly:

A few of our railways are continuing [1911] the use of an American (sic) type of engine known as the 'Atlantic'. They are, in my opinion, the most unsatisfactory engine that has been introduced into English practice, owing to the disturbing effects on the permanent way and bridges, compared with the four-cylinder, six-coupled modern express engine...[5]

A year later the Institution of Locomotive Engineers heard a similar argument from a less conservative source, H. Woodgate-Dearberg, in a contentious address 'On the Standard-isation of Large Passenger Locomotives'[6] which questioned the efficacy of a 4-4-2, as opposed to a 4-4-0 or 4-6-0:

> *It is difficult to see why some designers have so consistently clung to the 4-4-2 design which, regarded from an engineering point of view is a wasteful design…nothing more than a glorified single wheeler, capable of splendid work, and at times indifferent work also.*

Woodgate-Dearbearg thought the future lay with the 4-6-0, preferably a 4-cylinder simple version after which railways ought to 'eliminate all other designs of older machines as they wear out.' A railway world reliant on 4-6-0s would cause 'talk about electrification to die a natural death.' Some support for this line of argument came from a prestigious source present at the meeting: F.H. Trevithick, former CME of the Egyptian State Railways who had compared 4-4-2 and 4-6-0 performance carefully, and had no doubt of the superior pulling-power of the latter.

Stout defenders of the Atlantic remained, like Theodore Ely and A.W. Gibbs of the Pennsylvania. As late as 1926 there was some touchy correspondence in the British *Railway Gazette* when R.G. Peckitt, a firm Atlanticist and CME of the Egyptian State Railways stated that the Egyptian Atlantics which 'were designed by me' were superior to 4-6-0s 'which, though better at getting away from a station were not as satisfactory as a 4-4-0 between stations' and that the latter were 'underboiled in rough weather.' Supporting correspondence came from Hugh Reid, Managing Director of NBL, and a supplier to the ESR who thought that 'it is the 4-6-0 in this case [Egypt] which has been superseded.'

Past Noon: the Measure of Decline

In the year of the St Louis Exposition, 1904, about 370 Atlantics were built, 260 of them in the USA; in 1900 the equivalents had been ninety-six and forty-two respectively. Atlantic output continued to grow to 1906 when world production reached 423; USA: 303. It held for a short while before falling away. In 1910 world production was 164; USA: eighty-nine. It then slipped ever-downwards. In 1915, for the first time since 1893, the USA manufactured no Atlantics and only fourteen were delivered elsewhere. Thereafter only a handful were produced; none in 1919, none again in 1922. There was a large order for Egypt in the mid-1920s, and from then on little until the end in 1939 when the last Atlantics appeared, six streamlined flyers for the Belgian State Railways. For data on Atlantic production over the years, see note 7 at the end of this chapter.

Except for some special orders the game was up after 1912 – even though by some criteria the Atlantics' finest hours were yet to come. In general, why the startling growth to 1906, and the precipitate fall thereafter? The early Atlantic achievements, very solid and well-publicised built up strong momentum. Atlantic output up to 1906 resulted partly from the power of managerial fashion; certainly there was some insufficiently examined procurement of Atlantics by railways that might have benefited from a more general-purpose type of machine like the 4-6-0. Some of the post-1906 Atlantic market was sustained by engineers or administrators who remained loyal to the Atlantic idea, preferring to dwell on its merits, and to play down or seek ways of remedying its defects, people like Gibbs and Peckitt.

Even the extraordinary E6s class of the Pennsylvania (1914), quite able to see off many contemporary Pacifics, could not buck the trend. As they rolled out of the Juniata shops at Altoona, Pennsylvania, the first wave of unwanted Atlantics was being shunted off to the scrap heap: two notoriously unsuccessful 4-4-2s on the Malmö-Ystad Railway in Sweden.

Although many Atlantic performances were astonishing, and it was amongst the most elegant of locomotives, there was no escaping the fact that whilst it had strong lungs it also had slippery feet; its potential was more limited than the first wave of enthusiasm had suggested.

Notes for Chapter 4

1. On the Saxon State Railways a V (often in Gothic or *Fraktur*) denoted a *Verbund*, or compound class.

2. K. Gölsdorf: 'Lokomotivbau' in *Geschichte der Eisenbahnen der österreichisch-ungarischen Monarchie*, 1908; reprinted in K. Gölsdorf: *Lokomotivbau in Alt-Österreich 1837-1918*, 1978.

3. *Railway Magazine*, May 1903.

4. see Chapter 3, Note 6.

5. Dugald Drummond: *Extract from address to LSWR Engineering Society...*, 1911. Drummond may have been influenced by the furore over the North British Railway Atlantics (Scottish, not English; he ought to have known!) but his points are well taken. McIntosh of the Caledonian, another Scot, thought the Atlantic had not been a conspicuous success anywhere.. (*Cassier's Magazine*, March, 1910) although had tried his hand at three 4-4-2 designs.

6. *Proceedings* of the I Loco E, 22nd November, 1913.

7. **Atlantic production: 1905-13**

Year	USA	Rest of world	Total
1905	184 (51%)	176	360
1906	303 (72%)	120	423
1907	187	147	334
1908	49 (26%)	138	187
1909	79	86 (52%)	165
1910	89	75	164
1911	30	56 (65%)	86
1912	8	2	10
1913	2	23 (92%)	25
Grand totals	931 (53%)	823 (47%)	1,754

Chapter 5
Atlanticitis and the
Search for a Cure

The Rough Riders

Of the two endemic flaws of the Atlantic: its *uncertain adhesion*, and its *rough riding*, the latter was the less serious and has generally taken second place in the concerns of commentators and railway operators. It was the engine crews who suffered the inconveniences of the 'Atlantic wag', not passengers, still less the office-bound railway administrators. To some extent the roughness was a function of velocity, a flaw which might have been masked in a plodder. The Atlantics' tendency to sway about at speed did not render them seriously unstable. Apart from shoving crews about, the main problem resulting from this sinuous movement was a reputed (and disputed) tendency to spread track slightly and possibly to accelerate wear and tear more quickly than might otherwise be the case. Positive-thinking people made a virtue of the problem, claiming that the roughness assisted the fireman by shaking down coals in the tender, or distributing them in the firebox.

Some Atlantics were notoriously more rough than others: in the USA, the Norfolk & Western, and the Southern 4-4-2s were well-known offenders; the early Lancashire & Yorkshire Atlantics

Norfolk & Western: *one of this great steam road's less successful forays; No.600 (Baldwin 1903) at Norfolk, Va, in 1917; the seven-strong class J were poor riders and insufficiently flexible for their operators. Five were later superheated, however.* Photo: Harold K. Vollrath.

rode poorly at first, similarly the GNR large Atlantics. O.S. Nock wrote in an oft-quoted passage about a footplate trip on LNER No.4456, an Ivatt Atlantic (*The Great Northern Railway*, 1958):

> *What a ride she gave us! With her rolling, and swaying, and much sharp 'tail wag' we had a high old time on the footplate; her 'tail wag' was transmitted to the tender. No coal pusher was needed on this engine! After each spell of fast running the footplate was ankle deep in Rossington 'hards'.*[1]

The generally excellent Egyptian Atlantics suffered a related problem:

> *The 4-4-2s swung a bit…you noticed the strain of getting 400+ tons moving by a sideward rocking. Exactly like the GWR 'Prairie' tank 2-6-2Ts…[which] 'wagged' their boilers getting away on inclines. The ESR weren't so much rough as rollers, but…you hung on to the cabside, or tender-brake (or something)…*[2]

The Netherlands State Railways Atlantics (Beyer, Peacock, 1900 – five engines) may have been among the worst offenders in spite of having inside cylinders which are often cited as a source of stability in that they reduce the tendency of a locomotive to 'hunt' from side to side when compared to outside cylinders. The Dutch Atlantics had to be soon demoted to slow passenger and freight working. The discomfort to the crew of working on a locomotive that swayed about at speed may have been mitigated slightly for the engineer on the American 'camelback' 4-4-2s who rode near the centre of the locomotive, not far from the point around which the mass was swaying. But even this perch had its discomforts; it was cramped, it could be simultaneously hot and cold and it offered minimal protection against flailing rods which, if they fractured, could pulp the engineer in a trice.

Dutch Atlantic: *originally No.995, here as No.2001 of class PO[2], one of the five Beyer, Peacock 4-4-2s built for the Netherlands State Railways in 1900; an example of the rare inside-cylinder sub-species of Atlantic. A large machine for its day, with 7ft driving wheels and Belpaire firebox, but too unsteady for express work from which it was soon demoted; nevertheless, later superheated.* Photo: H.R. Norman.

Many causes of this rough riding were cited, some approaching mutual contradiction. Also, different classes of Atlantic may have been rough riders for different reasons. Commonly found explanations have included the wheelbase being too long and rigid or, more usually, too short; rear axles mounted in pedestals giving insufficient play to trailing wheels, particularly the earlier, inside-bearing, variety; some bogie designs contributing to rigidity by having a limited self-centering capability; connecting rods which drove an axle too near the centre of mass of the loco-motive (the majority of Atlantics, particularly in America, drove the rear pair of driving wheels); unsteady tenders; too much rear overhang. Inferior track could amplify any of these problems.

The muster of smooth riding Atlantics was not inconsiderable and may throw some light on the problem. Europe's earliest Atlantics on the KFNB were reputedly good riders, as were most Austrian Atlantics – all of which had drive to the front axle. The KFNB machines also had outside bearings and some lateral play for the rear axle.

The Nord Atlantics were fabled easy riders and had the superior self-centering 'Alsatian' bogie adopted successfully by the GWR in the UK. They also had 4-cylinder drive, and there is enough evidence to suggest that 3- and 4-cylinder Atlantics with steadier torque and well-balanced motion were easier riders than their 2-cylinder sisters.

The 3-cylinder GCR Atlantics rode well, but the 2-cylinder GCR variety were notoriously rough with an excessive hammer-blow. One of them was selected for the *Bridge Stress Committee* tests of 1923 on the grounds that it would thump bridges good and hard. It was run over forty-six bridges located in many parts of England. Like other 2-cylinder Atlantics tested (GNR large Atlantic and an NBR class I, later C11) it imparted much more of a shock to structures than the altogether smoother-riding former NER class Z Atlantic, a 3-cylinder model.

The Atlantics of the NWR in India had their riding dramatically improved when their inside-bearing trailing axles were moved 1ft back and replaced by outside Skefco roller-bearing axleboxes; this was done in 1940, after thirty-three years of hard riding.

An even better way to improve riding qualities, employed mainly in the USA, was to mount the trailing wheels on an improved two-wheel trailer truck. An example of this is the Player truck used by Brooks Locomotive works on its 4-4-2s, or the of 'delta' form Kiesel truck and its derivatives used by the Pennsylvania after initial experiments on the mighty and generally good-riding E6s class of 4-4-2s of 1914.[3]

Radial rear trucks on Atlantics had a long history; after 1914 they were common on new machines and rebuilds. The largest and fastest of the final-phase Atlantics, the Milwaukee Road *Hiawathas* (from 1935) were given delta trailing trucks and had drive to the front axle. They were famously stable: anyone so interested could ride in their cabs and take notes standing or sitting comfortably at 100mph; smoother riding than that is hard to imagine.

Wheel Slip

The chief technical problem of the Atlantic form was, however, the tendency of the 4-4-2 to 'lose its feet' and slip, mainly on starting.

What was the point of so much speed and style if the locomotive could not get going in the first place? Thus, of the GNR 'large Atlantics' in their later, LNER days:

The big loads emphasized the poor starting characteristics of these engines (and of most

'Atlantics'), for with carrying wheels fore and aft the weight on the coupled wheels was an uncertain quantity and starting on an upgrade was a correspondingly uncertain operation. An Ivatt 'Atlantic', superheated and in good condition, having run from London on time with the 'West Riding Pullman' could occupy three minutes covering a quarter of a mile between a signal stop and Wakefield Westgate Station... (W.A. Tuplin, *British Steam Since 1900*. 1969).

As trains became heavier the problem grew until it was the main cause of the Atlantic's rapid replacement by its rivals, and consequent demotion to mundane duties, or to storage, or to the scrapyard.

An Atlantic with drive on only four of its ten supporting wheels is clearly more prone to traction loss when hauling a train of given weight than another locomotive where all the wheels are driven, such as an 0-6-0 or an 0-8-0. This is the 'factor of adhesion', (also adhesion, or adhesive factor). It is determined by dividing the tractive effort on the coupled wheels by the weight of the locomotive. On good, dry rails the maximum tractive effort of a 2-cylinder steam locomotive ought not to exceed one-quarter of the weight borne by the driving wheels; the limiting adhesion factor is about 4.3. A 3- or 4-cylinder locomotive with a more even steady torque on the driving axle, might manage with an adhesion factor of 3.5. Also, adhesion deteriorates quickly on greasy rails or in severe frost.

Working within these bounds a designer has *either* to hold back on tractive effort – not popular with operators who seek locomotives with strong pulling-power in order to shift heavy trains quickly – *or* to increase the weight bearing on the driving wheels, not popular with civil engineers who need to keep down the expense of ways and works, especially of bridges and track. They do not, therefore, welcome locomotives with great weight concentrated on their driving wheels, particularly when the effect of this weight is amplified by the effects of reciprocating motion, generally worse in 2-cylinder engines like most of the Atlantics.

Attempted Palliatives

Engineers tried to increase the factor of adhesion of the slippery Atlantics, or to live within its limitations, with varying degrees of success:

(i) There were traditional ploys like *sanding* the track to increase adhesion, and *starting gingerly*. Neither technique guaranteed a cure for slippage but both might reduce the chances of its occurring. It was certainly unwise to open up an Atlantic throttle hard and sharp on starting:

I have often thought how completely misleading was the caption [of a painting depicting an L&Y 4-4-2 departing from Poulton-le-Fylde]...'Sound and fury: No.1419 storming away....' No driver with anything of a load would attempt to 'storm away' from a station stop. (O.S. Nock, *British Locomotives of the Twentieth Century* on the frontispiece of Eric Mason's 'otherwise admirable' *The Lancashire & Yorkshire Railway in the Twentieth Century*).

The secret of starting an Atlantic was a soft touch on the regulator. Many drivers were well aware of this; some raised it to a high art like Alf Aylwin who, in getting LB&SCR Atlantic

Highflier: *Lancashire & Yorkshire No. 1405 of the first batch of 1400 class Atlantics leaving York on a Manchester express, early XX century. The stark presentation of these engines concealed some technical devices of note: Joy's valve gear; steam driers and the largest wheels of any Atlantic at any time: 7ft 3in diameter.* Photo: H Gordon Tidey.

No.421 under way, was wont to 'creep away with only a breath of steam' from the Brighton terminus. To the group of spectators – the public, and fellow locomotive men who gathered to witness the ghostly departure, Aylwin would point towards No.421's chimney and, cupping his ear, call out: 'Can't hear her, you can't hear her.' How did he do it? At least one of his colleagues theorised that, since Aylwin only had thirteen minutes to reach Keymer tunnel, he must surely have opened out once out of sight of the Brighton station platforms. However, no one heard the resulting pyrotechnics, and the smokebox of No.421 was singularly free of char, a sign that it been driven with a gentle hand.[4]

There was an interesting variation on this technique: *setting back* (American: *bunching the slack*). By reversing the locomotive very slowly and slightly a driver could squeeze the carriage couplings of the train in such a way that on restarting, the locomotive took up the slack, carriage by carriage and therefore started the train *seriatim*, not all at once. The buffer springs, where used, aided this movement slightly. In the USA the looser central couplings of the carriages meant that this move, an Atlantic engineer's favourite, could jolt passengers noticeably. So common was the practice amongst the drivers of Ivatt large Atlantics that it had its own word: *poling*, from the technique of heaving back the long reversing lever (the 'pole' in GN usage) into reverse gear by way of setting the engine back on its train. With a heavy train, or on a difficult day, the process might have to be repeated more than once.

A famed race of virtuoso drivers, the *mecaniciens* of the Nord in France also made clean, quiet departures with their superb de Glehns, aided by the characteristics of 4–cylinder compounds which gave good, even torque on starting and, like Aylwin's Atlantic, were generally soft-spoken as they got under way. The drivers' skill was all the greater since a de Glehn, working with simple expansion on all four cylinders (a starting arrangement available to drivers), had a tractive effort that might rise to a massive 45,000lb. This could result in severe bouts of slipping unless controlled with great insight and experience[5]. Seasoned Atlantic drivers the world over knew that 'gently does it' was the secret of getting an Atlantic under way:

> *The ESR [Egyptian State Railways] were mostly level...and always had a dry rail...drivers coddled the Kings [ESR Atlantics], always starting away gently to avoid slipping with four driving wheels...*[6]

But even accumulated skill and experience could not disguise the fact that ultimately, as trains grew heavier the problem grew worse.

(ii) *Increasing the weight bearing on the driving wheels*: this solution was strictly curtailed by the weight limits set by civil engineers. Because the Pennsylvania had high track standards, the E6s Atlantics (1914) could bear 133,300 lbs (59 tons) on the drivers, in practice 64,500 lbs (nearly 29 tons) on the front driving axle, and 68,800 lbs (over 30 tons) on the rear one, an adhesion factor of 4.86. The E6s were famously 'adhesive', but this kind of solution was only available to railways able to command great resources. The British had to work within a maximum axleload of 18-20 tons; the Austrians 14 tons. Another possibility was to increase the weight on the driving wheels temporarily as the locomotive started, then to redistribute it so that the driving axle weights were lighter on the open road. This was the so-called *traction increaser* tried initially on the NYC, later on the Santa Fe and the St Lawrence & Adirondack, on ten and two Atlantics respectively. But the device added to the complications of design and maintenance and was a blind alley. Attempts to increase the weight bearing on the drivers sooner or later generated further problems such as risking bent crankpins, or sluggish performance.

(iii) Adding *temporary, extra driving wheels*: an even more complicated solution which clashed with the engineers' dictum that 'if it looks right it is right.' It came in two forms. A Bavarian 4-2-2 (Krauss, 1895) was equipped with a temporary, spring-loaded, driven axle to be raised or lowered between the bogie and main driving wheels, thereby becoming a 4-2-2-2, a courtesy Atlantic with double the effective weight available for adhesion (15 tons raised to 30 tons). On the Palatinate Railways an unorthodox Atlantic (Krauss, 1900) was given a powered axle between the free-running bogie wheels which increased adhesion by 47%, or so it was claimed. These temporary axles were not merely lowered, but actually 'pressed' on to the rails.[7]

(iv) Another 'temporary driving axle' plan was the *booster*, the powered trailing axle, first used by the NYC on an Atlantic in 1919. In the UK the LNER experimented with boosters on Atlantics, starting in the first year of its existence (1923) when its new Chief Mechanical Engineer, H.N. Gresley, had a Franklin booster from the USA fitted to former GNR Atlantic No.1419. The booster had two 10x12in cylinders and drove the trailing axle through spur gearing. It operated at low speeds only, adding a further 8,500lb to the

Atlantic with booster: *LNER class C9 No.727 (originally NER class Z, NBL, 1911) one of two 3-cylinder Atlantics of class C7 so converted in 1931. The Stone booster articulated the locomotive to the tender. It could assist starting, or cut in at 25mph with occasionally spectacular results, but too late in the day to save the Atlantic project.*

starting tractive effort – but at a cost of nearly five tons extra weight. With the booster the engine could cope well with an 18-coach train climbing up the stiff gradients from King's Cross terminus to London's Northern Heights. Bob Howe noted, however, (*British Railway Journal* No.57, 1995) that extended use of this device strained even a free-steaming Atlantic boiler. The booster, like the main engine could slip on occasion, particularly if steam were applied too hard, and the rough riding problem endemic with Ivatt Atlantics was aggravated. The booster was removed in 1934.

Gresley tried again with two former NER class Z Atlantics, Nos 727 and 2171, which were smoother-riding than the Ivatt 4-4-2s. He proposed to mount the rear of the locomotive on an articulated, booster-driven truck linking the engine to the tender. Was the result an Atlantic or a 4-4-2-2, or what? Another fine point for taxonomists. The transformation added nearly 6,000lb of tractive effort. The transformed Atlantics could start 746-ton trains on the level, compared with 496 tons without the booster. They worked on normal duties between York and Edinburgh, but the expensive boosters did not add commensurate sparkle to their performance and were removed 1936-1937; the locomotives were scrapped five years later.

The booster'd Atlantic was more successful in the USA. The best-known user, the Southern Pacific, converted four Atlantics (Sacramento and Los Angeles shops, two each 1927-1928) later putting them to work on short-run offshoots from prestigious long-distance trains. The *Sacramento Daylight* and *San Joaquin Daylight* were drawn by booster Atlantics.

(v) Another technique was simply to add more Atlantics to a train, *double-heading*. The Pennsylvania was a heavy user of this uneconomic approach; it would even triple-head passenger trains, for example using three E3a Atlantics to take the *Pennsylvania Limited* up and round the 1.4% grade of the Horse Shoe Curve (Altoona-Gallitzin, a rise of 1,000ft in just over 11.5 miles). Double-heading with Atlantics was occasionally employed in the UK, particularly by the LNER. In Egypt with railways at full stretch during the Second World War, an Atlantic might be coupled to a venerable double-framed 0-6-0 but, at the insistence of its crew as the leading engine since Atlantic prestige was at stake. Double-heading was an impressive sight but sooner or later the obvious question would arise: why not construct one powerful locomotive able to do the job?

(vi) The '*more powerful locomotive*' might be a more puissant Atlantic. Every 'improved' Atlantic class was of this kind; thus the GNR large Atlantics were an improvement on the 'Klondykes'; each fresh Pennsylvania Atlantic class was an advance on its predecessors; the E3 on the E2, and so on. The Prussian S9s were stronger than the S7s; the Paris-Orleans de Glehns on the converted Fourquenot 2-4-2s.

But even the Pennsylvania's eighty E6s engines, constructed in 1914 after some five years of planning and evaluation to produce the supreme 'classic' Atlantic could only buy time for the Atlantic form. In spite of their success the Pennsylvania was to run five times as many K4 Pacifics (425 locomotives) as its E6s Atlantics. Other strong supporters of the Atlantic in the USA, the Santa Fe and the NYC abandoned the type quickly once the superiority of 4-6-0s and Pacifics was clear. The NYC ordered no more 4-4-2s after 1907; already an operator of Pacifics it started an order that same year for 152 more from Schenectady and was soon acquiring them in squadrons.

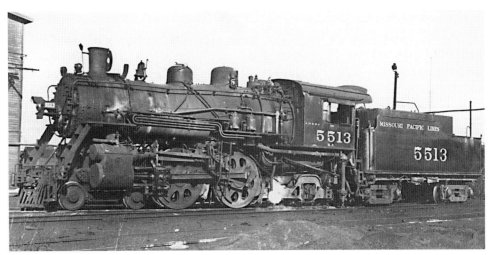

Modernised: *Missouri Pacific No.5513 of class A-79 (Alco Brooks, 1907) once bearing inboard valves and Stephenson gear, now sporting outside valves and gear, disc drivers, cast steel delta truck with booster, exhaust of which pokes up between stack and bell; original 6ft 7in drivers reduced to 6ft 1in for fast freight work in the flatlands; Van Buren, Ark, January 1946.* Photo: Harold K. Vollrath.

(vii) One way of upgrading the Atlantic in the face of this competition was 'if you can't beat them, join them', convert a 4-4-2 to a 4-6-0 thereby increasing its adhesion. There were some successful conversions of this kind. The Egyptian State Railways even ordered a special 'convert-ible' Atlantic from Brooks, deliberately designed for easy transformation to a 4-6-0 should the 4-4-2 type be found wanting. In the 1930s the ESR carried out some 4-4-2/4-6-0 conversions but with mixed results. The Santa Fe altered ten Atlantics to 4-6-0s in 1904; in Austria the State Railways similarly converted some of the KFNB Atlantics in 1913. The Swedes changed a few of the mettlesome class A Atlantics into handsome 4-6-0s in the 1920s and 1930s; the Paris-Orleans planned to convert all its de Glehn Atlantics into 4-6-0s in the 1920s, but did not proceed owing to electrification plans. An unusual Atlantic conversion took place in Denmark where eight Danish class-P Atlantics metamorphosed into 4-6-2s, a drastic change which required boilers to be lengthened by a ring resulting in a rather crowded-looking but successful Pacific. The Buenos Ayres & Pacific 4-4-2s were similarly converted after only seven to nine years.

In the UK the GWR carried out a series of famous conversions, of a 4-6-0 *into* an Atlantic, and of just over a dozen Atlantics into 4-6-0s, but this was a part of G.J. Churchward's comparative evaluation of 4-4-2s and 4-6-0s rather than an example of any latter-day disillu-sionment with the 4-4-2 type. The typical 4-4-2/4-6-0 conversion was applied to existing machines, a trading-in of Atlantic sprightliness for the surer-footed qualities of the 4-6-0. In the long run, building new ten-wheelers was found to be a better policy, and that is what took place.

(viii) A less successful development of the 4-4-2 was to add to its power by converting it to, or building from scratch a 4-4-4, in effect an Atlantic raised to a higher power. A de Glehn Atlantic of the Nord was amplified in this way, and further examples appeared in Germany, Canada and the USA.[8]

(ix) *Improving starting torque*: the three- and four-cylinder Atlantics had a more steady torque, particularly on starting. Herein lay part of the success of the 4-cylinder de Glehn Atlantics, the 3-cylinder NER class Zs or the Prussian Atlantics which were 4-cylinder compounds, as well as that rarest of birds, the four-cylinder simple Atlantics.[9] But multiplying cylinders (or adopting compound expansion) to obtain a more steady turning moment than was possible with a simple 2-cylinder machine only diminished the risk of traction loss, it was no guarantee against it. It also added to complications, original cost and maintenance charges. The GWR drivers, unfamiliar with the huge tractive effort which might be exerted by de Glehn compound 4-4-2s on starting, could cause 'massive slippage'[10] on occasion. When one of the excellent 4-cylinder compound 4-4-2s of the NER (class 4CC) was being tried out on the NBR in 1908, an attempt to start it out of Hawick on a drizzly day caused it 'to slip extremely violently and sheer both outside crank pins.'[11]

There were palliatives but no enduring or economic cures for the Atlantics' lack of adhesion. The large capacity of their fireboxes raised possibilities which were vitiated by their being light of foot, the very quality which made them attractively swift when once they got under way. This was the Atlantic conundrum, inescapable physics, and no engineer found a satisfactory solution to it.

Notes to Chapter 5

1. *Hards* were coals much favoured by British locomotive men; *Rossington* – a famed Yorkshire colliery, not far from Doncaster the birthplace of the GNR Atlantics. For fuller details on coal classification, see Stopes classification of bituminous coals.

2. Private communication from Mr Bert Dyke.

3. For a detailed history of the rear truck, especially in the USA, see Alfred W. Bruce: *The Steam Locomotive in America*, 1952; also P. Ransome-Wallis (ed): *The Concise Encyclopaedia of World Railway Locomotives*, 1959; for the woes of Atlantics, wheel slip in particular, and proffered cures, see W. Reuter and C. Bock: *Eleganz auf Schienen*, 1982.

4. See F. Rich, *Yesterday Once More, A Story of Brighton Steam* (1996).

5. See M. Rutherford *Great Western 4-6-0's At Work* (1995), embodying *Halls, Granges and Manors at Work* (1985) – the de Glehn 4-4-2s could be mettlesome starters in the hands of GWR drivers used to working single-expansion Atlantics of lower tractive effort.

6. Bert Dyke, see Note 2.

7. Ernest F. Carter *Unusual Locomotives* (1960), and Franz P. Flury, *Dampflokomotiven und ihre Bauteile* (1976).

8. Almost curiosities; Prussian 3-cylinder compounds with all-enclosed bodies, front-cab drive, and a return crank on one outside cylinder (like G. Stephenson's *Locomotion*) referred to as the *Möbelwagen* (furniture van). In the USA there was a rough-riding 4-4-4 for the Philadelphia & Reading (1915) later converted to an Atlantic, and a Baltimore & Ohio locomotive with a high-pressure water-tube boiler (1935). Most of these locomotives of well-balanced appearance suffered advanced Atlanticitis, although there was one rather more successful specimen, the Canadian Pacific *Jubilee* class (1936) which ran for many years, 'modern locomotives... but in an understated, typically Canadian manner', Gordon E. Lloyd 'Homage to a Jubilee', *Classic Trains*, Fall 2000.

9. There were very few of this Atlantic sub-species: the GWR *North Star*; two on the British GNR; two on the Chicago, Rock Island & Pacific, and the Tasmanian double-Atlantic which had two sets of four cylinders.

10. M. Rutherford, *op cit*.

11. P. Atkins, '*The Four-Cylinder Compound Atlantics of the North Eastern Railway*', *Back Track* Vol 11, 8, August 1997.

Chapter 6
Atlantic Afternoon

The First World War affected the distribution and ownership of Atlantics. The Atlantic as a design was in terminal decline before 1914, ironically the year in which it first demonstrated its remarkable capacity to be 'born again'.

The 'Apex of the Atlantics' – Pennsylvania Class E6s

Although the flaws of the 4-4-2 were well known, so dramatic had been its effects on train speeds and technical development that some engineers searched for solutions other than adopting 4-6-0s or Pacifics outright.

One such engineer was Alfred W. Gibbs (1856-1922), General Superintendent of Motive Power of the Pennsylvania's 'Lines East', 1903-1911, and the road's first and only Chief Mechanical Engineer, 1911-1922. Like G.J. Churchward, of the UK's GWR, he had a receptive mind. He liked to chat *incognito* to engine crews at stations where he 'asked their opinion of his engines, listened carefully to any criticism, and enjoyed more frequently voiced praise.'[1]

Gibbs was not an uncritical Atlanticist; his wide range of designs included electric loco-motives, 4-6-2s and a heavy 2-8-0 freight engine. He concluded after a close study than a super-Atlantic was better suited to the easier grades prevailing on the Eastern segment of the Pennsylvania, the 'Lines East'[2] than a 4-6-2. His case was sound: the Atlantic was a locomo-

The Big E: *Pennsylvania class E6s No.1397 (Altoona, 1914) rushing the ten steel cars of the* Manhattan Limited *at 70 mph, August 1914 – last month of the old era; engineer, Oliver P. Keller.* Photo: Frederick Westing, *Apex of the Atlantics.*

tive of proven sprightliness, less expensive to build and maintain than a Pacific; Gibbs' predecessor as Pennsylvania's motive power chief, Theodore N. Ely put it succinctly: 'We think that every pair of drivers adds complications of machinery and friction.

Gibbs envisaged an Atlantic capable of starting and hauling fast trains of heavy steel coaches with ease. But what of 'Atlanticitis'? The Pennsylvania had excellent track, roadbed and bridge structures which permitted high axleloads. On the E6s Atlantics which resulted from Gibbs' calculations and designs, this ran to 30 tons, the highest on any Atlantic to date. Before embarking on series production of the proposed super-Atlantic, Gibbs had a prototype constructed, tried out on the road as well as the test plant at Altoona; that which had once graced the St Louis World's Fair, 1904. This engine, No.5075 was designated class E6 (the 's' was added in later years to denote 'superheated'; 5075 in its original form used saturated steam). After extensive tests and further prototype construction the E6s went into full production, April–August, 1914.

The Pennsylvania super-Atlantic embodied many recent improvements as well as tried-and-true arrangements. Its huge boiler, based on that of the class H8 2-8-0, had a Belpaire firebox which was not common in the USA, although popular with the Pennsylvania. Gibbs had been early in adopting the precise, accessible and relatively light Walschaerts valve-gear; largely through his advocacy, 352 of the E3d Atlantics on Lines East, and 55 on Lines West were already so equipped and the E6s class now used it. The firebox rested on a 'KW' patent truck based on the Kiesel delta-truck but with a frame cast as a single item of great strength. These improvements were there for all to see; others like the 'Goodfellow nozzle' (a blastpipe orifice named after the Altoona test plant foreman) were concealed. The sum total of these devices was a locomotive well able to 'boil water' in large amounts. The E6s No.51 evaporated 44,628 lbs of water per hour when on test; one hp per 2lb of 'dry Westmoreland County bituminous coal'; 1,200hp from each pair of driving wheels – *indicated* hp in each instance. For the record, an E6s had 23.5x26in cylinders; 6ft 10in driving wheels; a grate area of 55.19sq.ft; and a weight of nearly 109 tons (see Appendix 3 for comparative tables). The E6s was a heavy-weight which could crowd on the steam like no other Atlantic, and few other engines of its day.

It was soon apparent that this Atlantic, 'a product of the test plant' according to the British journal, *Engineering* (1914) was a record-breaker, well able to compete with Pacifics. A high factor of adhesion permitted the E6s Atlantics to pull hard at low speeds without fear of slipping; further tests demonstrated that they could walk along slowly with large trains when necessary: at 14mph and in full gear (82% cut-off) they exerted a drawbar pull of 30,917lbs. At speeds in excess of 50mph their drawbar pull exceeded that of the experimental and potent K29s Pacific.

The E6s class were quickly and successfully at work on crack expresses such as the *Congressional Limited*, and the *Broadway Limited*. When the effects of the Great War began to be felt and there were passengers standing in the aisles of 12 and 14 car trains, the super-Atlantics took it all in their stride. They were popular with the public, and a source of wonder to those who closely observed trains, like the young Frederick Westing:

> *I could never see enough of them...fresh from Altoona...with their shining jackets of Brunswick green...they'd come East with a heavy train behind them with machine-gun like exhausts...Westbound they were equally impressive as they worked a train up to speed with a staccato accompaniment of sharp exhausts. Especially was this so in the dark night when the open firedoor threw a reddish glow wide and skyward.*[3]

When the E6s Atlantics appeared on the original Atlantic racing ground, the Atlantic City run, the rival Philadelphia & Reading became seriously worried. They rushed, unwisely as it turned out, into producing a quick answer to the E6s challenge in the form of an extended Atlantic, a 4-4-4. Four were built hurriedly in 1915; they soon manifested chronic Atlanticitis, particularly in their bad riding at high speed. All were converted equally quickly into Atlantics a year later and given Hodges' patent two-wheel trailing trucks to steady their passage on the permanent way.

The E6s did, not, however signal a serious, sustained rebirth of the Atlantic. Their success may have delayed the Pennsylvania's development of its logical successor, the K4 Pacific[4] but it could not delay it indefinitely. The K4 embodied many E6s features, its greater adhesion and mechanical stoker gave it great advantages over a hand-fired 4-4-2. The K4s had also appeared in 1914, although it did not go into series production until 1917. The E6s class continued to perform well for many years, but they were gradually demoted to lighter duties. For all their excellence they could not start and run the 1,200 ton train of the 1920s and 1930s with the sure-footed competence of a K4.

Reparations

The last E6s emerged from Altoona just as the Great War broke out in Europe. In the aftermath many of the European Atlantics were caught up in the confusion of post-war settlements, treaties, boundary shifts and sundry discontinuities. Boundary changes in the former Austro-Hungarian Empire resulted typically in a stud of Atlantics remaining where it had previously operated, but within the railway network of a new state. Thus fifteen of the KFNB Atlantics, Europe's original class of 4-4-2s, were taken over by the Czechoslovak State Railways (CSD), as were the eight Atlantics of the Austrian North-Western, the ÖNWB. Four of these were already based in Czechoslovakia; the balance were sent up from Vienna where they had become surplus to the requirements of the new and truncated Republic of Austria.

Poland also inherited a further ten KFNB Atlantics, and ten more virtually identical ones from the former Russian line, the Warsaw-Vienna Railway, which now ran in Polish territory – all twenty were treated as one class, numbered in continuous series.

The Polish State Railways (PKP) also inherited a solitary Austrian 4-cylinder compound Gölsdorf Atlantic, Austrian class 108[5] The remaining twenty-four of this fine class went to Czechoslovakia, suitably so in that eleven of them were products of excellent Czech workmanship having been built in Bohemia, 1905-1910.

The most curious post-Versailles[6] Atlantic locomotive settlement was the strange story of the Transylvanian Atlantics. The Romanian state railways (CFR) took over seven Hungarian Atlantics, one Austrian '108' and a lone Prussian S9 (Altona No.909). The ways in which these locomotives were acquired are indicative of the chaos prevailing in Eastern Europe at the time. The Hungarian locomotives were operating in Transylvania, fomerly part of the kingdom of Hungary. The Austrian engine, operating on the *Carl Ludwig Bahn* in Galicia was 'liberated' by Romanian troops passing through Rezszow; the Prussian Atlantic, brought in the wake of a German army of occupation, and put to work by the *Militar-General-Direktionsbezirk Bukarest* was abandoned when the troops left.[7]

Although most of these re-allocated Atlantics continued to serve the lines to which they had been designated in the days of Austria-Hungary, under the terms of the Versailles settlement Germany had to make 'reparations' to the allied victors of the Great War. France and Belgium were awarded railway rolling stock amongst other materials. This involved large numbers of locomotives including Atlantics, following a stocktaking survey by the 'Armistice Locomotive Committee.' Belgium received seventeen of the Prussian S9s; in France the Est got ten S7s and four S9s; the Etat received ten of the Baden 4-cylinder compounds and the Alsace-Lorraine railways one old Prussian S7. Ironically no Atlantics had been operated by the 'Elsass-Lothringen' railways when they were part of the German Empire. These allocations were a small part of the total – the Est received some 140 Prussian 0-8-0s, for example; altogether France received 2,095 German locomotives; the Atlantics were but a drop in this ocean, just over 1%.

Scrapping Begins: the Great Atlantic Purge

The Germans may not have been too sorry to let the Atlantics go in the postwar settlements. In his *Compound Locomotives*, John van Riemsdijk writes of the Prussian S9's that 'they were, for the most part, cunningly off-loaded onto Belgium and France as reparations after 1918.' The Germans, fully aware of the Atlantics' limited potential with an adhesion weight of only 33 tons out of nearly 75 tons total engine weight, had ceased developing the 4-4-2 after 1910. Those Atlantics which had not been off-loaded as reparations were classified in the '14' series of locomotives by the new state railway system in 1924, but twenty-seven of the S9s had been withdrawn by then, and the rest were scrapped shortly thereafter. The Baden 4-4-2s went in 1925; the Saxon ones 1925-29; the Bavarian Atlantics 1925-1927 – the two Baldwin pioneers had already been withdrawn in 1923.

Prussians (I): *one of the S7 varieties, No. 708 a de Glehn 4-cylinder compound at Strassburg (then) in December 1912.* Photo: Kelland Collection, BRC.

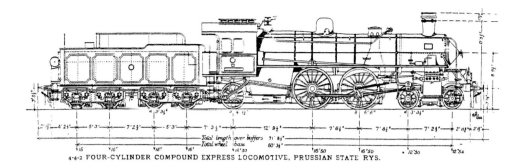

4-4-2 FOUR-CYLINDER COMPOUND EXPRESS LOCOMOTIVE, PRUSSIAN STATE RYS.

Prussians (II): *elevation of KPEV S9 4-cylinder compound; 99 locomotives built by Hanomag, 1908-1911, grate area nearly 43sq.ft and Pintsch gas lighting. Most S9s used piston valves, this model had the Lentz variety.*

This was the earliest mass-elimination of Atlantics, although not the first of all. In Sweden, the problem-strewn twins of the Malmö-Ystad Railway had been scrapped in 1915 after a life of only eight years. Canadian railways flirted but briefly with the Atlantic concept and withdrew their few Atlantics from 1917. The pattern was more complex in the USA where the ownership of 4-4-2s was divided between nearly seventy railroads. Some lines rebuilt or improved Atlantics, squeezing a few more years' useful life out of them. Others were more ruthless and junked them, sometimes because they preferred to invest in more modern stock, sometimes because dwindling traffic did not justify their retention, particularly during the Depression.

Circumstances brought about different policies on the same road depending on such variables as the size of particular classes, mileage logged up, potential for improvement, and traffic patterns. The Chicago & North Western used about half its ninety-one Atlantics for many years as commuter-haulers in the Chicago area. They were withdrawn gradually, 1936-1954, but there were still ten of these Schenectady pioneers (built 1901-1908) steaming in 1952, representing a good return on capital invested. The Milwaukee Road, not having the C&NW's homogeneity of a single class of Atlantic, weeded out superannuated locomotives class-by-class; with three or four exceptions its entire stock of seventy Atlantics was withdrawn by 1931. If the Milwaukee Road seemed to have written off the Atlantic project altogether this was not so; a world-class surprise lurked just around the corner.

Other large Atlantic users began writing off their stocks. The Pennsylvania started in 1924; three classes were extinct by 1940, although some of the E6s super-Atlantics lasted until 1953. Withdrawal often took place over a long period because some Atlantics found niches for which they were well suited, particularly after rebuilding or improvements had enhanced their performance. The Santa Fe Atlantics faded away 1925-1953, two of the smaller classes went in quick succession, the 256 class (Baldwin, 1903) of four in 1925-1927, and the 1550 class (Baldwin, 1905-1906) of twelve engines in 1925-1930.

A few Atlantics made way for electrification. This was the final fate of the Paris-Orleans Fourquenot rebuilds during the 1920s; the electrification on Britain's Southern Railway displaced the Brighton Atlantics down the pecking-order although they still kept their

BALDWIN LOCOMOTIVE WORKS

Balanced Compound Atlantic Type Locomotive, 1904

Class 10-24-44¼-C-102 — Code Word, RECOSIAMOS — Road No. 507

GENERAL DIMENSIONS

GAUGE . . . . 4′ 8½″
CYLINDERS . . 15″ and 25″ x 26″
Valve . . . Balanced Piston
BOILER—Type . . Wagon Top
Material . . . Steel
Diameter . . . . . 66″
Thickness of Sheets, 11/16″ and 13/16″
Working Pressure . . 220 lbs.
Fuel . . . . . Coal
Staying . . . . . Radial
FIREBOX—Material . . Steel
Length . . . . 107 15/16″
Width . . . . . . 66″
Depth . front, 75⅞″; back, 67⅜″
Thickness of Sheets, . sides, ⅜″
back, ⅜″; crown, ⅜″; tube, 9/16″
Water Space,
front, 4½″; sides, 5″; back, 4″

TUBES—Material . . . . Iron
Wire Gauge . . . No. 11
Number, 273 . Diameter, 2¼″
Length . . . . 18′ 10″
HEATING SURFACE—Firebox, 190.0 sq.ft.
Tubes . . . 3015.0 sq.ft.
Firebrick Tubes . . 10.0 sq.ft.
Total . . . 3215.0 sq.ft.
Grate Area . . 49.5 sq.ft.
DRIVING WHEELS—Diam. Outside 79″
Diameter of Center . . 72″
Journals . front, 10″ x 10½″
back, 9″ x 12″
ENGINE TRUCK WHEELS—
Diameter . . . 34¼″
Journals . . . 6″ x 10″
TRAILING WHEELS—Diameter . 50″
Journals . . . 8″ x 12″

WHEEL BASE—Driving . . 6′ 10″
Rigid . . . . . 15′ 9″
Total Engine . . . 30′ 3″
Total Engine and Tender, 59′ 6½″
WEIGHT—On Driving Wheels, 101,420 lbs.
On Truck, front . . 46,920 lbs.
Trailing Wheels . 45,420 lbs.
Total Engine . . 193,760 lbs.
Total Engine and Tender
about . . 358,000 lbs.
TENDER—Number of Wheels . 8
Diameter of Wheels . . 34¼″
Journals . . . 5½″ x 10″
TANK—Capacity . Water, 8500 gals.
SERVICE—Passenger.
Radius of curves, 16 degrees.

Evolution on the Santa Fe (Above): *from a Baldwin Catalogue No.507 of 1904 (head engine of class 507) a typical AT&SF 4-cylinder balanced compound with drive to front axle and consequent long, rangy appearance; class withdrawn 1925-1943.* (Below): *a rebuilt 4-cylinder compound 'Bull Moose' No.1483, now a 2-cylinder simple with rear coupled wheel drive and cross-compound air pumps, Kansas City, Kansas, November 1938.* Photo: J.R. Quinn.

Light engine, poignant: an L&Y '1400' in its latter days as LMS No.10310; the disproportionaly small trailing wheels more obvious from this angle. To the unsentimental categorisers of the LMS these engines were classed as 2P, fairly low in the power stakes, but the big-wheeled elegance remained to the end. Photo: Stephenson Locomotive Society.

Newhaven boat-train duties for many years. In India the electrification of the GIPR Ghat lines had a similar domino effect; its Atlantics migrated to the North Western Railway. The last Belgian Atlantics, the last to built anywhere, were displaced by electrification.

In the USA the majority of Atlantics lasted for about thirty years, some like the E6s attained nearly forty years. Some lines were more ruthless; most of the Union Pacific Atlantics survived about twenty years; some of the Southern Pacific 4-4-2s only a dozen years – although others lived much longer, particularly if rebuilt. A middle-of-road record might be offered by the Baltimore & Ohio whose Atlantics lasted about thirty-five years, or the Wabash, also about thirty years. The more thorough the rebuilding, the longer the Atlantic life span. The CB&Q, for example, rebuilt its P2 class (Rogers, 1902-1903) in 1915-1917 and some lasted, in the guise of a new class P5, until the late 1940s.

Generally, 4-6-0s lasted longer but thirty years on average was a fairly typical lifespan for a passenger locomotive, a figure which held good in Europe also. The 'Hitchin Case', a legal contest and Court ruling of 1906, suggested 30.4 years for a steam locomotive's 'reasonable' working life, although fast-moving passenger engines expected shorter lives than slower freight locomotives. The LMS, for example, estimated thirty years' lifespan for an express passenger locomotive, fifty years for a non-superheated goods or shunting locomotive.

In the UK the LMS itself withdrew the Aspinall L&Y Atlantics 1926-1933; they were no part of its motive power policies. On the other hand, the penurious LNER, the largest owner of British Atlantics, husbanded its capital stock carefully and gave the historic 4-4-2s a longer lease of life than might have been the case with a more prosperous concern. The largest of its stocks, the Ivatt large Atlantics inherited from the GNR, lived out the inter-war period successfully; most were still in steam in 1945. The last did not retire until two years after nationalisation (1948) as British Railways No.62822.

This retirement was marked by running a fully-booked special excursion on 26 November 1950. Ivatt's son, himself an eminent engineer, attended the occasion with sundry other VIPs including R.A. Riddles who was effectively Ivatt's latter-day equivalent on British Railways. The driver, J.C.B. Burgess (fireman: C.E.H. Fox) was handed a message by the stationmaster at King's Cross for his opposite number at Doncaster:

> They [GNR Atlantics] helped to make the East Coast route justly famous and no doubt that tradition will go on in yet further brilliant pages of our railway history.[8]

Which, against the odds, it did.

The LNER retired the North British Atlantics in the late 1930s, but most of the NER 4-4-2s soldiered on until after the Second World War, some to 1948 as did the majority of Great Central 4-4-2s which it also inherited; one or two of these made it to 1950.

The collapse of the Atlantic empire 1925-1940 came about partly because the railway administrators of Germany, Europe's largest employer of Atlantics, decided their day was over, but mainly because the principal Atlantic homeland, the US railroads, wrote off so many 4-4-2s. But before the end there was a stirring tale of a brief and brilliant renaissance.

Notes to Chapter 6

1. Frederick Westing, *Apex of the Atlantics* (1963).

2. The Pennsylvania was divided into two sections; the hillier 'Lines West' (ie, of Pittsburgh) had their own Motive Power Department, something of a satrapy headed by David W. Crawford who favoured the 4-6-2. The two segments of the Pennsylvania even adorned their locomotives differently: 'Pennsylvania' on the tenders of Lines East engines; 'Pennsylvania Lines' on those of Lines West.

3. Frederick Westing, *op cit*.

4. See Brian Reed, *The Pennsylvania Pacifics*, 'Loco Profile 14', 1971.

5. Or did they? In *The Steam Locomotives of Czechoslovakia*, 1995, Paul Catchpole lists this Atlantic as former Austrian 108.14. But this is also the engine stated [see Note 7 below] by Gottfried Wild to be the Austrian 4-4-2 taken over by Romania. Another mystery for railway history-detectives.

6. The term is a generic convenience; the Eastern European treaties and settlements were numerous.

7. See Gottfried Wild: 'Atlantics and Pacifics in Romania', *Locomotives International*, Vol 7, 33, June 1996.

8. 'The Last Ivatt Atlantic', *Railway Magazine*, January 1951.

Chapter 7
Renaissance & Fading Away

Improvements

Between the world wars, despite the general decline in the numbers and status of Atlantics, there were two major developments: the improvement of existing stock, and two last, remarkable additions to the Atlantic family.

Superheaters

> Forney's *Catechism of the Locomotive*:
>
> Question 379: *What is the advantage of using superheated steam in a locomotive?*
>
> *Answer.* By avoiding cylinder condensation...the loss of heat is prevented, and a saving of steam consumption is effected. [1]

To Brian Reed, the practically-experienced historian of the steam locomotive, the superheater was 'quite probably the greatest single advance in steam locomotive practice since variable expansion of steam was introduced in 1843-1844.'[2] Although the concept of superheating steam had long been known, the Schmidt superheater of 1897 is usually accepted as the first practical device of the modern type.

One early variety, the Aspinall smokebox superheater, was tried out on an L&Y Atlantic, No.737 in 1899. Thereafter, introduction of the superheater on Atlantics and many other locomotive types was generally haphazard, not assisted by a long and earnest debate amongst engineers as to what advantage to take of its properties: whether to increase cylinder power, or to obtain the same power as before but with a lower boiler pressure, and hence reduced maintenance costs. Ivatt on the GNR opted for the second alternative, and rather late in the day at that. The last ten of his large Atlantics, built in 1910, were fitted out with 18-element Schmidt superheaters, and their boiler pressure cut from 175lb sq.in to 150lb sq.in. Performance improved, but not so much as when Ivatt's successor H.N. Gresley (who took the alternative, high boiler-pressure line on superheaters) installed 24-element superheaters and raised pressure to 170lb sq.in. Eventually all the GN Atlantics were given generous and highly effective 32-element Robinson superheaters thereby demonstrating the full potential that lay locked within these engines.

By 1932 the LNER had sufficient confidence in the superheated Ivatt Atlantics to cut ten minutes off the London-Leeds section of the Atlantic-hauled *Queen of Scots*, a Pullman express. In 1935, Cecil J. Allen reminisced about the irruption of the new, superheated Atlantic on the transport scene:

> *Of all my Great Northern journeys, I cannot help thinking that pride of place belongs to the extra-ordinary run tabulated when Ivatt Atlantic No.1452 – the first superheated Atlantic to run on Great Northern metals – was attached at Doncaster to a 58-axle train…Most remarkable of his [Driver Codd's] work was starting out of Retford and Grantham, attaining 40.5mph…and 38mph up 1 in 200 grades…but even more phenomenal, perhaps, was the minimum of 45mph at Stevenage…[3]*

One year later Cecil J. Allen happened to be on an East Coast express hauled by a 4-6-2, which failed at Grantham. A venerable but superheated Atlantic was attached and off they went like a rocket. More than once Allen had to look out of the window to be sure that he was being hauled by a 4-4-2 which actually gained time with a train of 585 tons. Later in the same year, the sprightly Edwardian locomotive responsible for this feat (LNER No.4452, Doncaster, August 1910) brought the crack *Silver Jubilee* from Doncaster to London, King's Cross, 156 miles in 139 minutes.

This impressive transformation was replicated elsewhere. Slightly fewer than 400 Atlantics had superheaters installed when new; a further 1,323 locomotives had them added later in life.[4] Aspinall's Atlantics had only modest superheaters, or rather 'steam-dryers' which became effective in saving about 3.5lb coal per mile after the engine had been worked hard for fifteen or so minutes. The earliest Atlantics to be built with integral smokebox super-heaters, the more potent variety of the apparatus, were the Swedish class A Atlantic of 1906, designed with a view to fuel economy which was important to a system which had to import its coal from the UK. After 1916 no Atlantics were built without superheaters – but only ninety-nine more Atlantics were to be built in any case.

Great Northern: *an Ivatt 'large Atlantic' coming North out of London like the hammers of Hades, LNER No.3274 of class C1 (originally GNR No.274, Doncaster, 1904) given an 18-element superheater by the GNR in 1920, and the last to receive the 32-element Robinson superheater from the LNER in 1934. This locomotive, here admired by flat-capped train-watchers, lasted until 1946; ten years earlier (aetat.32) it had covered Welwyn-Hitchin eleven miles in twelve minutes thirty-nine seconds, touching 86mph.*

Other Devices

The Atlantic rebuild of the 1920s in the USA had a superheater added and as a consequence outside piston valves, usually actuated by Walschaerts or Baker valve gears.[5] Atlantics were the beneficiaries, and occasionally the victims, of other attempted improvements like booster engines and feed-water heating. Nigel Gresley of the LNER was a pre-eminent Atlantic experimenter. In addition to the booster he tried unusual superheaters (twin-tube model, 1915); steam-operated water pick-up gear (1929); Worthington, Dabeg and ACFI feed-water heating (1926-1928), and Lentz poppet-valves (1933), but these initiatives were confined to a few locomotives only.

Later in the 1930s there was a vogue for streamlining steam locomotives. Gresley toyed with the idea of so treating an Ivatt Atlantic, No.3279 in 1936.[6] The PLM in France encased some of its pre-1914 veteran Atlantics in a well-styled streamlined casing, putting seven of them to work on 200-ton Paris-Lyons expresses which they were expected to run at an overall average of 64mph (102.5km/h). The coaches of this *train aerodynamique* were also reconditioned. The PLM's assistant chief engineer, M. Parmantier noted that tests demonstrated 'our Atlantics, already thirty years old, and with a maximum cylinder horsepower sustained of only 1,400, could only haul a four coach train on the level at 140km/h if the whole train was streamlined.'[7] The 'Crampton trap' closed on this bold enterprise and it ended after four years; its popularity led to longer, heavier trains and consequently haulage by Pacifics.

Streamlining: *nine of this PLM class of twenty Atlantics were streamlined in the 1930s (two by SNCF which classed them 221.B) given superheaters and modernised draughting arrangements; here one is embarking on a test run, probably 1935.*

Nord Atlantic: *an improved de Glehn 4-4-2, 2.659 (SACM 1902) given Lemaître blastpipe, large chimney and smoke deflectors (1936) for operating high-speed light expresses such as* l'Oiseau Bleu. Photo: H. Fohanno.

The Nord experimented more modestly by modernising the front ends of two de Glehn-du Bousquet Atlantics. These famous Atlantics had already received superheaters, many of them in 1912; two of the first thus improved (5148 and 5154, SACM 1902) now had Lemaître five-orifice multiple-jet blastpipes installed (1936) and, because of the softer exhaust which resulted, two large 'elephant ear' smoke deflectors. The outcome was of strikingly modish appearance and gave good performance. 'Mercury' writing in the *Railway Magazine* of March, 1937 was enthusiastic:

> [Far from reaching the end of its effective life' Atlantic 2.659 was used] *with entire success on the very fast* North Star *and* Blue Bird [Etoile du Nord; Oiseau Bleu] *non-stop expresses between Paris and Brussels...Examples of the performance of No. 2.659 have appeared recently in our French contemporary,* Transports...*On the 4.20 pm* rapide *from Turcoing to Lille, Arras and Paris, with a heavier load of 359 tons, No.2.659 ran the 41 miles from Arras to Longueau in 38.5 min., start-to-stop...but weather conditions were very bad with squalls of wind and rain which...reduced our speed to 10mph partly, no doubt, due to limited adhesion...and consequent slipping.*

New potency, but old, familiar problems.

The last major Atlantic improvements took place a long way from the racing-tracks of the *Silver Jubilee* and *Oiseau Bleu*. One of the most thoroughgoing Atlantic rebuilding programmes was undertaken in India by the NWR which had acquired thirty-eight of the E/1 class Atlantics

(NBL, 1907-1908) from the Great Indian Peninsula Railway in 1932-1933 and put them to work on Delhi-Lahore fast trains. The GIPR had already improved them by fitting superheaters. Twenty-eight of these locomotives were then taken in hand at the Moghalpura works of the NWR. Under the direction of Harold Hinton-Cooper they received new and strengthened frames. Their typically Atlantic proneness to running hot bearings on the rear, inside-bearing, axle was cured by fitting outside roller-bearings and hopper ash-pans. Improved springing combatted their tendency to roll about at speed. This extensive and successful work brought about a virtually new Atlantic, classed E/M by the NWR; one of the group went on to be the longest-living of all Atlantics and now reposes for all to see in the Delhi Railway Museum.

Renaissance on the Milwaukee Road – The *Hiawathas*

And with speed it darted forwards...And the evening sun descending (Longfellow)

The ultimate development of the Atlantic as a high-speed machine, and the star of its brief renaissance, took place on the Milwaukee Road in the USA which acquired four ultra-Atlantics, 1935-1937 – amongst the fastest land machines on the planet in their day. Stiff competition lay at the root of this enterprise, as well as the Milwaukee Road's well-established culture of lateral thinking in the face of adversity. This now included rivalry from air and motor traffic as well as competition from neighbouring lines: the Burlington had started to run its *Zephyr* diesel trains; the C&NW tempted travellers with a prestige steam-hauled express, the *400* (400 miles between Chicago and Minneapolis-St Paul in 400 minutes).

Swift of foot: *oil-fired Milwaukee Road* Hiawatha *(No.1 of 1935) arrows across the plains at a comfortable 100mph or more, the last, largest and fastest class of Atlantics in North America or anywhere else; steady as planets. A crescendo of orange, grey and maroon and it is gone.*

The engineers' solution was an Atlantic raised to the highest power, hauling a short, light-weight and streamlined train. The resulting locomotive was huge by previous Atlantic standards; it would have dwarfed the UK's largest express locomotives, the LMS 'Coronation' 4-6-2 streamliners, for example. It weighed 125 tons, ran on 7ft driving wheels, had a grate area of 69sq.ft, and a boiler pressure of 300psi. To keep servicing stops to a minimum, the *Hiawatha* Atlantics, as they were named (*Swift of foot was Hiawatha* according to Longfellow) had large, 10-axle tenders weighing 110 tons, carrying 13,000 gallons of water and 4,000 gallons of oil fuel. Their performance at very high speeds may have been enhanced by the streamlining which was then enjoying a vogue; in any case there was good publicity mileage in this arrangement, further enhanced by a startling colour scheme of grey, black, orange and maroon.

There were four *Hiawathas*, Milwaukee Road class A. They embodied virtually all the important lessons learned in the long evolution of the Atlantic; they ran on roller-bearings, had a radial rear truck, and drive to the front axle. The driving wheels bore 62.5 tons, but on track which had been greatly improved, in anticipation of the new trains, with rails of up to 131lb/yd resting on twenty-four inches of fresh ballast. The locomotives not only moved with fabulous speed, they were amongst the most steady and comfortable express locomotives ever constructed.

The *Hiawathas*, which could raise over 3,000hp, moved 430-ton loads easily in excess of 100mph; their trains (also called the *Hiawathas*) frequently hovered around that speed in a general service which soon proved to be phenomenally popular. Starting in May 1935, the *Hiawatha* trains (later, *Morning Hiawatha, Afternoon Hiawatha*, etc) carried 138,000 passengers by the end of the year, mainly on the 412-mile Chicago-Twin Cities route which they traversed in 6.5 hours, later even quicker. This success soon ran into the Crampton trap. Trains became larger and assistance was occasionally required in the form of extra trains hauled by 4-6-4s and older 4-6-2s. The two sets of locomotives ran an excellent service with a 93% punctuality record, which might have been better but for the severity of the North American winters. In 1938 the Milwaukee Road ordered six semi-streamlined 4-6-4s (class F7) to shoulder much of the *Hiawatha* duty, although the Atlantics continued to haul the Twin Cities expresses to 1946, after which they transferred to the *Mid-West Hiawatha* (Chicago-Omaha-Sioux Falls). The F7s then fell into the same trap and were supplanted by diesels; by the end of 1951 all steam *Hiawathas*, Atlantic or 4-6-4, had gone.

Thus departed Hiawatha…To the Land of the Hereafter

The renaissance was short but memorable and it demonstrated the Atlantic paradox as clearly as ever. The passing of the *Hiawathas* left the usual legacy of enigmas which surround the Atlantic type. Were they the fastest of all locomotives? This is contentious territory. The LNER A4 Pacific *Mallard* holds the official world speed record for steam locomotives at 126 mph, but reliable sources have spoken of *Hiawathas* running capably at 120mph, where the calibration on the speedometer ran out. Alfred W Bruce (*The Steam Locomotive in America*, 1952) stated that during time-schedule stabilising runs '…the hand of the speed indicator was often reported against the pin at 128mph. Exactly what maximum speed was reached is not known – but it was plenty!'[8] The high plume of exhaust from the *Hiawathas*, familiar from many photographs has been explained variously as an outcome of good streamlining design, running at high cut-offs or possibly by a high blast-pipe pressure. The *Hiawathas* employed the 'Goodfellow tip' blastpipe introduced on the Pennsylvania E6s class. These and other minor mysteries remain, but one assertion can be made safely: the *Hiawathas* were the fastest of a fast breed.

The Belgian Atlantics: the end of the line

The mainstream of Atlantic development did not end with the *Hiawathas* but with a small class of flatland racers built for the Belgian State Railways in 1938. Like the *Hiawathas* they were designed to rush short, lightweight trains with minimum station stops; in this case Brussels-Ostend, seventy-one miles in one hour with a single stop at Bruges. The kind of market, even the kind of world for which they were designed, collapsed swiftly in 1939 with the outbreak of the Second World War and the German occupation of Belgium. The immediate postwar world of austerity and hard-won recovery had little place for 'flying varnish' so, although for a short period they held the world's start-to-stop speed record for steam power, the Belgian class12 Atlantics did not reach their potential for long.

They were the last Atlantics to be built anywhere, except for the miniature 4-4-2s. They were of an unusual but successful design, engineered by M. Notesse, streamlining by M. Huet. Unlike most European locomotives they had bar frames for ease of access to their inside cylinders which were another oddity by mainland European standards, designed to dampen the Atlantics' propensity towards oscillation at speed. Piston valves and related gear were mounted outside. The streamlined casing, painted sage green with thick yellow stripes, was cut away drastically at appropriate points to give access to this curious, but logically-disposed, motion.

It was appropriate that the last Atlantics like the very first – the Strong locomotive of 1888 – were individualistic. Atlantic design ended as it started; something out of the ordinary.

Belgian Atlantic: *State Railways No.3308 of class 6 (Cockerill, 1905) based on the de Glehn system, but with strong Belgian influence: prominent capuchon, large Belpaire firebox, Walschaerts valve gear.*

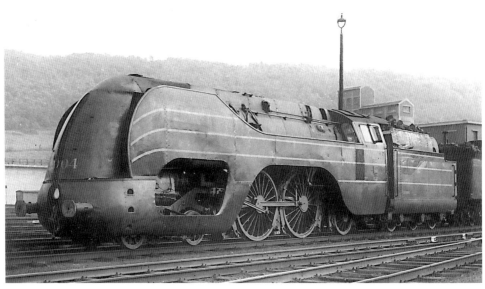

The Atlantics' last throw: *SNCB/NMBS semi-streamlined 4-4-2 (Cockerill, 1939) for light, high-speed expresses; a good example of Belgian originality with inside cylinders, outside valves and gears, and bar frames; alas war conditions prevented these engines from sustaining their full potential.* Photo: R.K. Blencowe.

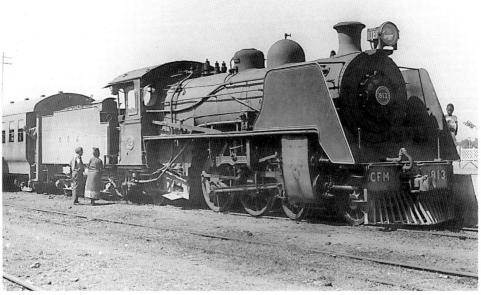

Last of the Line: *Mozambique CFM No.813 photographed by A.E. Durrant at Nampala, 16 July 1969; journey's end for the morning train from Nacala and Lumbo; one of the last Atlantics in operation.* Photo: Mrs Christine Durrant.

Into the Sunset

On 12 July 1912, GCR Atlantic No.364 *Lady Henderson* (Gorton, 1906) a 3-cylinder compound of timeless elegance finished in Brunswick green with freshly burnished brass mountings, drew the Royal Train from Grimsby to Immingham for the grand opening ceremony of the Great Central's new dock. Thirty-five years later, at the end of the 1939-1945 war, it ended its days running the Humber ferry trains to and from New Holland, occasionally grubby, and sometimes tender first because of a shortage of turning facilities. In the intervening years it had worked the Leicester-London expresses and, in the depressed 1930s, it spent some time tallowed-down in storage. As LNER No.2897 it was withdrawn in 1947 after a career which mirrored the rise and fall of the Atlantic type.[9]

The later careers of the former North British Atlantics offered a less dramatic contrast. Reclassified class C11 by the LNER they continued to haul Royal Trains until the mid-1930s, as well as the *Northern Belle* tourist train (1933 onwards) and various expresses and semi-fast passenger trains. Until gradually displaced by LNER Pacifics from 1928, they dominated heavy passenger work on the demanding Waverley Route (Carlisle-Edinburgh). They could be found, for example, on the 12 noon Edinburgh-Carlisle express as well as the 6.15 am Carlisle-Edinburgh all stations 'Parliamentary' which, *inter alia*, called at lonely Whitrope Siding to pick up the children of railway families for their school at Riccarton Junction, among the most isolated railway communities in Europe. But by 1937 they all had gone, save one intended for preservation.

In their declining years Atlantics were put on week-end excursions, stopping and secondary trains, fish trains (which required speed) and even freight trains, for which they were not suited given their high combustion rates and tall driving wheels designed for long bursts of great speed. The Illinois Central experimented by converting eleven Atlantics for freight and branch-line work in 1942-1943, but without success.[10]

In the UK, some of Ivatt's GN Atlantics survived to the time of nationalisation; they had continued to haul important passenger trains of the second rank between the wars: until 1935, the *Harrogate Pullman*, later the *Queen of Scots*; the *Yorkshire Pullman*; and until 1937, the London-Cambridge 'Beer Trains' (more properly, the *Garden Cities and Cambridge Buffet Expresses*). But thereafter they gravitated to secondary trains, and excursions. After 1945 rows of them could be observed outside locomotive sheds, 'cold' and unemployed. The seventeen remaining at nationalisation did sterling work on early-morning workmen's trains: 'Wonderful engines, still so elegant and taking it all in their stride, but so dirty...'[11]

The Brighton Atlantics were the last of the British fleet of 4-4-2s in full-time steam and they went out in style. One of them, No.2038 *Portland Bill*, drew the first 'Continental Express' for civilian passengers since the outbreak of war, on 15 January, 1945 – even before the war ended. Perhaps an Atlantic taking a boat train South was reassuring evidence that some kind of sanity was returning.

The last of the Brighton Atlantics was British Railways No.32424 *Beachy Head* (Brighton, 1911). On 13 April 1958 it took the *Sussex Coast Limited* organised to mark the occasion of a last Atlantic run from London Victoria-Newhaven Harbour. One of its nameplates was later presented to the Mayor of Eastbourne.

To complete our sad tales of the death of Atlantics: apart from the *Hiawathas*, the last Atlantics to be built in the USA were two for the Pittsburgh & Shawmut in 1919. The last 4-4-2s to be

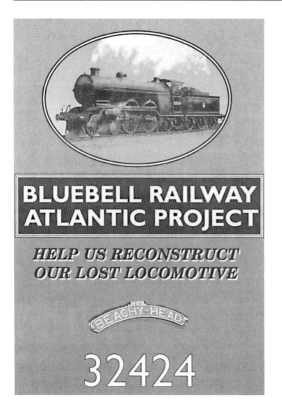

Atlantic Phoenix: *the recreation of a Brighton Atlantic around the boiler of an Ivatt large Atlantic, discovered in 1981. The Bluebell Railway Atlantic Project, based on volunteer effort, sent out this appeal in 2001, maintaining the century-old craft of assembling Atlantics.*
Courtesy: Bluebell Railway Atlantic Project.

built in Europe, apart from the Belgian flyers, were for the Egyptian State Railways in 1926. The last to operate in Europe were the well-maintained, sweetly-running Danish class P Atlantics which ceased their work in 1963. The last Atlantics to operate regularly in the world were the CFM 4-4-2s in Mozambique. These four 3ft 6in gauge engines (Henschel, 1923) ceased operations in 1978. Gölsdorf's last Atlantic ceased running in Austria in 1935; in Czechoslovakia in 1949. By then, to judge from photographs they were long past their pristine best, with stalactites of grease descending from running boards, leaky glands and other features that would not have passed muster in Gölsdorf's day. Egypt started withdrawing ('siding' in ESR parlance) its Atlantics in 1942, although India did not finish this process until 1970 when the most venerable Atlantic of all (once GIPR No. 922 of 1907) ceased to work.

The concept of a 'decline and fall' of Atlantics, or any other locomotive is problematic in any case. Did not a week-end excursion train to Cleethorpes or Bridlington do quite as much for human happiness as the *Queen of Scots*? What is essentially ignoble about a Grimsby fish train? Did not the all-stations stopping train which took children to school at Riccarton Junction contribute as much to enlightenment as the Brighton 'Stockbrokers Special'?

Nor did the Atlantics disappear without trace. Their memory is well-preserved, even fragrant, enshrined in photographs, memoirs, scholarly tomes, popular histories and reminiscences. Miniature Atlantics still steam forth, and in Sussex a dedicated group of people have laid plans and commenced work on rebuilding an LB&SCR Atlantic around an Ivatt large Atlantic boiler. A good dozen Atlantics still exist, most of them are well-preserved and admired in museums around the world.

Some Atlantics, far from fading away, strode into history. When the last Ivatt Atlantic (BR No.62822) was due for withdrawal it was put to work on an *Ivatt Atlantic Special*, the 11.00 a.m. King's Cross-Doncaster train, Sunday 26 November 1950. The event was suitably draped in a 'London Particular' fog of impenetrable thickness. Later, in bright sunshine the locomotive touched 75 mph, still game. Staff lined up to pay respects as the whistle-shrieking Atlantic passed New England shed, an old Atlantic haunt. They did the same at Grantham, very much in the manner of saluting the passing of a friend, or hero.

Notes to Chapter 7

1. Forney's *Catechism*...Third Edition, 1911.

2. Brian Reed, *Modern Railway Motive Power* (1950). Another controversial 'first' – types of superheater had been tried out by R&W Hawthorn in Newcastle upon Tyne, 1839, and by J.E. McConnell on the LNWR, 1852.

3. 'British Locomotive Practice and Performance', *Railway Magazine*, July 1935

4. Reuter & Bock, *Eleganz auf Schienen*; estimate 387 Atlantics were built with superheaters *ab initio*.

5. Superheating a locomotive raised problems with the lubricants of the time as well as with the slide-valves which characterised many early Atlantics; piston valves were superior in this respect.

6. LNER No.3279 was the rare 4-cylinder Ivatt Atlantic which was rebuilt into a potent 2-cylinder engine with improved steam passages and long-travel valves; see John F. Clay, 'Britain's Most Modern Atlantic', *Journal* of the Stephenson Locomotive Society, June 1967. The detailed *Locomotives of the LNER*, Part 3A (RCTS, 1979) cites No.4420 – a suitable number for an Atlantic – as the chosen streamliner, however.

7. J.T. van Riemsdijk, *op cit*. See also a detailed paragraph, Anon, 'Overseas Railways' *Railway Magazine*, September 1937.

8. Contentions can go further: the fabled PRR 6-4-4-6 was stated to have touched 140 mph on occasion, but since this was in breach of ICC regulations it was not a matter to be bruited about. See article by A. Haas, *Lok Magazine* 42, and by A.F. Cook, *Journal* of the SLS, April 1979. Many Atlantic records, especially early ones, have long been contentious for various reasons: insufficiently formalised; technically dubious; arguments tinted by subjectivism, etc. See John F. Clay, 'Foolish Legend but Honourable History', *Railway World*, Aug and Sep, 1976, and W. Reuter, *Rekordlokomotiven. Die Schnellsten der Schiene, 1848-1950*, 1978.

9. Another Atlantic mystery; the RCTS survey of LNER locomotives, *op cit*, states the Immingham loco-motive was No.364, but David Jackson, *J.G. Robinson: A Lifetime's Work*, 1996 notes it as being No.365.

10. See Chapter 15 for details.

11. Reminiscence of one who dwelt by the Northern Heights line in those days.

Chapter 8
Stopping for Water

Testing, Testing

The Atlantics, being at the cutting edge of technical development, exemplified many technical issues of their time, particularly scientific testing. Locomotive testing has roots almost as old as the locomotive itself: George Stephenson devised a simple test for the pulling power of a locomotive in 1818; Charles Babbage, inventor of the mechanical computer, helped to design an apparatus for the GWR (1838) which measured tractive effort, distance and speed. The famous Rainhill Trials of 1829 were really the original 'comparative test' between different locomotive types. The Atlantic entered a world which had inherited and refined these processes considerably; it was also in the first wave of the new, scientific testing wherein lay the future of locomotive design. The Pennsylvania E6s was amongst the first test-bed designed locomotives, and Atlantics figured strongly in the original fully-detailed comparative reports made available to a wide public, the St Louis World's Fair tests of 1904.[1]

On test: *Pennsylvania No.89, (class E6 becoming E6s) having its performance tested following the addition of a superheater, Altoona Test Department, 1913. The hydraulically-retarded supporting wheels can be discerned below driving and trailing axles, the latter borne in a built-up Kiesel truck later supplanted by an integral cast-steel KS delta truck.* Photo: erstwhile PRR.

Most Atlantics underwent typical running-in tests and many were tried out on road tests in traffic or harnessed for tests to a dynamometer car, but the outcomes of these tests have often been lost. Ken Hoole stated in *The North-Eastern Atlantics* (1965) 'unfortunately the records of most of these trials were sent for salvage in 1941.' He managed to unearth some old Log Books, so discovering the range of NER Atlantic road tests over the years: seventeen entries from comparative tests in 1906, to the testing of a class C7/2 Atlantic equipped with poppet valves, May 1935 – one of the latter-day attempts to improve and modernise the 4 4 2.

The 1906 comparative tests were between a new 4-cylinder compound Atlantic, class 4CC, a 2-cylinder Atlantic (class V) and others: a 4-4-0 and a 4-6-0. The 1935 test required the use of a counter-pressure locomotive, a fellow engine so managed as to present an invariant load on the 'testee', up hill and down dale; a form of road test pioneered by the Polish engineer A.O. Czeczott in 1921, taken up by the LNER soon afterwards.

The Prussian State Railways carried out exhaustive tests before adopting Atlantics; first, in 1901, it pitched de Glehn 4-4-2s built by Grafenstaden against a von Borries design by Hanomag. The outcome was that the majority of its S7 Atlantics were of the Hanomag variety. Its later S9s were tested against the improved S6 4-4-0, hauling identical trains between Wustermark and Hanover in 1909. The S9 demonstrated that it was superior in most respects with heavier trains and ninety-nine were duly constructed.

As tests become more precise they took place under carefully controlled conditions. The problem then arose of the extent to which simulating conditions of the 'real world', the rough-and-tumble outside the test plant or the dynamometer car could be simulated. When former NER Atlantic No.2206 was fitted with a French ACFI feed-water heater (1926-1928) and duly tested, the Chief Test Inspector expressed doubts about the realism of an assessment which he considered too brief and too narrow in range:

> *When men are moved about from one engine to another, as they are under present conditions, they lose interest and we might as well resign ourselves to the fact that they will not use these appliances if they can help it...I fear that having regard to human nature we shall be disappointed...*[2]

Which turned out to be the case.

An important trial of 'real world', long-run comparative tests involving Atlantics took place on the GWR in Edwardian times under the guidance of the railway's Locomotive, Carriage and Wagon Superintendent (later, CME) G.J. Churchward. A gifted pragmatist and member of a now defunct social species, the English gentleman, he had a certain directness of manner, a tendency towards understatement and the art of listening carefully to other people whatever their status; he was thus a talented learner also. If Nord compound Atlantics were as brilliant as it was claimed, then close investigation was required; Churchward persuaded his directors to purchase a de Glehn compound, duly shipped in dismantled form to Swindon after initial steaming at the SACM works. Churchward inspected the parts as they were unpacked: 'this is watchmaker's work' he is reputed to have exclaimed in admiration at the French workmanship, high praise from a Swindon engineer. Two more French Atlantics, of the slightly larger Paris-Orleans type were acquired later for similar comparative assessment.

Test run: *engineers, officials et al on the occasion of a test run by No.811 of class In (later class 203) an Atlantic of the Hungarian State Railways, 1906. This fine 4-cylinder compound with conical smokebox door to the fore, Vanderbilt tender to the rear and V-shaped cab front, had drive to front coupled wheels with steeply-angled connecting rods in order to make room for a generous firebox; grate area: 41.7sq ft (3.90 m^2).* Photo: MÁV.

Anglo-French: *the historic GWR No.102, La France (SACM, 1903) a de Glehn 4-cylinder compound in its final form (1923-1926), French frame and machinery, Swindon No.1 boiler, plain cast-iron chimney and outside steam pipe, of slightly bodged appearance, leading to hp cylinders. A locomotive from which much was learned by those willing to learn.* Photo: W.H. Whitworth.

The young Victor Bayley, later to become a senior railway engineer of the Indian Raj, was working himself in as a Swindon draughtsman, doing his turn in another Churchward innovation, the new GWR dynamometer car coupled behind the first of the GWR French Atlantics, *La France*:

> I remember one astonishing run between Swindon and Paddington with a heavy train…the performance of the locomotive was recorded on a moving reel of paper…There were several senior officials in the car and I still remember the tense silence of the little group round me as the clicking pens told their astounding story…It was a magnificent feat and the Great Western…was hard put to it to reply. However, the upshot of the tests was that…there was nothing to choose between La France *and the English product….Churchward was not satisfied, however.*[3]

There was more than one agenda in these GWR tests: for a start, was compounding superior to single expansion? Churchward designed a 4-cylinder simple Atlantic (No.40, later *North Star*) and ran it against the compound 'Frenchmen'. Secondly, was the Atlantic the engine of the future or the 4-6-0? The 2-cylinder 4-6-0 (No.171, *Albion*) was pitted against the French machines and converted for a short period into an Atlantic so that comparisons would be fair.

Swindon built thirteen convertible 2-cylinder Atlantics in 1905 to run against similar 4-6-0s on demanding parts of the system. Comparative tests in June 1905 saw the new GWR Atlantic No.171, *Quicksilver* working against the equally new 'ten-wheeler' No.178 *Kirkland* on the dreaded 1 in 42 gradient of Hemerdon Bank, hauling London Paddington – Plymouth expresses. Both locomotives were successful, but Churchward became convinced that the greater adhesion of the 4-6-0 gave it a decided advantage. The Swindon Atlantics had relatively narrow fireboxes designed to burn good-quality coal. Unlike Ivatt's wide-firebox 4-4-2s the GWR Atlantics were quite literally 4-6-0s with rear coupled wheels replaced by a trailing axle.

Churchward, a farmer's son, was fond of the adage: 'if you wait for the grass to grow green, the horse will starve.' The tests were concluded as soon as he was satisfied. Henceforth the GWR was to be a railway of simple expansion locomotives with two or four cylinders. The GWR Atlantics were accordingly converted, or reconverted, to 4-6-0s by 1914.

Churchward also admired certain American designs and techniques which he embodied in his own work. He was, moreover, said to be a friend of Alfred W. Gibbs, father of the E6s and another supporter of scientific testing.[4]

The principal player in the Pennsylvania testing team was Charles D. Young, Engineer of Tests. Much of the Altoona test plant had made its debut at the St Louis World's Fair in 1904. As a contribution to the 'compound or simple?' debate, the St Louis enterprise had included a series of tests between different Atlantics, both simple and compound, and between different forms of compound. Although partisans interpreted the test results according to their own lights, the Cole compound repeatedly generated greater indicated horsepower and was considered the more straightforward design of the contestants. None of these locomotives could be called 'simple' in either sense of the word, the *relative* simplicity of the Cole machine was an important consideration in American eyes; it was 'a good railway job.'[5]

The NYC&HR compound, No.3000 was also matched against a Pennsylvania 2-cylinder simple Atlantic, class E2a No.3266. Conclusion: 'The steam distribution of the compound was less satisfactory at high speed than the simple', which is not the same as asserting that compounding *per se* necessarily involves inferior steam distribution.

There were some methodological problems at St Louis: most tests were between saturated-steam Atlantics, but the Prussian Atlantic had a Pielock superheater. There is fairly clear evidence that the testers were insufficiently familiar with the French de Glehn Atlantic to draw out its full potential. Nevertheless, the St Louis tests with the Pennsylvania plant represented a major step forward in executing and publicising the scientific testing of steam locomotives.

In addition to the famous E6s tests, Young oversaw many others. They were openly available, well stocked with data and offered straightforward conclusions – an 'executive summary' in later parlance. They also covered many detailed aspects of locomotive working. For example, testing Atlantic No.3266 once more (1911), Young reported that it could emit 16-23lbs of sparks from its stack in one hour, and in the same period deposit 52-58lbs of cinders and char in its smokebox. It was the work of Young and his team that led to the design of the Goodfellow nozzle which enhanced performance of the E6s Atlantics '[we] recommend some form of nozzle...to give better draft conditions than the present circular nozzle' (*Tests of a Class E6s Passenger Locomotive*, Pennsylvania RR, 1913).

A particular form of road test was the 'indicator test' whereby some engineers, preferably young and hardy ones, sat or crouched in a temporary shelter at the front end of an engine, protected from burns by thickly-lagged steam pipes, and keeping notes with mounting numbness. Old photographs show smart young Edwardian engineers in bowler hats, white collars and overcoats ready for the fray of indicator tests; LB&SCR Atlantic No.39 (Kitson, Leeds, 1906) was so tested. Nearly forty years later, in 1943 two Brighton Atlantics were involved in another kind of road test, in this case of the road itself. The engines picked their way gingerly over the temporary repairs to the London Road viaduct in Brighton, recently breached by six German fighter-bombers on a hit-and-run raid. A sharp contrast to the days when the Marsh Atlantics spun the *Southern Belle* with its elegantly attired passengers down to the Sussex coast.

One young engineer who was involved with Atlantic tests on the GNR in Ivatt's day was Oliver Bulleid, later CME of the Southern Railway. Ever anxious to advance the cutting edge of locomotive technology, he was inspired by the results of draughting tests in the USA[6] to construct an unusual, wide chimney for large Atlantic No.251. It worked well, but Ivatt was unimpressed and ordered its removal. Bulleid was set a more conventional task, to measure the rolling resistance of a 'coasting' large Atlantic. Coming down the gradient from Stoke at 49mph with steam shut off, it settled down to a steady 31mph. However, if steam was cut off at 20mph it then accelerated or 'ran up' to a steady 31mph, *ergo* 'they took 11.2lb per ton as representing the resistance of an Atlantic...which was just as good as any other figure' – a vintage example of the breezy style with which Bulleid was apt to provoke orthodoxy.[7]

Thirty or so years later, towards the end of his career on the Southern Railway, Bulleid designed a weird double-ended locomotive driven by two power bogies containing sleeve-valve steam motors (the 'Leader' locomotive). Would this kind of valve actually work on a steam locomotive? An old Brighton Atlantic, now SR No.2039 *Hartland Point* (once LB&SCR No.39, of indicator-shelter fame) was chosen as a mobile test-bed for the experiment. Whilst he was about it, Bulleid had the engine fitted with a Lemaître multiple-nozzle blastpipe with an accompanying dish-shaped chimney – not unlike his youthful Doncaster essay into improved draughting. Unique in form and appearance amongst Atlantics, indeed amongst all locomotives, *Hartland Point* could be found working its three-coach train around southern England, but the sleeve-valve system was touchy and raised as many problems as it solved.[8]

Test bed: *a much-transformed Brighton Atlantic, BR No.32039* Hartland Point *(once LB&SCR No.39 of 1905) as test-bed for experimental sleeve-valves and Lemaître multiple-jet blastpipe; outside Brighton works, 1948; ingenious, inelegant and none too successful.* Photo: Lens of Sutton.

This was the last and possibly the most unusual of the Atlantic tests. In one sense the Atlantic was itself an experiment to be tested, an experiment with ambiguous, inconclusive results. Nevertheless, important lessons were learned from the 'Atlantic project' about adhesion, and the advantages of the large firebox as a water-boiler.

Counterfactual Atlantics – the 4-4-2s That Never Were

The testing of Atlantics at least took place in the 'real world', whatever that may be; but what of that shadowy realm in which Atlantics remained purely conjectural? Counterfactual history – what might have happened 'if it had been otherwise' has become sharper in recent years.[9] Under careful control it can offer a useful, if hypothetical, way of gauging the importance or 'inevitability' of choices that were made, of that which did happen.

The most potent counterfactual Atlantic was Karl Gölsdorf's proposal of 1881. Had it been constructed it might have advanced express passenger engine design by a lustrum or a decade. The Americans and French would probably have been interested; the British possibly not as they were about to flirt with a revival of 4-2-2 'singles' and are occasionally prone to bouts of finding problems for every answer, but who can say?

Nearly twenty years later French engineers proposed two curious Atlantics. One, on the Paris-Orleans had twin boilers and the Durand et Lencauchez valve gear (based on the Corliss arrangement) – 'un projet trés remarquable' in the judgement of Sauvage and Chapelon in their classic, *La Machine Locomotive*, 1946. The other proposal (Ouest Railway, 1900) was for a singular Webb-type compound with three inside cylinders involving a complex transmission. The idea was drawn up and signed by the Ouest's Administrator, R.M. Dufresne and has been fully described by John van Riemsdijk in the *Journal* of the SNCF Society, No.98, 2000.[10] The locomotive was to be named *Lord Roberts*, after the Ouest's chairman.

There were also some British might-have-been Atlantics. The Locomotive Superintendent of the South Eastern & Chatham Railway, the suitably-named Harry Wainwright, had to cope with severe boiler-scaling in his locomotives which ran on hard water from chalk-bearing strata. He sketched an Atlantic around the least troublesome boiler design used on the SE&CR, that of the class C 0-6-0. Ten Atlantics were to be built at Ashford in 1903, in something of a rush, to combat the scaling crisis. The chemists came up with a better answer – water softening systems – and the Atlantic idea was dropped. Then, in 1907 Wainwright seems to have toyed with a Churchward-type plan, building and comparing two sets of similar engines, 4-4-2 and 4-6-0, but the driving axleloads were considered too large in the view of the Civil Engineer, and the plan faded.

Counterfactual Atlantic: *the proposed Caledonian Railway 4-cylinder compound 4-4-2 designed by J.F. McIntosh, 1905 and recreated here by the artist, Robin Barnes. A singular engine with high-pitched boiler, low running plates and long eccentric rods. Flanked by two real-world singularities: a last surviving Conner outside-cylinder 0-6-0, and No.781, a Barclay industrial-type tank engine.* Courtesy: Robin Barnes.

The Caledonian Railway also looked seriously at the Atlantic idea on three separate occasions. In 1901 and again in 1905 J.F. McIntosh, the CR Locomotive Superintendent, outlined schemes for robust, inside-cylinder 4-4-2s. He received authorisation for the 1905 set but it was not implemented. Another 1905 scheme was for a compound Atlantic with 6ft 6in driving wheels and four cylinders in line. The notion of a fairly complex compound ran counter to the CR style of no-nonsense locomotives built like battleships and able to be driven hard. The non-existence of the CR and SE&CR Atlantics is regrettable from the aesthetic standpoint; both railways presented exceptionally good-looking engines to the world. Ashford was renowned for excellence of line and finish, and a CR express locomotive decked out in ethereal blue, sounding its siren-horn has had few rivals in engineering aesthetics.[11]

In 1901, the very dawn of the Atlantic era, *The Locomotive* ran a short article, with illustration, of a 'Chautauqua', a proposed Atlantic of advanced design with de Glehn compounding, a fiercely conical smokebox door, outside bearing rear axle and an V-shaped cab 'similar to the practice of the PLM Railway in France.' Precisely which railway or country was to benefit from this fine locomotive was unclear; the details had been sent in by 'a continental engineer correspondent.' The engine, which combined French, Palatinate, Hungarian and Swedish features remains in the counterfactual universe.

So also did another unusual proposal coming at the very end of the era, for a large Garratt 4-4-2+2-4-4 or 'double Atlantic', like the Tasmanian original but for the standard gauge. A Swindon boiler was amongst the various GWR touches to the locomotive in an outline drawing accompanying the idea, which appeared in the *Proceedings* of the Institution of Locomotive Engineers, 1916, (*The Garratt Locomotive* by H. Woodgate-Dearberg) and which would surpass 'anything hitherto attempted in this country as regards power.'

Occasionally counterfactual 4-4-2s may form in the mind as a result of a misunderstanding. In Nik and Helma Mika's admirable *Railways of Canada, A Pictorial History* (1972) we learn that the Quebec, Montreal, Ottawa & Occident Railway opened in 1877 'using Atlantic-type engines with eight-foot drivers.' If this were so it would not only put the date of Atlantic invention back four years but also establish a new technical record for the type. Similarly, there has been a persistent rumour that the last Tsar of Russia, Nicholas II, had a private stud of three Atlantics kept in St Petersburg and maintained by the Nikolai Railway for the imperial train. There were, in fact, three special imperial locomotives built for the Tsar by Cockerill in Belgium[12] but their relatively light weight (48 tons) points to their being 4-4-0s – and there is no hard evidence of Atlantics in Tsarist Russia except for the Austrian-type series run by the Warsaw-Vienna Railway. The QMOOR and *Tsarskiye* Atlantics remain enigmas, therefore.

The last major counterfactual plan for Atlantics was the Pennsylvania's putative class E8 of 1936, child of the 1930s fashion for fast, lightweight trains. The ultra-Atlantic was to be adorned with a nickel-plate boiler shell, be stoker-fired and have roller bearings on all axles. The idea was dropped when electrification was decided upon.

A counterfactual variant of interest to railway cognoscenti is of locomotives which *were* built but which turned up in unexpected places. For example, the pages of the *Journal* of the Stephenson Locomotive Society in 1979 contained speculation about the likelihood of a Lancashire & Yorkshire Atlantic climbing the Shap gradients of the LNWR, a line for which they were not designed and which lay a considerable distance from their habitual territory. There is evidence that one of these unusual Atlantics drew Carlisle race specials in 1903-1904[13]. But the correspondence centred on a frustratingly incomplete photograph of a down passenger train at Crewe, *c*.1920, hauled by an LNWR 'Jumbo', No.901 *Hero*, and an L&Y Atlantic. After exploring a wide range of possibilities in a well-informed correspondence, notes on the reverse of a duplicate photograph by its original taker (W.H. Whitworth) seemed to clinch the matter: that the L&Y Atlantic, No.1414 was on a Windermere train and would therefore have left the West Coast main line before the great inclines.

A better-known Atlantic-wandering resulted from Great Central Railway's promotion policy. The general manager, Sam Fay, was keen to publicise his company's fine-looking and prestigious Atlantics on long-distance passenger runs, if agreement could be obtained from other companies. Relations with the GWR were good, so some GCR Atlantics made forays as far as Plymouth with excursions from Manchester. One of them, No.197 tried to brave the 1 in 42 rigours of Hemerdon bank alone, and with a heavy train, but it had to be assisted.

The LNER, in its early years, organised a range of workings whereby Atlantics from one constituent company ran on the metals of another, sometimes in comparative tests, sometimes in the normal course of business. But this kind of activity lacks the bite and spice of genuine counterfactual history, where Caledonian compound 4-4-2s tackle Beattock. Perhaps in another cosmos, they do.

Was there an 'Atlantic Mania'?

The existence of known counterfactual Atlantics suggests that others may have been envisaged, but that they did not advance much beyond ideas or sketches. Rous-Marten recalled a meeting with Ivatt at which the famous Atlantic-designer showed him an early sketch for a 4-4-2 on paper with a date stamp bearing the mark of Inchicore Locomotive Works, of the Great Southern & Western Railway of Ireland. This had been Ivatt's employer before he moved to the GNR at Doncaster in 1895. Had he once outlined an Irish Atlantic, or was this only a convenient sheet of drawing paper?

Why did so many American railroads purchase Atlantics relative to the rest of the world? In the USA about sixty-seven railroads ran Atlantics; the two major Canadian lines did also, albeit in very small numbers. Twenty-three roads owned ten or fewer Atlantics, some only acquired one or two. The mighty Northern Pacific bought only three; the Norfolk & Western, ten. In some cases it seems a mystery why they were bought at all. George W. Hilton in his definitive *American Narrow Gauge Railroads* (1990) thought that the one-off 3ft gauge Atlantic (Baldwin, 1902) of the Washington & Plymouth was 'the greatest anomaly among narrow gauge locomotives...no wheel arrangement might seem so inappropriate to narrow gauges...' Some railroads tried out a few Atlantics by way of evaluating the type; others may simply have bought them uncritically, hearing of their great achievements. Also, in America locomotive building was a large-scale commercial business concentrated in the hands of a few manufacturers who could 'hard sell' their products, for example when Schenectady sent a new wide-firebox C&NW Atlantic to Saratoga Springs for the Master Mechanics to see and admire at their Convention.

In Britain the large railways generally built their own locomotives, or designed them for others to build. The Atlantic-promoting techniques of Baldwin or Brooks were largely absent in this milieu which was (*pace* Churchward and a few others) rather conservative in Atlantic times. Of the major British commercial builders only one, North British Locomotive produced Atlantics on any scale, mainly for British-owned overseas railways, and the NBR at home. Kerr, Stuart constructed a solitary 4-4-2 for the Taokow-Chinghua line in China. Beyer, Peacock of Manchester, 'locomotive builders to the world' built the Garratt double-Atlantics (two for Tasmania, eight for Argentina), the five unsuccessful 4-4-2s of the Dutch State Railways and seven Atlantics for the Great Central, not much compared with the Baldwin legions.

Individual engineers or procurement officers had a good deal to do with the adoption, or lack of it, of Atlantics: Robert Garbe of the Prussian State Railways was pro-Atlantic, as were Ivatt, Gölsdorf and Gibbs. Dugald Drummond of the LSWR did not like them, S.M. Prince of the Reading thought they were over-rated, but tried some just the same. Overlaying the views of the engineers there was the hype of manufacturers and the popular and professional media. It is probably safe to say when viewed objectively that in America more Atlantics were built than were strictly justified by the needs of railroads. Elsewhere, Atlantics faced greater resistance and, in any case, the gentle but inescapable imperatives of 'the geography of loco-motion' generally restricted their adoption and use to a few lines where their talents could be employed to their best advantage.

Although the phrase 'Atlantic mania' has been employed by some writers, if the Atlantic project is placed in context it hardly justifies the term; more a 'passing fashion' perhaps. In 1903 when that fashion was well under way 844 Atlantics had been built in the USA, about 40% of the total ever constructed there. This was about 2% of all American locomotives at the time (*c*.41,000). After holding for a short while the proportion dropped quickly. Of the sixty-seven railroads using Atlantics about half a dozen might be said to be heavy users (100 or more machines) and most of the 'light users' were trying out the Atlantic rather than buying it uncritically. Very few railroads went in for unsuitable Atlantic investment, maybe ten at the most. There were only thirty-five of the world-famous Nord Atlantics, 1.7% of all Nord locomotives (1,993) in 1910. Even so, the impact of this modest company of Atlantics was very great indeed both in engineering and 'PR', publicity terms, and it lasted as long as the steam locomotive did.

Virginian individualist: *the last Baldwin Atlantic (June, 1916) with the smallest driving wheel diameter for a new standard-gauge 4-4-2 in the USA (5ft 6ins); the sole passenger engine for the Interstate Railroad, a short, coal-hauling line in the mountains of Virginia. A set of paradoxes symbol-ised by its outside Southern valve gear distributing, however, saturated steam through slide valves.* Photo: Harold K. Vollrath.

Notes to Chapter 8

1. For early testing theory and practice, see Michael Rutherford, 'Measurement Not Mystification' in *Back Track*, Vol 9, No. 8, August 1995

2. K. Hoole, *op cit,* p81

3. Victor Bayley, *Nine-Fifteen From Victoria*, 1937.

4. But there is some doubt about Churchward's having visited the USA. Perhaps Gibbs made the pilgrimage to Swindon. The two had much in common including an ability to listen to other people and a penchant for thorough, long-run testing.

5. E.C. Poultney, *British Express Locomotive Development 1896-1948*, 1952.

6. By Professor Goss of Purdue University, the home of another testing plant, and a major seat of locomotive theory.

7. *Proceedings* of the Institution of Locomotive Engineers, March-April, 1914.

8. Kevin Roberston, *Leader: The Full Story*, 1995. Sleeve valves on steam locomotives were not entirely novel; they had been essayed on Cecil Paget's 2-6-2 constructed at the Midland Railway works, Derby, in the early years of the century. Bulleid's sleeve valve had complex evolutions; it rotated and reciprocated simultaneously, describing a figure-of-eight path as it worked.

9. See Niall Ferguson (ed), *Virtual History, Alternatives and Counterfactuals*, 1997. Fictional use of the form is common, see Paul Seabury, 'The Histronaut' (*Fantasy and Science Fiction*, Vol V, 1, Dec 1963) in which a CIA agent uses a time-machine to travel to Germany, 1917 to waylay the 'sealed train' bearing Lenin to Russia. Memo to archive-beavers: was Lenin's train Atlantic-hauled at any stage?

10. Robin Barnes depicted the outcome of the P-O plan in the following number of this *Journal*.

11. See D.L. Bradley, *Locomotives of the South Eastern and Chatham Railway*, 1961; C.P. Atkins, *West Coast 4-6-0s At Work*, 1981.

12. A.D. de Pater and F.M. Page, *Russian Locomotives*, Vol I, 1987.

13. See Eric Mason, *The Lancashire & Yorkshire Railway in the Twentieth Century*, 1954; an Atlantic with 7ft 3ins driving wheels tackling Shap must have been a sight to behold. Other L&Y Atlantics made it to Windermere on occasion, long before the affair of the Preston photograph.

Chapter 9
The Unexpected

A locomotive like the Atlantic, intended for fast running, was bound to catch the public eye as a result of its work on rapid expresses, stunts, sudden emergencies, and dashes here and there. It was mainly in the first quartile of the twentieth century that the Atlantics were in the limelight because of their prestige and capacity for sustained speed with light trains such as extras and specials. Like the reporter of old, the Atlantics had 'mingled with the mighty.' Or was it that the mighty enjoyed the inestimable privilege of mingling with Atlantics?

Fast running raises risks; nevertheless the Atlantics had a creditable safety record. They were involved in accidents but none was attributable to the *design* of the engine. The usual suspects were at fault: carelessness, weather, flawed materials, misunderstandings, 'Acts of God', and so on. But first, the alarums and excursions.

Specials

Not all Atlantic forays were necessarily headline-catchers. There was one such early example: the *Stafford incident*. Stafford lies on the main London-Carlisle 'West Coast Route' to Scotland, which in 1900 was part of the London & North Western Railway, the 'Premier Line' which had, as the Scots put it 'a guid conceit of itself.' For most railway purposes Stafford was an LNWR town, its station the haunt of the blackberry-black locomotives built in Crewe. But Stafford was also the terminus of a secondary, somnolent GNR branch line from Uttoxeter, treated with some condescension by the local officials of the LNWR. One Monday morning in 1900 they got the shock of their professional lives: Britain's largest express engine, the apple-green 'Klondyke' Atlantic, GNR No.990, prestigious and very obvious, had slipped into the GNR bay platform. It only stayed long enough to make a point before moving away, cross country back to Grantham and the GNR main line.

The strategy behind this Atlantic raid has given rise to speculation. A likely cause is that H.A. Ivatt, No.990's designer, a man with a droll sense of humour, had started his engineering career on the LNWR at Stafford and was gently showing that a 'local lad had made good.' Since the LNWR was going through a period of some difficulty with its traction policy, frequently having to double-head its main line expresses with under-powered locomotives, the original 'Klondyke' drove the point home, sharply.

Fifteen years after the Stafford incident the GNR and its Atlantics were taking part in a massive war effort. One of the large Atlantics, No.1442, once star of the Imperial International Exhibition, White City (1909), was the immaculate 'Royal Engine', kept for hauling Royal Trains, now having to take its share in mundane wartime tasks. In June 1916 it was to play an important role in the incident of the *Kitchener special*, part of a concatenation of events which, for connoisseurs of failure, exemplify perfectly Murphy's Law at its most ironic.[1]

Pomp and circumstance: *NER No.1792 of class V hauls the LNWR Royal Train over Robert Stephenson's High Level Bridge spanning the Tyne, 10 July 1906. Its chief passenger, King Edward VII having just opened a second bridge (named after himself) is returning to York; as LNER No.2937 of class C6, this was the last 'Gateshead Infant' to be withdrawn, 1947.*

Field-Marshal Lord Kitchener, Secretary of State for War in 1916, had convinced himself that his presence in St Petersburg, then the capital of Britain's faltering ally, tsarist Russia, might improve the organisation of war effort on the Eastern Front. Together with his entourage he set off from London's King's Cross station, bound for Russia, via Scapa Flow. GNR 'Klondyke' No.252 was ready with a four-coach special to speed the party northwards; large Atlantic No.284 would take over at Grantham, en route for York. However, on arrival at King's Cross it was found that the Foreign Office papers had been sent to Euston (LNWR) by mistake. Kitchener was in an almighty hurry so his train set off leaving the Foreign Office specialist, O'Beirne to speed to Euston and catch up afterwards. The GNR quickly arranged a 'special' of two coaches in the charge of the Royal Engine, No.1442. So fast did this superheated Atlantic run that it caught up with Kitchener at York; King's Cross to Grantham had averaged 65.5 mph.

All to little avail: Kitchener and his party including O'Beirne and his papers were lost at sea when their transport, the light cruiser HMS *Hampshire* struck a German mine off the Orkneys.

Atlantics were often given the duty of pulling *Royal Trains*. The epitome of the age was an immaculate Smith compound 4-4-2 of the NER taking King Edward VII on a royal progress in his superbly-appointed train: Newcastle upon Tyne to Edinburgh 17 September 1906 in the fastest time to date. A month later Queen Alexandra was similarly taken from Edinburgh to York; and just under a year after that the King once more, from York to Edinburgh 'at express speeds.' In the course of these stylish dashes up and down Eastern Britain the Smith compounds would pass their birthplace, Gateshead Works. The locomotives' makers lived in the nearby smoke-encrusted terraces reaching down to the coaly Tyne; an ironic juxtaposition.

In 1901 the Duke and Duchess of York (later King George V and Queen Mary) made a 12,000 mile imperial tour, including the Dominion of Canada. Their 'handsome train of nine vestibuled cars, splendidly equipped' ran for part of the way behind the ultimate *rara avis* of the Atlantics, one of the only three Canadian Pacific 4-4-2s, a Vauclain compound constructed by the CPR in its own shops. Eleven years later the Duke was Emperor of India, holding an imperial durbar at Kotah; *The Locomotive Magazine* noted that a Great Indian Peninsula Atlantic had the honour of hauling the 'Supplementary Royal Train' thither. In 1915 Eastern Bengal Atlantic No.255 took the Viceroy of India and his suite to open the Ganges Bridge, there and back from Calcutta in imperial splendour at an average 55mph.

These martial, royal and imperial progresses could be emulated by the general public if they had the wherewithal to pay for the service. One example was the 'Coyote Special', better known in railroad history as *Death Valley Scotty's Special*, an episode which brought considerable fame to the Atlantic family.

On 8 July, 1905, in the Los Angeles office of John J. Byrne, General Passenger Agent of the Santa Fe lines East of Albuquerque, a customer appeared attired in a rough serge suit, blue shirt with red tie, cowboy boots and a wide-brimmed hat: Walter Scott, aka 'Death Valley Scotty'; a 'character', professional eccentric, and a man before his time – a century later he would be a celebrity, famous chiefly because well-known. He asked how long it took to reach Chicago by rail; Byrne told him that the record was nearly fifty-eight hours. On being asked if it could be done by a special train in forty-six hours, Byrne thought that it might, at a cost of $5,500. Scott peeled the sum off, mostly in $1,000 bills and the AT&SF was in business.

Scotty's special left La Grande station, LA at 1 p.m. the next day. The train (baggage car, dining car, and Pullman car *Muskegon*; in all 170 tons) was to be relayed by fast express engines to Dearborn station, Chicago. It covered the 2,265 miles in forty-four hours, fifty-four minutes, hauled by a series of nineteen locomotives eight of which were Atlantics, mostly the Baldwin 'balanced compounds' then popular with the Santa Fe. They belonged to the 507 or 542 classes and acquitted themselves well; it was claimed that No.510 touched 106.1mph between Cameron and Surry and average speeds were 55-60mph. On the last leg (Chillicothe-Chicago) No.517 suffered an overheated crankpin at South Joliet, soon rectified. More seriously, No.530 knocked out a cylinder head at Kent, but only four minutes was lost before 2-6-2 No.1095 replaced the errant Atlantic.

Scotty worked hard at the publicity potential of his express. A press despatch sent from the train told of a fine meal 'at 60mph' which included a caviare sandwich *à la* Death Valley, and porterhouse steak *à la* Coyote. Scotty assisted with firing the locomotives; on entering Dodge he wired President Theodore Roosevelt:

> An American cowboy is coming east on a special train faster than any cowpuncher rode before; how much shall I break the transcontinental record?

For whatever reason, TR (who was ambivalent about railroads) did not respond. But Scotty reached the Windy City at record speeds and had all the publicity he needed. So too did the Baldwin Locomotive Works, which published full details of the stunt made possible by its products. It added the names of all engineers involved, but not their firemen.[2]

The careful research of Frederick Westing[3] does tell us, however the name of the fireman on another legendary Atlantic flyer, the *Lindbergh Special* of 1927, the prince of coal shovellers, Fireman A. Hayden.

After completing the first solo transatlantic flight, Charles Lindbergh returned to the USA on USS *Memphis* which arrived at Washington Naval Yard on 11 June 1927. Movie cameras recorded the return of the hero, his acclaim by immense crowds, and a formal welcome by President Calvin Coolidge. The race was on to get the films developed and to New York in time for showing in cinemas that day. A co-operative effort by the International News Reel Company and the Pennsylvania Railroad won the race. The film was developed en route in a darkroom fixed up in a standard baggage-express car on Extra 460 East, a special hauled by the E6s Atlantic, No.460.

The 'Lindbergh Special' exceeded 100mph and reached Manhattan Transfer, 216 miles from Washington at an average speed of 74mph, hauled on its last leg by an electric locomotive. It arrived at Pennsylvania Station, New York nine minutes later, 3.21 p.m. and the films were being watched by cinema-goers on Broadway fifteen minutes later.

Not content with reporting the facts, the press created some news by claiming that Dixie Tighe, the only woman on the special had been riding in the 'cabin of the locomotive.' She was accordingly posed in the cab of a Baltimore & Ohio Atlantic (No.1434) which was obligingly standing at Washington just before the departure of the Pennsylvania special. The press may have thought that the laity would not distinguish a Pennsylvania 4-4-2 from a B&O one; assuming that reporters realised that there was a distinction to be made in any case.

In their last years the duties of Atlantics were more mundane than the glitzy world of specials and imperial trains, but they had their moments. A seasoned railwayman recalled that in wartime-occupied Egypt an Atlantic double-headed a heavy troop train with a 2-6-0. Coming the opposite way a 'Robinson' GCR-type 2-8-0 became derailed at some catch points. Attempts to re-rail it by coupling to the Atlantic merely wrenched out the coupling hooks. Next, chains were tried; they worked after a fashion but caused the 2-8-0 to crush the sleepers as it moved back on to the track. At length, with jacks, and a crane produced by ever-resourceful Americans, wrongs were righted and the trains went on their way.[4]

In the early twenty-first century another former railroader, once a young brakeman on the Missouri Pacific , recalled a venerable but game Brooks Atlantic (No.5522 of 1907) doing its turn on a 30-gondola ballast train, creeping along near Morrilton, Arkansas. Having unloaded the ballast, the 4-4-2 was turned on a wye and returned to base with a solitary, aged caboose. There was one oncoming train in the 70 miles ahead, so they returned at Atlantic speed hoping to eat up the miles before having to wait 'in the hole' for a meet with the other train. The last leg involved five miles in as many minutes and included a tunnel into which the Brooks engine plunged with its caboose. The crew held on: 'The sound was as if we'd hit a brick wall' The pressure imploded all the glass windows of the cupola; 'shattered pieces covered the floor...'[5]

Accidents

Atlantics were involved in many accidents, but their safety record was generally good and certainly comparable with other types of locomotive which tended to be driven *à l'outrance*.

Most accidents were slight mishaps, such as the occasions when LB&SCR No.37, an accident-prone engine, fell into the Brighton turntable pit during a snowstorm (17 February 1906); or suffered a left-hand driving wheel shifting on its axle, fortunately at low speed (11 May 1908); or was backed heavily on to a London express waiting in Brighton station, damaging a carriage which had to be removed (29 November 1914); and then again on 17 June 1918 when a driving wheel tyre broke between Earlswood and Horley. On this occasion No.37 was moving at great speed, hauling the 3.10 p.m. *Southern Belle*. The results could have been catastrophic but fortunately the engine stayed upright on the tracks and its crew stayed calmly at their posts.

A similar hairsbreadth escape from catastrophe occurred at Buddon on the Dundee and Arbroath Joint Line (LNER and LMS) on 28 June 1924 when LNER Atlantic No.9868 *Aberdonian* (formerly of the NDR) dragged a partly derailed train at 60mph before the fireman noticed what was amiss. Five out of twelve coaches remained on the rails and of the 200 passengers, only five complained of shock.

The mishap-prone sister of LB&SCR No.37, No.40 was less fortunate. On 29 January 1910 she was racing Northwards near Stoats Nest with a Pullman train (3.40 p.m., ex-Brighton) when the last six vehicles derailed and slewed across the tracks; one hit a platform ramp and five passengers were killed. Two passengers waiting on Stoats Nest platform were buried in the debris, but fortunately they survived. A bogie wheel shifting along its axle on one of the coaches was believed to be the cause, by fouling the bogie frame and working into red heat before mounting a check-rail and derailing the carriage.[6]

One of the worst Atlantic accidents in Britain involved the GNR large 4-4-2, No.276 which derailed at Grantham, 9 September 1906 causing fourteen deaths including the engine crew. The cause of the tragedy remains a mystery, 'the most mysterious major accident in railway history' according to L.T.C. Rolt[7]. Atlantic No.276 on the 'down mail', was due to stop at Grantham to unload and take on mail at about 11.00 p.m.; all signals were correctly set. Instead of slowing down the train continued at about 45mph through the station and on to a curve which took the Nottingham branch from the mainline; the points for this branch were still set following the passage of a heavy mineral train. The Atlantic swept round the curve at such a speed that its tender derailed, causing the engine to skew across the track. The coaches then smashed into it. One theory was that its driver had perhaps had a heart attack, and his fireman (a promising Doncaster premium apprentice, R. Talbot) had not noticed in time; both were killed.

In rare cases two Atlantics struck each other, as at York, 19 August 1919. NER class Z Atlantic No.2198 was approaching York station and struck a class V/09 Atlantic No.701, the driver of which had over-run signals. Human error also caused NER class Z Atlantic No.720 to strike the rear of an empty stock train at Auckland Junction (19 December 1921) and, detached from its tender, to roll down an embankment. The porter in charge of a local shunting operation had neglected both to place a tail-lamp on the stock train and to tell the signalman that he had put the train on the main line – the signalman believed it was still tucked in a siding.

More tragically, when coaches were being shunted at Darlington, 27 June 1928 the driver of the 4-6-0 concerned over-ran two signals and put his carriages athwart the main line, in the path of a crowded Scarborough excursion train bearing down behind class Z1 Atlantic No.2164 at about 45mph. In the resulting smash, the worst in Britain involving an Atlantic, twenty-five passengers were killed in telescoping coaches. Fourteen of the dead were from one County Durham mining village, Hetton-le-Hole. The Atlantic, a tough bird (NER Darlington, 1914) was duly repaired and survived to be the last operational NER 4-4-2 of them all, withdrawn in December 1948.

The deaths of these excursionists and other passengers may have been poignant, but the more frequent injuries and mortality of railway staff have tended to receive less attention and comment in general railway history. For instance, an equally moving tale of disaster occurred on the LNER main line, again near Grantham, on 19 January 1936. Two NER Atlantics (Nos 2198 and 2199) returning light to York overshot three sets of signals at danger and ran into the rear of a ballast train, killing eight permanent way staff.

At Burntisland, in the dark, small hours of 14 April 1914, the East Coast express (London–Aberdeen) hauled by NBR Atlantic No.872, *Auld Reekie* had a crew comprising driver John Dickson 'one of the most reliable drivers in the company's service', and fireman McDonald with 'an absolutely clean record' (both statements from Colonel Mount, Board of Trade Inspecting Officer). It proceeded swiftly under signals worked by a strictly-living teetotal signalman. Not ostensibly very promising circumstances for a crash, but by a combination of minor signalling confusions and errors, *Auld Reekie* struck a glancing blow to a goods engine backing from the main line, leapt off the track and came to rest on its side in the soft earth of Lundin Links golf course. Dickson and McDonald were killed under the jack-knifing tender.

The general judgement given by the Scottish railway historian John Thomas with regard to the NBR Atlantics would, however, hold good *mutatis mutandis* for all British 4-4-2s: 'Considering that the Atlantics were employed continuously on high speed trains traversing difficult routes for thirty-three years their accident record was commendable. In none of the few accidents in which the class was involved was any fault attributed to the engines.'

This would apply also to the excellent class P Atlantics of the Danish State Railways, even though one of them was involved in one of Denmark's worst rail accidents on 1 November 1919. Atlantic No.904 ran into a passenger train waiting in Vigerslev station. Restored to working order it sallied forth for a long career, and was one of the few P class to be selected for conversion to a 4-6-2 (class PR). In its new Pacific guise it suffered a head-on collision near Brorup exactly thirty-two years later to the day after Vigerslev. This time DSB drew the line and it was scrapped; like LB&SCR No.37 it seems to have been an unlucky, even jinxed, engine.

The elements have been a major cause of railway woes. Another Atlantic twice involved in accidents was Lancashire & Yorkshire No.1404, the victim of a minor crash at Sowerby Bridge. Four years later (30 November 1907) it ran into a stationary cattle train at Bamber Bridge, in thick fog. The destruction was considerable, the Atlantic's bogie was torn off and its massive front end stove in; the victims were twenty pigs. On 18 March 1915 L&Y Atlantic No.1394 sped the Leeds-Fleetwood boat express through the worst blizzard for many years. Much of Lancashire was whitened out. The frost and weight of the snow interfered with the movements of a distant signal near Rochdale causing the Atlantic's driver (J. Moon) to keep up speed. He ran into a standing train, losing his own life in the resulting collision, which destroyed large quantities of rolling stock, and took several other lives.

On a December evening in 1916 there was an accident 'of the new type' in the USA: the anthracite-burning Camelback Atlantic No.2463 (Baldwin, 1900) of the Lehigh Valley Railroad ran into an automobile on a grade crossing near Geneva, NY. The car was crushed out of existence; the Camelback fell on to its left side but was soon back at work. What else could be the outcome when the hammer meets the egg? There had been many such accidents before and multitudes more were to come.[8] There exists an old flashlight picture of the

Aftermath: *22 October 1903, L&Y Atlantic No.1404 on a Leeds-Liverpool express punched a tank engine right through Sowerby Bridge tunnel (660 yards), miraculously no lives were lost although a good deal of frame-straightening was called for.*

tragedy encapsulating a great deal. The Atlantics, for all their grace, seem elephantine beside mere motor cars. But despite their faults they were generally very safe custodians of travellers. Could the same be said of the motor-cars that replaced them? The statistics suggest not.

The great steadiness at speed of the Tasmanian 'double-Atlantics' may have caused the accident at Campania, 1916 when the Launceston-Hobart express derailed, killing the driver and seven passengers. Poor track may have been the cause but the Garratts rode exceptionally well and the driver may have underestimated his speed. The administrators played safe and put the double-Atlantics on to freight work.

Safety on railways depends on an accumulation of wisdom, custom and practice which is built into legislation and rule-books. How far the Atlantics contributed to this cumulative expertise is hard to say but in one respect their contribution was important. By raising the average speeds of prestige expresses in well-publicised ways and doing so with, generally, a high degree of safety they demonstrated that high speed was not of itself dangerous. The Atlantics have other claims to fame, but this was an important one.

Notes to Chapter 9

1. Murphy's Law: *if it can go wrong, it will*, refined (Gumperson's Law) into: *the unexpected always occurs when least convenient.* The Kitchener incident provided other vivid demonstrations of the law, mainly after the party had left the mainland.

2. Baldwin Locomotive Works, *Record of Recent Construction, No.56*, 1906. In all fairness it noted that two of the engines were products of the Rhode Island Works, Alco from 1906.

3. Frederick Westing, *op cit.* The PRR had run similar specials before; to rush an opera singer from one concert to another, and a loquacious politician between consecutive rallies; see G. Freeman Allen, *The Fastest Trains in the World*, 1978.

4. See Chapter 5, note 2

5. Clifton E. Hull, 'Just in time' *Trains*, June 2000.

6. D. L. Bradley, *The Locomotives of the London, Brighton & South Coast Railway, Part 3*, 1974; Bradley cites both Nos 40 and 41 as being involved at Stoats Nest; No.41 was the locomotive in question.

7. L.T.C. Rolt, *Red For Danger*, 1955. Although the Grantham accident cannot be ascribed to locomotive design, the Ivatt Atlantics had swing-link bogies which tended to 'dig-in' the wheel flanges on sharp curves in contrast to the 'Alsatian' bogies of the Nord Atlantics which opposed initial sideways movement with countervailing, spring-loaded pressure. The Grantham Atlantic stuck well to the rails, it was its tender which came adrift and derailed it.

8. Grade crossing accidents have been a global tragedy, but particularly serious in the USA; 4,000 people died in this way in 1902, nearly 14,000 in 1919. The increasing use of motor cars played a part in this grim statistic, as did accelerated trains. Thus the Atlantic was thus an engine of destiny, in a more sinister sense. See John Stilgoe, *Metropolitan Corridor, Railroads and the American Scene*, 1983.

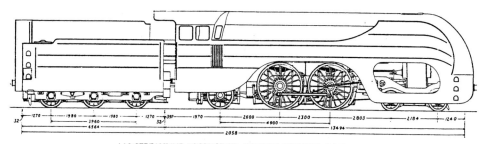

4-4-2 STREAMLINE LOCOMOTIVE, BELGIAN NATIONAL RAILWAYS.

Belgian semi-streamlined Atlantic (Cockerill, 1939) the last 4-4-2s to be built.

Chapter 10
Some Atlantic People

Women and Atlantics

An engine I remember well is No.990. My father took my sister Dorothy and me to the station to see her first run through. We stood on the main up platform near the bookstall. 'Here she comes!' father said; and a tall slim silver-grey engine with a very long train swished quietly through the station…It seemed ghost-like, somehow to me at 10…

The words of Ivatt's daughter Marjorie, later the wife of Oliver Bulleid and mother of H.A.V. Bulleid who recorded her words in his *Bulleid of the Southern*, 1977.[1]

As the daughter an Atlantic-designing engineer, Marjorie Bulleid, *née* Ivatt was better-placed than most women of her day to have her consciousness raised about the finer points of locomotive design. She was born into a world where gender-determination of roles, interests and professions was immeasurably stronger than a century later. Under that old order, steam engineering was overwhelmingly a male sphere of interest. Even so, there exists an alternative or supplementary history of Atlantics perceived by women; the patchiness of its archive is itself instructive.

The first major conjunction between women and Atlantics occurred in the Great War when female labour was recruited to fill vacancies left by men who had gone to fight. At Low Moor on the Lancashire & Yorkshire, W Paterson, M.I. Loco.E.[2] observed the war had 'led to the introduction of female labour in the locomotive department…women have been usefully employed as fitter's labourers, general labourers, boiler washers, steam crane drivers…as well as for engine cleaning.' His point was made forcefully with an official photograph of an L&Y Atlantic (No.1406) completely covered by women cleaners, seventeen atop the boiler alone.

Similar conditions existed at Doncaster where women got the grease encrustations off Ivatt Atlantics, removing ash and char and preparing them for the road. Here, however, women also rubbed down, repainted and polished the Atlantics; photographic evidence exists (E.A. Pratt, *British Railways and the Great War,* 1921) of a kind which suggests that women of average height and size were better suited to the exiguous cabs on these engines than men. But driving and firing Atlantics was not for women workers; they filled only such niches as the patriarchal order saw fit.

Boundaries were extended slightly between the wars, mainly on miniature railways. Eleanor, daughter of the leading miniature Atlantic designer Henry Greenly assisted her father in his drawing office. Mrs Notter assisted her husband E.F.S. Notter, District Locomotive Superintendent at King's Cross and one of the great originals of his profession, to construct a superb model Ivatt Atlantic in the family home. Occasionally women took a hand at operation: there exists another photograph of a 6.5 ton Atlantic *Douglas Clayton* on the 15in gauge miniature railway at Hardwicke Manor near Tewkesbury, *c.*1935[3] resting at a water tower and being replenished by a well-dressed woman in a stylish hat.

Snippets of correspondence or reminiscences by women[4] hint at what might have been, or went largely unrecorded: 'We used to go down to the Tay Bridge station [Dundee] to see them [former NB Atlantics, identified by names] go through each afternoon; they were well-kept, beautifully kept…'; or an intriguing piece of neo-Platonism: '…big wheels and a great bark, just like an engine ought to be...' [a GN Atlantic]; and 'a work-horse, looks dependable, but heavy and even dangerous...' [of an Hungarian Atlantic, class In].

In the main span of the Atlantic era women had to exist on the margins of 'Atlanticana', as passengers, observers, partners of the main players. As the interesting vestiges of discourse quoted above suggest, the world remains the poorer.

Atlantic Firemen and Tallow-Pots

The test of an LNER 4-4-2 (number not cited, but a former NER engine) was reported by Sir Nigel Gresley to the Institution of Mechanical Engineers, 1924; he stated that in one hour it consumed 71.1-103.7lbs of coal per square foot of grate. If it were a class V or Z this would imply up to 1.25 tons of coal per hour. When the class V 4-4-2s were young (1906) a journalist[5] joined the footplate staff to see the working of Atlantic No.784, (Gateshead 1903). He reported that the cab was furnished with cushion-covered wooden seats; 'when running however, he seldom sits down', 'he' being Driver William Johnson of Gateshead. But who kept the tons of Shilbottles moving into the firebox so that 'the coal, which is fairly soft, burned with but little smoke'? We are not told, although there was time to note such items as 'tremendous seas [which] could be seen breaking over Tweedmouth breakwater' as they neared the Royal Border bridge.

The hard-won skills of Atlantic drivers are rightly recognised, but what of the other, less publicised half of the team?

The most demanding of Atlantic firing jobs was probably that involving the Pennsylvania E6s class, which could develop up to 2,400 hp for long periods. Like most Atlantics the E6s class required firemen with unusually well-toned back muscles and unyielding stamina. Fortunately for once we have some names and details to hand.[6] Doyen of the E6s firemen was Norman Suhrie who had established his reputation by being the duty fireman at the St Louis World's Fair trials in 1904

Opinions differed amongst enginemen about how best to fire an Atlantic with its large firebox. Drawing on experience the two main schools of thought were 'little and often' during the journey, or heavy preparation before it, 'bank-firing'. A crack E6s driver, Martin H. Lee believed in the bank-firing system; being an old hand at firing he offered to teach his firemen the tricks of the trade. Not all took up the offer, however, since bank-firing required hard careful work and was generally frowned upon by Authority. But once done a fireman could leave the blazing mass of coals alone for a while, up to seventy miles on an E3d Atlantic, while he concentrated on his other duties: watching water gauge-glasses, keeping the boiler filled, and assisting the driver with signal-watching. Some drivers inflicted their own, occasionally idiosyncratic, ideas on the firemen, such as one who insisted that an E6s firedoor be kept ajar, and steam pressure maintained at 180lb sq in – 20lb sq in below the intended maximum. Authority did not like this eccentricity either; it reduced the drawbar pull, but it also lessened the risk of wheel-slip.

The Footplatemen's emblem:
*Atlantics of the GNR (left) and
Brighton Line (right) flank a
London electric tube train on this
ASLEF certificate of 1921; a
Trade Union document rich with
symbolism: peaceful doves, indus-
trious bees, worthy deities, and
the last cry in prestigious traction.*

In the UK we know more about the firing and footplate conditions of Ivatt large Atlantics than any other class of 4-4-2 mainly because there were so many of these engines. A consid-erable authority on the subject, not a railwayman but a scientist, was Dr W.A. Tuplin[7] who brought the subject alive with descriptions of actual and 'factional' footplate journeys. Younger readers (*Trains Annual*, 1965) were told of Tuplin's footplate journey aboard an Ivatt Atlantic from Nottingham to Sheffield.

> *It was normal practice to shovel heavy charges into the back of the wide firebox of an Atlantic
> and let it roll and shuffle wherever the vibration took it... 'little and often' is more troublesome
> for the fireman [however] I worked in a sequence of feeding four shovelfuls carefully through the
> fire-hole and then closing the trap...The men were amused by my use of gloves, uncommon in
> British firing practice at the time, but in placing coal into the back corners of the firebox one's
> hands come close to the flame, which with little-and-often firing is white and scorching.*

Tuplin recorded that the response of his Atlantic to a semi-skilled attempt at good firing was 'fervent and even embarrassing' with steam blowing-off noisily. He thought that merely watching a skilled fireman at work gave little idea of the 'job of swinging coal through a shallow slot in face of powerful radiation.'

Fettling up: *Atlantics looked well from many angles; here an NER class Z1 is prepared for the road c.1912; painted, lined out and polished in every nook and cranny. It is about to head the 12.20 p.m. Newcastle-Sheffield express, 'the fastest train in the British Empire', another Atlantic coup.*

In spite of the crew's hilarity about Tuplin's gloves, R.H.N. Hardy recorded[8] that

> *[on] the GNR Atlantics – during the war, some firemen were using a gauntlet on their left hand...but it got uncomfortable and a cloth was better in my opinion...I have often heard of drivers using aprons in their younger days...*

Another line on firing a GNR large Atlantic, from T.C.B. Miller, Chief Engineer (Traffic and Rolling Stock) of British Railways:

> *There was a particular technique in their firing; as soon as the pressure dropped by 5lb, eight shovelfulls were put on, one in each corner and four down the middle...[9]*

The first-hand experiences of an Atlantic fireman were posted on the web in 2001; Hal Hughes, who had once fired Atlantics on the Northern Railway in India recorded his experiences on a typical run from Saharanpur to Delhi; driver Mr Collis, second fireman Gurbux Singh; a team to guide the 'Queen of Locomotives' on her way. Firing techniques were described in close detail, for example:

...this is a knack one learns on an EM because the fire grate slopes down towards the tube plate and also due to the draught the coal gets pulled down towards the tube plate... I go over and open the firebox door and put on two shovels' full in each back corner of the firebox, four spread over the rest... (two just near the door and two sprayed from outside the door)...

Amongst the toughest of Atlantic firemen were those who fed anthracite culm into the Wootten fireboxed Camelbacks in the USA:

In 90 per cent of Camelbacks the fireman was out in the open with the scantiest of overhead protection; and all that guarded him from a sideways fall...was a chain...He was on the coal plate of the tender, and with each shovelful of culm he had to step on to the fall plate..between engine and tender...Under these conditions, with engine motion at its worst because of the long, heavy overhang, and the tender bucketing along behind...he had to shovel anything up to two tons of culm an hour from one vehicle to the other.[10]

Since some Camelback 4-4-2s had two fireholes, it helped if the fireman was ambidextrous. Statements about arduous conditions are, of course, relative – Ron Scott[11] thought that 'Firing [a GNR large Atlantic] was not difficult once the fireman had learned to ride the lurching gait of the engine.' A few Atlantics, mainly in America, were oil-fired and mechanical stoking developed too late for large-scale installation on time-expired 4-4-2s. The majority of Atlantics were hand-fired, coal-burning muzzle-loaders; firing their voracious fireboxes from a roughly oscillating footplate was hard, demanding and exhausting.

Closely Observed Atlantics: Watchers and Recorders

Charles Rous-Marten's publicising of the Atlantics' achievements in their early years contributed to their growing success simply by 'raising consciousness.' He was among the first of the guild of numerous railway people, amateur and professional, who observed and recorded the railways at work and gave their contemporaries an account of what was going on, as well as presenting posterity with a priceless, if necessarily selective, chronicle of 'how the railways were.' Rous-Marten founded the world's longest-running chronicle of such matters, 'British Locomotive Practice and Performance', published by the *Railway Magazine* from 1901. After his death in 1908, and a brief collegiate authorship, Cecil J. Allen carried the tradition forward until 1958; thence O.S. Nock, and latterly Peter Semmens. Allen and Nock both contributed to 'Atlanticology' first by carrying on Rous-Marten's critical record of Atlantics at work, later by writing retrospectively on the subject, for example in Allen's *British Atlantic Locomotives* (1968), and Nock's *Classic Locomotives, Great Northern 4-4-2 Atlantics* (1984); Atlanticists will long be in debt to them.

Many other people contributed to the Atlantic record. Baron Vuillet working in France and elsewhere put Atlantic performance (and much else) into a wide context. He had observed Nord Atlantics at work, as well as recording the near-legendary feats of the Milwaukee Road *Hiawathas*, in both cases from their footplates. Like other front-line specialists he drew on contributions from an army of well-travelled spies. Few activities, other than popular sports, have enjoyed so long and well-informed a scrutiny.

Early contributions to the record were often wordy in the manner of the times. Rous-Marten often used three words where one would suffice: 'The present able Locomotive Superintendent [Ivatt] of the Great Northern recognised very soon after his advent that the need had arisen for an absolutely new locomotive type and he, first among all British loco-motive engineers, introduced the 'Atlantic' design. No.990, the pioneer of this 'breed' has now twenty sister engines...' (*Railway Magazine*, August 1905).[12]

Allen knew the British Atlantics from their classic period, through the interwar renais-sance to their eventual demise. Looking back over 300 'Practice and Performance' articles in July, 1935, he recalled some all-time fine performances. These included the memorable run of GNR Atlantic No.1452, the first superheated 4-4-2 of its class, when 'no fewer than' 64 axles (490 tons) were whipped down from Doncaster to King's Cross, in booked time occasionally touching 77.5mph, a remarkable feat for the day. He praised the performance of an NER 4-4-2 in 1912 which kept excellent time with a packed 500-ton train, standing room only. In September 1921, long before the pyrotechnics of the 1930s revival, he found that 'the work that the 'Atlantics' can do when put to it is nothing short of astonishing...' In an article about NER and GNR 4-4-2s which included reference to a 600-ton load 'with heavy baggage literally to the roof' he remembered arriving at King's Cross ahead of schedule. 'Had I not timed it myself, I would never have considered it possible!'

The great stopwatchers had to be selective in their record. In summarising his Scottish experiences of 1926, for example, Allen admitted that his single LNER 'Waverley' route journey behind Atlantic No.9906, *Teribus* was 'one very dull effort' on the 1.05 p.m. from Carlisle to Edinburgh, the engine evidently not exerting itself and arriving at Waverley station a quarter of an hour late. But any attempt to generalise from such a journey, which Allen rightly declined to do, would be a text-book example of false induction. Other records demonstrate that the NBR Atlantics were performing excellently at the time. Allen himself noted, not for the first time and doubtless in vain, that the monthly articles instituted by Rous-Marten were not intended to be a topographical survey of all that occurred, but rather 'to keep readers...abreast of current developments in locomotive constructional practice, and of the capacity of locomotive types...as expressed by their work on the road.'

Like Rous-Marten, Allen received many records from private individuals, some of which he used. O.S. Nock recalled a meticulous amateur recorder A.F. Webber (a consulting engineer), who sent Allen details of an amazing Atlantic performance by the Grantham station pilot, a veteran 4-4-2 which took over the down *Flying Scotsman* from a failed Pacific and more than met the challenge. Allen apparently found the details unbelievable and set them aside; Nock – a friend of Webber – put the record straight in later years.[13]

Many of the private observers kept details to themselves, or within their circles. In later years, long after the Atlantics were gone, some of the data emerged to add to our knowledge of a typical (or occasionally untypical) 'day in the life of an Atlantic.' The *Journal* of the Stephenson Locomotive Society in the 1970s contained papers of this kind often in close detail. They included the use of former GNR Atlantics on the Great Central line between the wars; Atlantics on the Grimsby-Banbury fish trains, 1923-1942; the final runs of the Brighton Atlantics; details of SR workings of former Brighton Atlantics in the 1930s; and Lancashire & Yorkshire Atlantics in Halifax and beyond, 1912-1921. A paper on the latter described the daily working of Atlantics from four sheds (Leeds, Sandhills, Fleetwood, and

Newton Heath). From Fleetwood: 'A 4-4-2...worked the 1.23 p.m. from Fleetwood to Manchester, 3.40 p.m. out of Liverpool from Manchester only (4.25 p.m.)...'[14]

The British railway-observing record, although long-established, is not unique. The famous work of the *Hiawathas*, for example, was described by Eric Crickmay (a British resident in the USA); Robert Park of the Australasian Railway Circle; and a Frenchman, Baron Gérard Vuillet.[15] Vuillet was a seasoned veteran of Atlantic recording; the index of his *Railway Reminiscences of Three Continents* (1968) refers to the performance of Atlantics on the Nord; Paris-Orleans; PLM; Pennsylvania; Reading; Southern Pacific; Milwaukee Road; Canadian Pacific; Germany (Baden); and Belgian State Railways. Like his British *confrères* he acknowledged the work of others which had enabled him to gather data widely, for example crediting details recorded by J.T. Burton Alexander regarding an achievement by one of the short-lived Canadian Pacific compound Atlantics, No.210 which touched 87mph between St Eugene and Rigaud on 21 August, 1900 when hauling a 200 ton load of *The Metropolitan Limited* – certainly comparable with anything going on around Atlantic City at the time.

Vuillet's work was particularly useful in immortalising the flyers of the 1930s; the rebuilt Nord 4-4-2s; the jazzed-up PLM Atlantics; and the Milwaukee Road and Belgian stream-liners which upheld the Atlantic tradition of high speed with limited trains. His hopes of trav-elling on the footplate of Belgian class 12 No.1201 were unfortunately curtailed, 'the declaration of war shattered this plan' and he had to make do with a print-out from a speedometer record of her sister inside-cylinder Atlantic, No.1201. This was not the real thing but exciting enough: 81mph at the junction for Denderleeuw; 92 mph just after Ghent.

Another reliable eye for the *Railway Magazine* was 'our valued correspondent' in Denmark, Mr James Steffenson who reported (April, 1937) 'an unusually fast Danish journey' during which a class P2 Atlantic left Masnedsund eighteen minutes late with a 350-ton boat train and yet contrived to arrive one minute early at its Copenhagen destination. To achieve this feat it had touched 72 mph, which was over the generally permitted limit.

The same number of the *RM* drew attention to an article by C.E.R. Sherrington in its contemporary, the *LNER Magazine* in which the author described an exciting journey on the footplate of a *Hiawatha*. He had stepped off the footplate as clean as when he boarded it; could make notes standing at 102mph (bearing out Vuillet's observations regarding the extra-ordinary steadiness of these engines) and had reached Milwaukee two minutes early in spite of a strong north-east wind which caused the engineer (Mr Falconer) to apologise for not attaining the customary 108mph. Sherrington was impressed by the oil-firing system; the fireman's only shovel-motions being to place three sandfuls of coarse sand into the firebox every twenty miles by way of scouring out the fire-tubes.

But what did the Atlantic-hauled trains look like, sound like? What could one see out of the carriage windows? What awaited travellers at journey's end? The answers are quite as much part of history as the start-to-stop times of Atlantic working from Edinburgh Waverley to Dundee, or Cairo to Alexandria. If we want to savour those experiences we have to look elsewhere. The master of this rarer genre was J.P. Pearson whose *Railways and Scenery* (1932) presented a record-in-depth of travel in the last years of the *ancien régime*, long before mass tourism, airport delays, and duty-free forays were everyday experiences; before the exotic magic of distance evaporated and was gone.

Great Northern, USA: *No.1702 of the ten-strong class K-1 (Baldwin, 1906) at St Paul, Minn, in the Spring of 1935. Originally a Cole 'balanced compound', now 2-cylinder simple; bogie with disc front wheels, spoked to rear; Belpaire firebox typical of the GN, but rare in USA.; dark green livery with striking logo on tender. Smaller than average drivers, 6ft diameter for hard work in Montana; sister of No.1700 which attracted J.P. Pearson's attention back in 1913.* Photo: Harold K. Vollrath.

Pearson's journeys (1888-1913) fill three closely-printed volumes, 2,080 pages in all. It became fashionable to deride his work as a cross between Cecil J. Allen and Mr Pooter; meticulous attention to detail on the one hand, but an indiscriminate recording of trifles on the other, a 'vast and shapeless assembly, as rambling as the author's journeys themselves... a mad, bad, almost unreadable book.' (Bryan Morgan, ed, *The Great Trains*, 1973). This uncharitable and misleading passage[16] carries a rider: 'And yet it is indispensable to anybody who wants to know what it felt like to travel over the railways of fifty countries...[in] the years of their greatness.'

Pearson's work coincided precisely with the roaring years of the Atlantics. A reading of *Railways and Scenery* also demonstrates when and where the Atlantics started to give way in favour of 4-6-0s and 4-6-2s, particularly in the USA. His recording was painstaking but erratic (he occasionally failed to supply details of motive power, weights of trains, etc.) but he had few peers in bringing the Atlantic era alive with his wand of prose.

In 1907, for example, he took the morning train from Charing Cross to Folkestone, thence by the SS *Queen* to Calais (105 minutes crossing) to catch a Paris train. Almost as an afterthought we learn that the fourteen-coach train was hauled by an engine which 'bore the number 2662', no further details given. This was in fact a Nord Atlantic. The coaches were a scratch lot of four and six-wheelers; the side windows in Pearson's coach 'were not arranged... to move up or down.' Our *rapporteur* arrives in Paris on Bastille Day, 'The streets were thronged with dancers and merrymakers...and presented a most brilliant aspect, and an old familiar smell (that, I think, of French tobacco)... the white electric lights of the Place de la Concorde were most dazzling to the eye...' A Nord Atlantic on 14 July in the *Belle Epoque* of the Third Republic, brought alive! Three years earlier at Schifferstadt, Pearson had noted one of the famed inside-cylinder Palatinate Atlantics hauling five eight-wheelers and two sixes, a caravan of coaches from Berlin to Saarbrücken, Dresden to Metz, and Würtzburg (and Innsbruck) to Neunkirchen, 'Where in any other country could such an array of through coaches be beaten?' He kept a weather-eye open for informed commentary upon which to draw comparisons. He read Rous-Marten closely and felt that although his own experiences with Nord Atlantics, 'these wonderful de Glehn locomotives' were good, none equated with 'the observations of the late Mr Rous-Marten who had very special facilities arranged for him' and who had drawn attention to 'our English performances [which] at the time suffered terribly [in comparison].' This observation came immediately after a run behind Nord No.2646, 'one of the finest efforts of this celebrated type of locomotive', notably a rock-steady 70mph from Pont-Remy to St-Roch, 34km (21.25 miles).

A last sample of Pearsoniana from the New World, where he was an enthusiastic visitor on more than one occasion. In 1912 Pearson was en route to the Niagara Falls on a chilly April day; Buffalo lay under a steely blue sky, its sidewalks 'sloppy...with melting snow...we were compelled to invest in Canadian overshoes...' He took the 12.50 am train, five 12-wheelers and two 8-wheelers of Grand Trunk Railway ownership, behind a Lehigh Valley Camelback Atlantic, No.2414, class F2. The day car impressed Pearson, with its reversible seats upholstered in 'bright green figured plush', end panels in brown wood, roof panels in green, and narrow clerestory lights of brown glass which sent their muted gleam to glint on brass luggage racks. This supplied a suitable overture to his day at the partly-frozen falls, set in air 'like champagne' and with groves of trees encased in ice. But later in the day he found evidence of the new locomotive order when he moved on to Toronto behind a Grand Trunk 4-6-0, and thence with a 4-6-2 to Montreal. Like the Wootten-fireboxed Lehigh Valley 4-4-2 the entire *mise en scène* seems now to belong to another planet, but thanks to the well-meant efforts of Pearson it can be recreated in the mind.

Coda. An intriguing question: were Atlantics observed by the noted Czech close-watcher of trains and well-informed spotter of Bohemian locomotives, Antonin Dvořák? He lived long enough to have a good look at the KFNB and ÖNWB Atlantics, even the initial kkStB 108s, all of which worked in or near his home territory.

Early Atlantic: *Lehigh Valley No.664 of class F1, Baldwin 1896 – a camelback seen in pristine condition at Mauch Chunk, Pa – July 1896; one of the first fifty Atlantics.* Photo: Harold K.Vollrath.

Notes for Chapter 10

1. There exists in another of H.A.V. Bulleid's works, *Master Builders of Steam*, 1963, an illustration of two of Ivatt's great-granddaughters driving a fine miniature GN Atlantic, No.251.

2. *Proceedings* of I Loco E, 1918.

3. Clarence Winchester (ed), *Railway Wonders of the World*, *c.*1935

4. Assiduously collected by the author over the years.

5. 'North Eastern Locomotive Running', *Locomotive Magazine*, 14 April 1906, anon.

6. See especially Frederick Westing. *Apex of the Atlantics*, 1963.

7. W.A. Tuplin, 1902-1975, Professor of Applied Mechanics, University of Sheffield and with considerable industrial experience; a controversialist who did much to alert his large audience to the crucial importance of unglamorous fireboxes, grates and ashpans in the development of the steam locomotive.

8. *Journal* of the SLS 48, 582, May 1972.

9. Quoted in Colonel H.C.B. Rogers, *Express Steam Locomotive Development in Great Britain & France*, 1990.

10. Brian Reed, *Camels and Camelbacks*, Loco Profile 9, 1971.

11. Ron Scott, *G.N. Large Atlantics*, Loco Profile 30, 1972.

12. Not alone in employing familiar statistical pads, e.g. *no fewer than*, as in: 'But now there are no fewer than thirty more of the "Atlantic" type...' *Railway Magazine*, August 1905.

13. O.S. Nock, *The Great Northern Railway*, 1958.

14. The articles were, in turn: R.A. Simpson 'GNR Atlantics on the Great Central', August 1976; David Jackson and Owen Russell, 'Grimsby-Banbury Fish Trains, 1923-42'; Bruce I. Nathan, 'London to Brighton Non-stop', August 1978; Norman Harvey, 'Recollections of the Marsh Atlantics', May 1970; and J.E. Shaw, 'Memories of the Lancashire & Yorkshire Railway' Pt I, May 1970.

15. See for example *Railway Magazine*, April 1938.

16. Pearson was a kindly man whose journeys, far from 'rambling' were planned with excellent staff-work, and gave high value for money.

Chapter 11
Atlantics & Aesthetics:
the Atlantic as Art

Form, Function, Proportion

The Atlantic has been one of the select few of steam locomotives which has been singled out for more aesthetic praise than most. Writing of the Atlantics of the Reading Railroad, Robert K. Durham noted 'such elegant lines; such grace; from the pointed cowcatcher to the magnificent spoked wheels...' Seeing one of the original 'Klondyke' GNR 4-4-0s entering King's Cross at the head of a train, Walter Bell, consulting editor of *The Locomotive* turned away from a crowd admiring the LNER A4 Pacific streamliner *Silver Link* to gaze at the veteran C2: 'That' he said with feeling 'is a pretty engine.'

C. Hamilton Ellis, a notable expert on locomotive aesthetics, thought the Ivatt Atlantic was 'extremely handsome' and that the gaunt Lancashire & Yorkshire 4-4-2s if 'not quite a poem in steel' were surely 'the most imposing thing to appear on British rails in all the Victorian era.' He also thought the Danish class-P Atlantics, the end of whose careers closed the Atlantic chapter in Europe were 'the last of their beautiful race.' Robin Barnes, historian and artist of the locomotive thought Atlantics had 'an elegance of line which has never been surpassed.' To Cecil J. Allen there was 'one legacy which the Atlantic left us... it is of having bequeathed some of the most lovely locomotive lines ever seen in Great Britain...'

The encyclopedia of the Atlantics by Wilhelm Reuter and Claus Bock was entitled *Eleganz auf Schienen*, 'Elegance on Rails.' Robert K Durham again: 'Such beauty of line and form would not go unnoticed in the world of art and sculpture.' This was indeed an expression of the true form... The true artist of this time was the designer of these beautiful machines.'[1]

The theory and doctrines of industrial design in relation to steam locomotives are in short supply,[2] but criteria for judging locomotive elegance can be derived from some general considerations in particular that form should follow function, a necessary condition but not a sufficient one as the Bulleid Q1 0-6-0 suggests. Other conditions include a respect for good proportion, for a balance of parts and the whole; lines which flow and interact easily, sensitively; and the crucial quality of being the right size. All these conditions have to relate together as an entirety. Also the locomotive must please the eye when in motion as much as when still; and when still, fired-up, sussurating in a station just as much as when it reposes cold in a museum. Aesthetically and functionally a good Atlantic embodied controlled exuberance able to delight the souls who contemplated it; as near a perfectly-proportioned machine as one has a right to expect.

By the 1880s the locomotive designers had developed considerable sureness of aesthetic touch, particularly in Britain. Although usually well-trained in draughtsmanship, they were not primarily artists in the conventional sense. But even the earliest essays in locomotive design, the work of the pioneers, the Stephensons, Bury, Hedley, Norris, Haswell and others had an honest handsomeness which soon blossomed into well-proportioned machines. Generally the best-looking locomotives were the products of minds that had *not* received special training in art or objectified 'design' in its modern sense.

The Atlantic era arrived just as locomotive aesthetics peaked. In the hands of design teams led by engineers like J.G. Robinson of the Great Central, or Karl Gölsdorf in Austria, the 4-4-2 demonstrated the best qualities of the 'great tradition' of engine design. W.M. Smith, chief draughtsman of the NER remembered mainly for his technical virtuosity was another designer able to conjure up, apparently effortlessly, a lovely machine from the drawing board such as his class 4CC Atlantics. The Atlantic form enjoyed certain qualities of proportion, size, line and coherence, a pleasing sum of parts which gave it grace and interest even in the hands of average draughtsmen; it was curiously proof against slips of the potter's hand.

There were a few such slips, but these were more a falling-away from good taste than being intrinsically ugly or displeasing. The low, inside-cylinder, outside-frame 4-4-2 *Lady Cromer* produced by North British Locomotive for Egypt was a case in point as were the NBL's low-slung Atlantics for the Cordoba Central in Argentina. Some other narrow-gauge Atlantics inclined to dumpiness; some broad-gauge versions towards being gangly. The reduction of driving-wheel diameter on the Illinois Central freight Atlantics, and the low profile of the Stannary Hills machine in Queensland still maintained some of the style inseparable from the 4-4-2 form. It was not easy to arrange an aesthically pleasing Camelback Atlantic, but the designers at Altoona and Philadelphia did well in handling the conflicting lines and proportions of this unusual model.

These considerations held for miniature Atlantics also. David Moseley and Peter Zeller opined: 'Greenly's freelance design [for a 4-4-2] compared in beauty of form with the full size North Eastern Railway or Great Central Railway locomotives' (*Fifteen Inch Gauge Railways*, 1986).

Locomotive designers, working for any gauge, had to assemble the parts together into an attractive whole. This was less complex in Britain where the norm was a locomotive with inside valve gear, and no bells, feed-water apparatus, sand-domes, or steam-driven pumps to relate to the entirety. The tendency towards 'bolt-on extras' and mounting large outside piston-valves in the 1920s, particularly in the USA, could spoil the original balance of form which was the outcome of a single mind, or more usually, team.

With deference to neo-Platonists, in the absence of any 'one, true, and perfect' Atlantic as a criterion of excellence, it is not easy to establish agreement in this field. Thus, O.S. Nock contemplating an Atlantic designed and built for the Taokow-Chinghua Railway by Kerr, Stuart & Co. of Stoke-on-Trent (1912) commented:

> *If a competition were to be held for the most handsome locomotive ever exported from Great Britain one could well imagine that these Chinese 'Atlantics' would come well within the 'top ten'... Their lines have all the grace of British locomotive practice at its most elegant....*[3] But Steve Llanso, a widely-informed American source thought at first sight of this Kerr, Stuart model: *a matter of taste, one supposes. The boiler is pitched high, with a lot of air showing above the splashers, the capped stack and small cylinders seem undersized, and a Belpaire firebox never conferred smooth lines on a boiler...*[4]

Atlantic era: *classic shot of a classic engine, Wabash-Pittsburgh Terminal No.2001 (Alco, Brooks 1905) now at work on the Wheeling & Lake Erie, Fremont, Ohio, 1910 and still bearing its original number. Both roads were components of the Gould railroad empire which disintegrated after the 1907 financial panic.* Photo: Collection of Howard W. Ameling.

What an observer is used to seeing often confers a 'right' set of proportions to a familiar Atlantic, tending to cast others in a less favourable light. People who prefer the plain GWR style of locomotive would not agree with the Hungarian engineer's view that Swindon products looked like 'plucked chickens.'[5] To many British eyes, Hungarian engines looked overburdened with accessories and accoutrements; their otherwise superb Atlantics being spoiled by a large Pecz-Rejtö water-purifying cylinder perched on the boiler top.

The broadside view of an Atlantic showed up such infelicities of proportion as might be. A common weakness of design lay in the disposition of coupling and connecting rods, since drive was generally to the rear axle, and this could result in a bunched-up appearance particularly when the wheelbase was short. Atlantics with drive to the front axle appeared more at ease: the NER Z class, the Prussian S9s; the Austrian and Hungarian Atlantics; the Shanghai-Nanking 4-4-2 and some American exceptions to the rule, for example on the Santa Fe. Unlike many locomotives, it was strong in its rear three-quarter view as well as from the front quarters. Here may lie the secret of its looks: from whichever standpoint it was viewed, the combination of leading, driving and trailing wheels, particularly of large-diameter driving wheels (the norm for most Atlantics) gave the 4-4-2 a completeness of form lacking in the more abrupt configuration of a 4-6-0.

The different Atlantic forms threw light on the issue of locomotive aesthetics. The Prussian S9 class had a long, lean, low style imparted by setting the trailing axle far back, the better to accommodate a large firebox and well-aired, accessible ashpan. Two contenders for the most gaunt of Atlantics were the Lancashire & Yorkshire 1400 class, severely plain and with unusually high-pitched boilers, and Gölsdorf's stately 108 class for the Austrian State Railways. In both cases a master-touch with the splashers made the engine striking rather than plain: Aspinall (or possibly his Chief Draughtsman, Zachariah Tetlow) encased the massive 7ft 3in wheels of the 1400s in large double splashers with well-proportioned central slots for lubrication. The second series of L&Y Atlantics were better detailed with split hand-rails, narrow valances and a tighter sweep to the cab cut-out. In the Austrian 108s, Gölsdorf's flair for the controlled style showed itself in huge, horizontal splashers, open-sided and set high, eye-catchingly generous but knowing exactly where to stop. If the 108s had an aesthetic flaw, it lay in the relatively short distance between the rear driving wheels and the trailing wheels, offset by its chief cause, placing the drive on to the forward axle which gave an easy, graceful disposition to the driving and valve-gear array.

Atlantic wheel-proportions are a revealing study in themselves. Virtually all American Atlantics had bogie wheel diameters of 33in or 36in (838mm, 914mm). Elsewhere there was much greater variety, but in virtually all American or European Atlantics, the trailing wheels were notably larger. The driving wheels of most 4-4-2s, designed for high-speed work, were usually large, even very large and this added to the thoroughbred looks of the machine. The largest were found on the Lancashire & Yorkshire 'Highflyers', 7ft 3in (2,210mm), but these engines had relatively small trailing wheels of 3ft 7in (1,108mm) which spoilt their proportions. The early ACL Atlantics had exceptionally large trailing wheel diameters, 4ft 11in (1,270mm) and the relative proportions worked better. In the absence of a Vitruvius or Palladio of the locomotive to offer guidance on correct proportions a pragmatic line must be taken. Most Atlantics had driving wheels 1.4-1.6 times the diameter of the trailing wheels. The ACL ratio was 1.44; the L&Y, 1.9 (the largest). Some early American Atlantics had exceptionally low ratios arising from huge trailing wheels, for example on the Wabash, Lehigh Valley and Milwaukee Road. The golden mean which looked good was about 1.54. Chicago, Rock Island & Pacific class A-24, a Brooks Chautauqua of 1901, for example was attractively proportioned in this way.

The Dutch Atlantics had exceptionally large drivers, 7ft (2,134mm) but their double frames, a great rarity on Atlantics, hid the effect. The Shanghai-Nanking Atlantics of 1914 had 7ft driving wheels, their effect masked by the overall height of the engine. The lower-lying Atlantics, such as the Stannary Hills 4-4-2, or the Cordoba Central quintet (NBL, 1907) had small, 3ft driving wheels, as did the Nippon Tetsudo, Cape Government (both 4ft 7in diameter) and the unique 3ft gauge Washington & Plymouth Atlantic (Baldwin 1902, driving wheels 2ft 3in). These Atlantics hardly had the racehorse look about them, but they still exhibited good proportions.

The Nord Atlantics not only had a delicacy of line and form which belied their considerable power but also well-proportioned valve gear motions which demonstrated the harmony of mobile geometry. But for an honest expression of brute power, a large-boilered Pennsylvania E6s could hardly be bettered for forward-hunched, bisonic force either at rest or on the move.

Individual touches of form and function enhanced the attractions of Atlantics. The Prussian and Hungarian 4-4-2s, for example, had conical smokebox doors, the *spitzer Rauchkammertür*, said to improve gas circulation and draughting within as well as lifting exhaust without. In line with the railway's policy the *Südbahn* Atlantics in Austria had an inverted saucer-shaped object over the whistle, the *Schallteller* , which deflected sound around the locomotive so as not to waste energy by alerting the fowls of the air to an oncoming train. The Paris-Orleans 2-4-2 conversions had sloping slide-valves actuated by the elegant evolutions of a Gooch valve-gear, and every American Atlantic was adorned with a fine bell, often well-burnished in the Atlantics' golden age.

J.G. Robinson of the Great Central who thought that a chimney, like a hat, 'completed the locomotive'[6], it was a sensitive crowning touch to a locomotive's design. They differed in form from the plain parabolic stovepipes in the USA, seen to good advantage on the Santa Fe Atlantics, through copper-capped GWR versions and emphatically capuchoned Belgian designs to some huge spark-arresting devices on the ÖNWB, known colloquially as the *Nachttopfschornstein*, chamber-pot chimney. The Danes embellished smokestacks with a broad band bearing the national colours; the Swedes' were black, showing large brass locomotive numbers. All Atlantic chimneys told the trained eye something about the nationality and ownership of the locomotives upon which they were mounted.

Many early American Atlantics, particularly the Brooks Chautauquas, had a lightness of form resulting from their spidery bar-frames, high-pitched boilers and large driving wheels. In time, boilers became much larger in diameter. When this feature was combined with driving wheels of normal Atlantic size, or smaller, the outcome could be a much beefier-looking locomotive, although still fairly well-proportioned: the Santa Fe 'Bull Moose' Atlantics, the Northern Pacific class N1 (Baldwin, 1909) with 6ft driving wheels or the Pennsylvania E6s (driving wheels 6ft 3ins).

Only streamlining, which affected fewer than twenty Atlantics, could spoil the tension of strength, delicacy and proportion which sustained the classic, graceful 4-4-2. The aesthetic outcome of streamlining had its defenders, although a machine which hid its technical logic and screened the parts that made up the whole, offered a narrower basis for aesthetic judgement than its unadorned fellows. The streamlined Atlantics were perhaps more interesting than refined.

A well-conceived Atlantic could be an expression of pure form quite as much as the products of formal, representational art. In the language of early aesthetics it was nearer to the 'sublime' than being merely 'charming' or 'attractive', qualities that rely more on emotional appeal. Unfortunately a good deal of aesthetic discourse has for a long time excluded the steam locomotive as an art form; their loss.

Can a locomotive (or a building or passage of music) 'express' some characteristic of its place or time. Was an E6s an expression of some essentially American quality, can-do pragmatism perhaps; or an Hungarian 203 the Magyar spirit, or an SJ class A the Swedish cast of mind? Were differences in Atlantic appearance merely the result of material causes, or did they demonstrate cultural differences? Occasional statements in locomotive histories suggest that many people believe that the 'geography of locomotion' expresses cultural factors as well as material ones, but perhaps we 'read in' these qualities.

Colour, Liveries

The majority of Atlantics were black because the majority of Atlantics were American and unlined black was the standard finish for many American locomotives. There were exceptions; the Rock Island Atlantics had boiler shells of greenish-black 'Russia iron' and graphite-silver smokeboxes; many Pennsylvania Atlantics were turned out in Brunswick green. Some other railways preferred black, for example the Lancashire & Yorkshire, which lined it out carefully in white and red. Gölsdorf set off his black Atlantics[7] with highly burnished brasswork, carefully limited in quantity.

One or two Atlantics were singled out for special paintwork (some blue Pennsylvania locomotives, and the Milwaukee Road *Hiawathas*, for example) but most Atlantics respected the general livery rule of their railways. Thus the Bavarian Maffei Atlantics were dark holly-green; the Prussian S9 class a dark sage green; the NER a brighter apple green. Nord 4-4-2s were chocolate (officially 'hot chestnut'). The Shanghai-Nanking Atlantic, actually delivered in mid-green came just after a period of painting some express locomotives in imperial yellow, a glowing hue which was kept for use with carriages. Egyptian Atlantics were finished in Burgundy; in India they might be presented in golden-brown (GIPR), orange-brown (EIR) or dark sea-green (BNR). The LB&SCR Atlantics narrowly missed being painted in a singular yellow, 'improved engine green'; an economy drive resulted in a livery of burnt umber which was rather suitable for a locomotive of Atlantic size, like the 'dark gamboge' of the North British.

What was the most splendid Atlantic livery? The GCR 'Jersey Lilies' have often earned the accolade, for example from Cecil J. Allen – who measured praise sparingly. They were finished in many coats of Brunswick green; frames, valances and cylinders in purple-brown, the whole lined painstakingly in black, red and white. Buffer beams were in vermilion and a neat, if elaborate, crest appeared on each splasher and the tender. For all that, the effect was one of thoughtful control, bearing out Goethe's dictum that 'it is in restraint that the master first shows himself.'

Like the Rock Island, the Swedes abandoned paintwork altogether on some boiler barrels of the class A Atlantics, preferring planished steel which looked well in snowy terrain, under milky-blue northern skies. Smokebox, cab and tender were, however, brass-bound black. No public relations image-creators lurked behind these manifestations of unpretentious good taste.

In the classic Atlantic era engine crews and cleaners usually took great pride in the appearance of their charges; the new Brighton Atlantic No.421 (Brighton, 1911) ran in works grey livery for its first two years. Its regular cleaner 'Boozer' Burrows (a teetotaller, so named by antiphrasis) was determined to keep up appearances and duly chalked its number on the cab-sides in a good imitation of LB&SCR expanded sans-serifs. Although Horatio Bottomley, editor of the popular magazine *John Bull*, poked fun at this ostensible sign of an impecunious Brighton line, it was actually evidence of an *esprit de corps* that oversized egos generally find hard to comprehend. Even in the depressed 1930s the charge cleaner at Leeds Neville Hill shed used a plain white rag to check that the LNER class C7 Atlantics (erstwhile NER class Z) were polished to perfection, without a spot of grease or dirt.

Pre-1914 Atlantics tended to be decked out in the adult colours of the old order: muted, restrained, sad; occasionally rich, never brassy. It remains an open question whether the spectrum of hues and tones beyond plain black was a necessary ingredient of an Atlantic's good looks. It was pre-eminently the shape, proportion and geometry of the Atlantic that underlay its beauty, for which reason the American, Swedish or Austrian 4-4-2s were in no way aesthetically inferior to the green or vermilion ones. Dirty, cold Ivatt Atlantics, lined up outside locomotive sheds awaiting withdrawal in the late 1940s, still demonstrated their good proportions quite as well as in their apple-green heyday. There is no settling this kind of argument, but the Atlantics supplied plenty of evidence for discussion.

Sounds

According to the history of the Canadian National Railways by Donald Mackay and Lorne Perry (*Train Country*, 1994) 'there were forty distinct sounds peculiar to the steam locomotive' – an assertion that might provide a good basis on which to assess knowledge of the iron horse. Some of these sounds were common to all Atlantics: exhaust beats; the hollow exhalation of blowers, brakes variously squealing or groaning; the clatter of driving and valve motions. Others depended where you were; Westinghouse pump beats were common in the USA, uncommon in the UK; bells and chime whistles sounded in America, but more rarely in Europe.

Most Atlantic-generated noises could be offered by a wide range of other engines – if there was one authentic Atlantic signature-sound it was the rapidly accelerated exhaust resulting from wheelslip. Reviewing an lp record of a former Brighton Atlantic, Peter Semmens noted: 'A burst of slipping again indicates the Atlantics' weakness in adhesion...'[8]

Most Atlantic harmonies faded with the winds that carried them. We have some knowledge of what a limited range, mainly of exhaust beats, sounded like, from the written record. In the UK the largest collection of Atlantics, of the LNER, has been well chronicled in this respect. Thus R.S. McNaught:

> No more diapason thunder could be imagined than that of the Reid Atlantics...when operating over the banks of the Waverley route. To hear Borderer or his brethren (those portly Falstaffs were never feminine) lifting a northbound express out of Galashiels was to experience locomotive effort at its most vociferous.[9]

This is borne out by John Thomas (*The North British Atlantics*):

> On a quiet night in Hawick people still awake in their beds could hear the Midland sleeper struggling into the hills after it had left the town. Long after the train had departed the snarl of the Atlantic could be heard in the distance...sometimes the exhaust might be broken by a thunderous slip. Then there would be silence followed by a slow beat as the Atlantic found its feet...

McNaught also described the 'deep-toned gruffness' of the L&Y Atlantics which seemed 'in ill accord' with their narrow smokeboxes. On one occasion he was able to compare this deep resonance of an L&Y Highflier with the 'asthmatical chiff-chaff' of its Doncaster contemporary, a Klondyke departing from Hull Paragon station simultaneously. The three-cylinder Raven Atlantics of the NER had a novel exhaust beat for their day, six exhausts per revolution of the driving wheels in contrast to the normal four. When the engine went fast the resulting sound was exceedingly rapid by existing standards: 'purring in a monotone like a two-stroke motorcycle.' Cecil J. Allen, struck by the urgent beat of the GCR 3-cylinder simple Atlantic No.1090 (converted from 2-cylinders in 1908) thought he was hearing 'a 4ft 6in goods or tank engine in tow.'

Not all NER Atlantics purred; No.2212 of class Z (Darlington, 1918) had Stumpf 'Uniflow' cylinders designed to raise thermal efficiency. One feature of the arrangement, very large exhaust ports, caused No.2212, and its 4-6-0 stablemate No.825 to fire off a deafening, staccato exhaust when at speed. Legend has it that the Uniflow locomotives raised egg production in the Vale of York by shocking poultry into higher productivity. The habit of driving GNR large Atlantics on

Staccato: *an NER class Z (LNER class C7) 3-cylinder Atlantic No.735 (NBL, 1911, withdrawn June 1945) sweeping along the East Coast Main Line with a seven-coach train in its heyday; triple-beat exhaust soaring up behind the capuchon chimney (Northumbrian: 'windjabber') – first of the class to receive Detroit sight-feed lubricator, mounted in cab; feedpipes can be seen under the handrail.*

about 50% cut-off, the very device that gave them their reputation for lively performance also caused a loud, rattling exhaust variously referred to by writers as 'peppering', or 'chirrupping', the 'centre of a moving circle of sound about four miles in diameter.'[10]

Compounds had their own exhaust characteristics. The Paris-Orleans 2-cylinder compound conversions offered half the exhaust beats of the more familiar 2-cylinder simple, disconcerting to unfamiliar ears. Compound exhausts were usually softer than those of simple expansion loco-motives. The de Glehn 4-4-2s, for example, seemed to flow along with effortless ease making little more sound than the sewing-machine clatter of their motion. At the other end of the scale the Pennsylvania E6s, epitome of 2-cylinder single-expansion brutalism, sounded their famous 'machine-gun roar' from Long Island to Chicago, and memorable it was.

Exhaust beats, or lack of them, were a good diagnostic tool for engineers, drivers and public alike. 'Question: *how many beats would you lose if you had a broken lap? Ans: I should lose one beat...*' (Thomas Pearce, GWR, *The Locomotive*, 1898). A well-trained engineman's ear could tell a great deal from various reverberations, wheezings, and irregularities of beat. But the least ambiguous locomotive sound, seemingly ever sounding in the middle distance during the age of steam, was the warning whistle.

Hear that lonesome whistle blow. McNaught expressed disappointment at the 'screechy little whistle' of the NBR Atlantics, in contrast to their bass, 'growling' exhaust, and the mellow NBR standard whistle-song. A shrill, even pipey, whistle was the aesthetic Achilles' heel of the otherwise elegant French Atlantics. The fullest and most glorious range of whistle-possibilities was found in the USA where the tradition of multi-toned instruments mounted on river steamers was coeval with, or even prior to, steam locomotion on land.[11]

Although the steam locomotive whistle was a British invention, Americans undoubtedly led the world in steam harmonics. At first, American locomotives echoed the British screech but the steamboat tradition soon shouldered it out of the way. By the mid 1860s the American locomotive whistle was 'a howling reservoir of sound, with an unearthly *(sic)* roar instead of a shriek' (*Engineering*, 26 July 1867). When the Atlantics came this reservoir was full, and its contents varied. The American Atlantics mounted between them anything from one to five toned whistles according to a range of designs: flutes, reeds, organ pipes set in many combinations, flat top, castellated and domed bells in gunmetal, brass and steel. The result was delightful to the human ear, a good warning to the world at large and as haunting as a gypsy air.

Notes to Chapter 11

1. Robert K. Durham, *The Reading Railroad*, 1997; C. Hamilton Ellis, *Classic Locomotives*, 1949 and *The Beauty of Old Trains*, 1952; Cecil J. Allen, *British Atlantic Locomotives*, 1962.

2. See Michael Rutherford, 'The Eye of the Beholder: The Beauty of Steam' in *Back Track* 13. 3 March 2000.

3. O.S. Nock, *Railways in the Years of Pre-Eminence* 1905-1919, 1971.

4. Private communication.

5. Quoted in Kalla Bishop, *Hungarian Railways*, 1973; the observation was ascribed to Béla Filovits, a noted Atlantic engineer himself.

6. A similar, and possibly earlier, phrase was also expressed in Robert Weatherburn, *Ajax Loquitur*, 1899. Ironically the well-shaped outer chimney casings of the Robinson Atlantics were removed to expose a crude flower-pot stack in LNER years, an offence to good taste which did no party credit.

7. Or dark blue, or with planished steel as in Sweden; sources differ.

8. P.W.B. Semmens on the Argo Transacord EAF 82, 45rpm mono; *Journal* of the SLS, Vol XL, No.473, Dec 1964.

9. 'The Voice of the Locomotive', *Railway Magazine*, Dec 1952.

10. Keith Farr, 'Atlantic Swells', *Railway Magazine* Nov and Dec 2000; W.A. Tuplin, *Great Northern Steam*, 1971.

11. Steamboat captains played whistle and siren variations on occasion, and some of their vessels bore *calliopes*, steam-organs which entertained passengers.

Chapter 12
Atlantics & Aesthetics: Interpretation

Poetry and Postcards

The Atlantic may have approached 'poetry in steel' but, as with railways as a whole, in practice it inspired little worthwhile poetry.[1] Atlantic-related poetry surfaced occasionally in literature. One of the *Railway Magazine's* early 'poems of the month', seven verses in all, was *An Ode to '1400'*, in honour of the new Lancashire & Yorkshire Atlantics: 'Oh! Give me of your strength, Fourteen Hundred!/ To run life's toilsome length, Fourteen Hundred!' The Burntisland accident on the NBR (1914) sprung the muse in Alex Brown; the six verses of *A Reminder of the Railway Accident at Burntisland*...were mainly in honour of the dead enginemen, but there was a reference to the locomotive: '*Auld Reekie* left her mighty track/And in the links was laid.' A few poets and versifiers paid compliments to the Atlantics, without really capturing their magic. In *Steam!* by Frederick Vanson (1985) there was a short poem to a *Brighton Atlantic, c.1938* which started 'Lone among the green electrics/She represents the age of steam/Here at London Bridge Low Level...'

Atlantic art: *Cyrus Cuneo's painting of a GNR Ivatt large Atlantic at speed. From Frederick Talbot's* Railway Wonders of the World. c.*1910.*

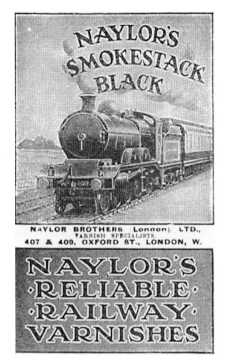

Atlantic imagery: *the 4-4-2s appealed greatly to PR departments in seemingly innocent times; GCR Atlantic (NBL, 1905) advertising industrial varnish; from NBR book* The Beauties of Scotland *(1913) a romantic association, Gretna was served by a short branch from the Waverley route; NBR No. 881* Borderer *depicted with a headboard for 'Gretna Green'; and a virtual Atlantic in sand with shell-like wheels (possibly a booster also?) from a GNR advertisement, c. 1910.*

The Atlantic was a godsend to publicists, particularly those of the GNR who worked the image of the large Ivatt Atlantic hard in advertisements, posters, postcards and on hoardings. A 'Klondyke' small Atlantic was even advertised *on* a locomotive (1903); the vast slab side-tanks of 0-8-2 No.116 were, for a short time, a mobile hoarding bearing a picture of an Atlantic-hauled train on the 'Express Route to East Coast'. Many railways publicised their Atlantics by means of postcards; the GCR and NBR in Britain, the NYC and Pennsylvania in the USA being amongst the most prolific. Formal paintings of Atlantics were more rare, but two good ones by T.H. Millar and Cyrus Cuneo were used in Frederick Talbot's *Railway Wonders of the World*. The former showed the cab of an Ivatt Atlantic at speed, and the latter a Brighton Atlantic throwing up a form of bow-wave to impart the idea of velocity.

Atlantics appeared on cigarette cards, biscuit tins, and even on stamps. Egypt issued commemorative postage stamps, in deep blue and black, (1933) to mark the Cairo meeting of the International Railway Congress, they bore a picture of one of the Peckitt 4-4-2s which were the mainstay of its express passenger work. Liberia, although not a user of Atlantics, used a GNR large 4-4-2 and a Baden State Railways 4-cylinder Maffei compound Atlantic in its 1973 'Historical Railways' series; about ten countries have issued Atlantic-stamps.

A singular and appropriate use of the Atlantic image was to be found above the District Locomotive Superintendent's offices at King's Cross, London where a two-dimensional Ivatt large Atlantic did service as a weather-vane. The wide use of Atlantics in representational art and advertising early in the twentieth century reflected the iconic status enjoyed by the 4-4-2. Although this artistic work may have drawn on the visual appeal of the Atlantic it did little to enhance it. As art, the Atlantic was sufficient unto itself.

The Naming of Atlantics

The Americans and French, once prolific engine-namers, abandoned this activity from the 1880s with the onset of more bureaucratic, cost-cutting forms of management and their penchant for employing numerical classification alone. The Prussians named no Atlantics although the Palatinate Railways awarded a few. The British oscillated between the total naming of Atlantic classes (GWR, NBR) and, on the dourly competent Lancashire & Yorkshire: nowt. British imperial administrators had a similarly uneven naming record. Nevertheless, such naming of Atlantics as occurred was a good indicator of contemporary mentalities, tastes and values, particularly those of the 'hegemonic culture' of the day. What that culture pronounced was one thing, however. The railwaymen had ideas of their own: for a list of Atlantic nicknames, see Appendix 5.

The world's first 4-4-2 *A.G. Darwin* was one of the few named Atlantics in the USA, as were the *Hiawatha* series, each of which bore the same name but with an individual number to distinguish it from its fellows. In the UK, the GWR in the South-West, and the NBR in Scotland named their Atlantics. The three GWR de Glehns bore witness both to their French origins, and to improving Anglo-French relationships: *La France*, *President* and *Alliance*. *Albion* was chosen as a counterpoint to *La France*. Some of the other GWR Atlantics bore the names of former broad-gauge locomotives, many from Scott's 'Waverley novels', part of a literary canon then widely shared but now largely evaporated. No.182 *Lalla Rookh*, was however an Indian princess; the eponymous heroine of one of Thomas Moore's poems. The name means 'Tulip Cheek', a charming thought for an Atlantic. The NBR named its Atlantics after Scottish locations, themes and people, occasionally in their vernacular versions, for example *Auld Reekie, Thane of Fife, Saint Mungo, Teribus*, and *Dundonian*, which had to be renamed *Bonnie Dundee* because a prominent lawyer took exception to what he took to be its commonplace tone.

The Great Central restricted Atlantic names to its 3-cylinder compounds which recorded the names and titles of prominent persons including *The Rt Hon Viscount Cross GCB GCSI*. Legend (or wags) had it that people not familiar with the complexities of the British honours system thought that the abbreviations referred to a Great Central order of chivalry; at the heart of the verbiage lurked Richard Cross, banker and politician. Other British railways were sparing with names, restricting them to special commemorations. The fledgling public-relations department of the Southern Railway sensed that interestingly-named locomotives might project a favourable image to the public and arranged the naming of its inherited LB&SCR Atlantics. They chose promontories and headlands in SR territory, some a long way from Brighton. All were double names like *Hartland Point* or *Beachy Head*; the obvious 'Seven Sisters', near to Newhaven where the Atlantic-hauled boat trains ran was, however, not selected.

In France the once imaginative tradition of locomotive naming was near its end[2] and only a small handful of French Atlantics were named. The Etat awarded place-names to its ten Baldwin 2-cylinder simple expansion Atlantics of 1900; *Ville-Francoeur, Paris, Trementines* and so on, perhaps to impart some French quality to American imports. In Germany, the Palatinate Railways alone named Atlantics, four of people and most topographical such as *Pfälzerwald, Inn, Neckar*. Elsewhere in Europe, only the Malmö-Ystad Railway in Sweden gave names, after two towns on its main route.

The imperial administrators of the Atlantic era were not short of self-confidence, even of brass neck, and thought nothing of naming Egypt's pioneer Atlantic *Lady Cromer*, wife of the British Proconsul. Later Egyptian Atlantics had names more appropriate to Egyptian history and culture such as *Rameses II; Amenhotep; Mohamed Ali El Kebir*. They had lengthy name-plates bearing their titles in Roman-lettered English and in Arabic. India had the fullest flowering of imperial nomenclature on its Atlantics; all forty of the Great Indian Peninsula class E1 Atlantics were named, not one of them after an Indian. Instead the GIPR had (among others): *Lord Clive, Warren Hastings, Dalhousie, Lord Elgin, Northcote*, and *Leamington*.

This scattering of names speaks of long-lost literary tastes, culturally neutral topography, the self-esteem of capitalists and imperialists, and of a particular slant on the interpretation of history. None honoured the people who designed, built or operated the Atlantics; but that was the way of it.

Smaller-Scale Atlantics

Virtually all Atlantics referred to in orthodox railway history have been full scale ones: 'twelve inches to the foot.' But a large number of Atlantics were built to smaller scales, most of them were concerned in one way or another with 'leisure'. They ran on private railways, on commercial lines largely devoted to tourism or, in their smallest form, as toys in drawing-rooms or attics.

In *A Survey of Seaside Miniature Railways* (1992), D.J. Croft listed 113 of these lines which have existed in the UK at one time or another; about one quarter of them ran Atlantics. A recent compendium listed about half-a-dozen miniature Atlantics still in regular steam at the

Heuristic Atlantic: *a superb scale model Hungarian Atlantic, MÁV class 203 built by apprentices at the MÁV main repair shops, Istvántelek, 1939-1941.* Photo: MÁV.

end of the twentieth century. Many more exist in private hands.[3] Miniature railways designed to carry passengers appeared in late Victorian times, notably in public parks in the USA. The British pioneer of the movement, soon to dominate the European scene was W.J. Bassett-Lowke of Northampton. His chief designer, Henry Greenly, was a well qualified engineer of broad talents who drew up plans for three classes of Atlantic which became the dominant miniature locomotive form before the Great War.[4]

Greenly's first Atlantic design, the *Little Giant* (1905) was based on general Atlantic principles, which were ideal for miniature railway purposes as well as being *de rigeur* in public perception as the latest, raciest of steam engines . The large firebox ensured steam production in generous quantities; the short rigid wheelbase enabled the locomotive to adjust to the sharp curvature of many lines, and its general sprightliness kept traffic on the move. The 'Atlanticitis' problem was mitigated by the level layout of most lines, and loads were relatively light and easy to measure and limit.

Most of the early public miniature railways had a 15in gauge; *Little Giant* originally ran on such a line at Blackpool.[5] It was completed in twenty-two weeks and tested on the Duke of Westminster's private line at Eaton Hall where it touched 26.4mph, equivalent to 100mph in a full-scale Atlantic. In its first week of commercial service it hauled nearly 10,000 passengers. For private use Greenly designed a smaller Atlantic (1910) for a 9.5in gauge railway. It was closely modelled on the GNR large 4-4-2s, then in their first flush, and was used by John Howey of Staunton Manor, Huntingdonshire, on his personal railway.[6]

By 1914 Bassett-Lowke had built fourteen Atlantics, half of them 'Little Giants'. Some went to private estate railways, others joined the company of Atlantics shown off at international expositions. *L'Entente Cordiale* worked a miniature railway at the *L'Exposition Internationale de l'Est de la France* at Nancy, 1909. The small-scale Atlantic scene also had its counterfactual history; Greenly met Karl Gölsdorf, himself an enthusiast for miniature and model railways in order to discuss the possibility of a line on Gölsdorf's estate, although what transpired has now been lost. The Great War dampened small-scale railway engineering for a period, and offered a curious footnote. After the Allied advance in 1918, the remains of a 'Little Giant' Atlantic were found in a quarry having apparently worked a *Feldbahn* in the trenches – another Atlantic mystery.[7] About the time war broke out Bassett-Lowke offered the final and most potent of the Greenly Atlantics. Like the E6s, or Northern Pacific class N1 it was a tough-looking locomotive with a large boiler and relatively small driving wheels (20in). One example, *Synolda*, was sold to a wealthy Yorkshire landowner, another was an original locomotive of the Ravenglass & Eskdale Railway in Cumberland,[8] but these fine engines marked the end of the Bassett-Lowke years of Atlantic design and construction.

The tradition continued elsewhere. An early and long-lasting centre of small-scale Atlanticism was located at Rhyl in North Wales, where the miniature railway commenced operations in 1911 with two Bassett-Lowke 'Little Giants'. In later years traffic grew vigorously and Greenly designed a further Atlantic type, six of which were constructed in Rhyl by the line's manager, Albert Barnes. Scotland has a long-lived small-scale Atlantic working

Barnes Atlantic: *Rhyl Miniature Railway No.101* Joan, *one of six Atlantics designed by Henry Greenly and built by Albert Barnes of Rhyl, North Wales – in this case in 1920. The 15in gauge RMR opened in 1911; here* Joan *(cylinders 4.25 x 7in, boiler pressure 120lb sq.in) hauls a trainload of the British taking their pleasures sadly.*

Freelance Atlantic: '*Life would be tolerable but for its pleasures*' *(Sir G.C. Lewis) – more glum Britons sampling an Atlantic-hauled miniature train; George E. Flooks' short-lived line at Bricket Wood, Herts c.1904-05; provenance of the sturdy Atlantic unknown.* Photo: W. Nicholls.

at Arbroath on Kerr's Miniature Railway. The Arbroath 4-4-2 *Auld Reekie* was based on an NER class V form, but was later converted to petrol-motor drive. Originally a *bona fide* steam Atlantic it can probably be classed as a unique sub-species of Atlantic.

Miniature Atlantic production declined after about 1930 although a hard core of support for the form remained. Two notable Atlantics of broadly American design were built by David Curwen for the Stapleford Park miniature railway in 1958; one of them, No.750 *Blanche of Lancaster* achieved a kind of immortality by bearing down on the actress Diana Rigg, tied to the track in time-honoured form in an episode of the popular British TV series *The Avengers.*[9]

Steam-driven miniature 4-4-2s were still operating at the turn of the millennia – a Parkinson/Hammond Atlantic, built in 1988 on the Great Cockrow Railway in Surrey (7.25in gauge) and the *Red Dragon* of the Lakeside Miniature Railway, Southport, a 15in gauge model by Moss/Walker, 1991. A 'Little Giant' (Bassett-Lowke, 1913) operates in the Vidam Park in Budapest. A web-surf in early 2001 gave news of similar American operations including a Baltimore & Ohio A-3 (built 1976, rebuilt 1988); an adaptation of a Southern Pacific A-6 built in Texas, 1978; and another B&O-inspired model, finished in 1993. An exceptionally fine New Haven Atlantic, built to run on 4.75in track was completed in 1998 and exhibited at the Montreal Live Steamers International Meet; the website recorded that 'she ran like a watch', entirely in keeping with the best Atlantic standards set by de Glehn, du Bousquet, Gölsdorf and Gibbs.

Model Atlantics

The underlying growth in prosperity which enabled some people to own a miniature Atlantic or to enjoy a brief holiday trip behind one, allowed other people, generally less affluent, and often including the very young, to own their own *model* Atlantic. As a mass-movement this started in the 1890s[10] and soon came to be dominated by German manufacturers. The leading maker, Märklin offered a range of models: a rough approximation of the GWR *La France* (gauge 1, 1906); and a 'Germanic' 4-4-2, 1909.[11] Another German manufacturer, Bing offered well-designed likenesses of an Ivatt Atlantic and a 'South German' Atlantic in the 1912-1913 season. Bassett-Lowke competed in Britain with some well-crafted Atlantics for wealthier clientele. Three were specially constructed for the 2in gauge railway at the Glasgow Exhibition (1911). These were accurate, albeit electrically-driven, representations of Atlantics from the NER (class V); a GNR, large Atlantic; and an NBR Reid Atlantic, *Tweeddale*.

Commercially-produced model Atlantics had a shorter innings than hand-crafted steam-driven miniature and model 4-4-2s, although one of the best-known publicists of very small steam-driven locomotives, L. Lawrence (under his *nom-de-plume* 'LBSC') designed, built and publicised model coal-fired Atlantics as late as the 1950s.[12] The demise of the model Atlantic paralleled that of the prototype original. It was symbolic that an attempt by the insolvent American model-makers Ives to revive interest, with a large, diecast and copper-plated Atlantic-hauled model train entitled *Prosperity Special*, was launched shortly after the Wall Street crash in 1929. It was not a success.[13]

Hand-crafted Atlantic: *a CCC&StL Atlantic (prototype, Alco, Brooks, 1903, the St Louis Exposition type engine) in walnut and ivory – then an acceptable medium – by Mr Warther of Dover, Ohio (1924). Other model or representational Atlantics have been made in brass, plywood, copper, tinplate, even ephemeral sand, or jelly.* Photo: Collection of Howard W. Ameling.

Model Atlantics: *advertised in a 1959 Rivarossi HO scale catalogue. Above: a Southern Pacific rebuilt A3 4-4-2 on a freight train.*

Below: *a Milwaukee Road* Hiawatha *by Bolla. Although both prototypes had long gone, the Atlantic appeal remained.*

Notes to Chapter 12

1. See Samuel Carr, ed, *The Poetry of Railways*.

2. The Paris-Strasbourg Railway, later the Est, had a *L'Atlantique* (1841), a 4-2-0 Crampton. The Baltimore & Ohio had the first *Atlantic* (1832), followed by the Birmingham & Gloucester which ran an American-built 4-2-0 *Atlantic* ; the Glasgow, Dumbarton & Helensburgh among others an *Atalanta*; the goddess, not the ocean; the Campbeltown & Machrihanish Light Railway had a narrow–gauge 0-6-4T *Atlantic* – and there were others, none of them Atlantics! See C. Hamilton Ellis, 'On the Naming of Locomotives' in *The Beauty of Old Trains*, 1952

3. Robin Butterell, Dave Holroyde, Simon Townsend, *Miniature Railways*, 1998.

4. E.A. and E.H. Steel, *The Miniature World of Henry Greenly*, 1973; Anthony J. Lambert, *Miniature Railways Past & Present*, 1982; and H. Clayton, M. Jacob and R. Butterell *Miniature Railways* Vol I, 1971.

5. *Little Giant* still exists (2002), rescued after a long life and many vicissitudes – the oldest surviving miniature Atlantic.

6. Later co-founder and operator of the Romney, Hythe & Dymchurch Railway, perhaps the most famous of the miniature lines but a Pacific, not an Atlantic operator.

7. Possibly the Nancy Atlantic; see E.A. and E.H. Steel, *op cit*.

8. By a set of curious chances, *Synolda* found an eventual home on the Ravenglass & Eskdale Railway (2001).

9. Fortunately, she was rescued by 'Steed' (Patrick MacNee).

10. Its origins were much older. For example Goethe was presented with a model of the *Rocket* in 1829, complete with rolling stock and rails. He presented it to his grand-children.

11. A later Märklin 4-4-2, in black and grey, was auctioned in 1998 for DM 6,000, say €11,400.

12. There was a long-running dispute between 'LBSC' and Greenly on the subject of fuels – Greenly allowed spirit-burning on pragmatic grounds; 'LBSC', a bituminous hard-liner would have none of it. Lawrence's best-known work *Maisie, Words & Music* described the construction of a miniature GNR large Atlantic.

13. The model Atlantic has retained its hold on public affection, particularly amongst scratch modellers. In late 2000, for example, three hand-built model Atlantics were wending their ways in the Ross-on-Wye miniature railway museum; one each from the L&Y, NER and GNR. They demonstrated to school children among others, the 'elegance on rails' of machines which had gone to the scrapyard half a century or more before they were born.

Chapter 13
Classes, Standards, Economics

Classification

Systems of classification raise interesting questions about the ways we try to impose order on disorder, to plan ahead for eventualities and to adjust as we go along. Formal locomotive classification came of age in the new century.

World-wide the alpha–numeric system preponderated for Atlantics mainly because it was the most common designation in the USA where nearly two-thirds of all Atlantics operated. The big users of 4-4-2s illustrate this: all PRR Atlantics were classified in the 'E' series, classes E5, E6, etc. Further refinements were straightforward: E6s, meaning E6 superheated, E3d – an E3 with Belpaire firebox. The Milwaukee Road employed 'A' for its 4-4-2s, starting with A1 in the late 1890s.

In locomotive matters the Santa Fe was a law unto itself. It designated a class from the number accorded to its first member ('class leader'). Santa Fe 4-4-2s, therefore, might be class 256 (after No.256, Baldwin 1903) or class 1480 (after No.1480, Baldwin 1910, the 'Bull Moose' type). There were other idiosyncrasies; the Chicago, Rock Island & Pacific awarded two classifications to its engines, an MP (motive power) designation, determined by mechanical details and refinements, and a 'Road Class' designation arising from operating qualities such as wheel designation, and tractive effort. A Rock Island Atlantic had two guises; for example some 4-cylinder compounds bought in 1905 were MP18, W24, the 'W' denoting 4-4-2.

The British scene was similar. The L&Y Atlantics were generally class 1400, after the first of their number. The GNR Atlantics were C1, irrespective of their being early Klondykes or later large-boilered versions. When the GNR became a part of the LNER in 1923 they were distinguished: C1 for the large Atlantics, C2 for Klondykes, part of the LNER's logical reclassification in which 'C' meant a 4-4-2, whether Atlantic or 4-4-2 tank engine.

The early French Atlantic classes were often designated by the serial number of the class leader. Because this number often embodied a reference to the number of driving axles (two in the case of an Atlantic) many French Atlantic classes commenced with a 2; Nord class or 'series number' 2.640 was, for example the famous set of de Glehn racers, led by Atlantic No.2.641. In Germany most Atlantics ran in Prussia which classed fast passenger locomotives 'S' (*Schnellzuglokomotiven*) hence its two Atlantic classes were S7 and S9. The Austrian State Railways used a numeric classification; in which 08 meant 'Atlantic'; the original series was 108; those inherited from the Austrian North-Western (ÖNWB) in 1909 became 208.

Generally the further East one travelled in Europe the more refined became the classification and numbering of locomotives, particularly as the years passed. The former ÖNWB Atlantics gravitated from their original classification XVIb, to 208 when taken over by the state, to 264.4 when they were transferred to Czechoslovakia. The Czechoslovak classification

BESA Indian Atlantics, (I): *the 'bog-standard' BESA 4-4-2, East Indian No.124 (class AP, Vulcan, 1908) with 2-cylinder drive to rear coupled axle; easy lines, workmanlike if lacking in originality.* Photo: Kelland Collection, BRC.

BESA Indian Atlantics (II): *BESA for the thinking engineer, Bengal-Nagpur No.408 (NBL, 1913) with de Glehn system of compounding waiting at Gondia, 1928 with a Viceregal Special. Once named* Duke of Connaught and Strathearn *this locomotive was in class KS, i.e. superheated K.* Photo: Kelland Collection, BRC.

system demanded great mental agility from trainspotters; individual digits referred to particular locomotive qualities and had to be processed mathematically. The Polish classification was similarly logical, if intellectually demanding.[1]

Plainer systems usually sufficed elsewhere: straightforward letters in India; a minor alteration in Western Australia (the R class 4-4-0s became Ra class when converted to Atlantics) and an unadorned 'E' on the Shanghai-Nanking Railway. The Cape Government Railways employed the ordinal classification of Atlantics; the Baldwin 4-4-2s of 1897 were '4th class'.

Great events in world history occasionally determined new classification or renumberings. After the 1914-1918 war the Weimar Republic set up a unified administration for German Railways, the *Deutsche Reichsbahn* which rationalised its 284 locomotive classes and their numbering. The scheme finally implemented in 1923 grouped express locomotives in classes 01-19; Atlantics were put in the 14 slot. A typical Atlantic might be 14.NN, the 14 being the *Stammnummer* (class number) and the NN the *Ordnungsnummer* or the number of the individual locomotive. Even after most Atlantics had been withdrawn the '14 niche' remained. Thus when Germany occupied Czechoslovakia and Poland in 1939 and its officials found some former KFNB Atlantics still at work there, they were redesignated class 14.0 by railway bureaucrats, impartial and precedent-bound as ever. These superannuated Atlantics did not, however, last long.

Standardisation

The complexity of class designation might not have been necessary had there been fewer types of Atlantic in the first place; about 250 classes. But the characteristics of the steam locomotive militated against a single, all-purpose type of machine for goods, passenger and mineral work. The traditional 'American' 4-4-0 came close to this for half a century but it was a type, not a standardised class. The same consideration applies to the British 0-6-0, half of the country's locomotive stock in 1914 and a reliable general workhorse. The Russians approached the all-purpose ideal most closely at the price of running some notably slow passenger trains with 2-cylinder compound 0-8-0s (class O, for *Osnovnoi*, basic).

Occasionally engineers or administrators tried to cut through the accretion of classes by establishing a basic stud of standard types. The idea had operational and economic attractions but it proved to be slippery in practice. In one sense, any Atlantic is a 'standard' type but from the time that Henszey tried to patent the new 4-4-2 notation, it sported many varieties, not only between countries but in the same country, and even on the same railway. There were many reasons for this within the 'geography of locomotion.' Some railways standardised locomotive parts such as boilers, interchangeable cylinders, and wheels. National and eventually international standards of measurement or component began to emerge. The GWR under Churchward developed this system to a high level. To standardise is not necessarily a great intellectual adventure or achievement; 'standardisation' may be inherent in the logic and economics of technology, or in the structure of the human mind (or both, which may be related). It has a way of asserting itself sooner or later.

But sometimes there were plans to impose absolutely standard, virtually identical classes of locomotive on meta-systems, whole collections of railways. Two of these initiatives came well within the Atlantic era and included the 4-4-2. The later standardisations did not; neither the

USRA attempt to standardise locomotives in the USA (1918); nor the German and British attempts, of the 1920s and 1950s respectively, included Atlantics; by these times the 4-4-2 was well out of fashion.

At the opening of the twentieth century the cost-conscious administrators of India and its railways warmed to the idea of locomotive standardisation, as did some of the exporters who supplied them. The engineers differed amongst themselves about the virtues claimed for standardisation, but they did not hold the ultimate reins of power. The Secretary of State for India got the business under way at the Calcutta Conference (1901) which invited British manufacturers to prepare designs for six standard locomotive types including a '4-4-2 Mail' engine of both 15 and 17 tons axleloads. Back in Britain, the Engineering Standards Committee had been established by leading professional organisations and amongst its committees was one for locomotives. The Secretary of State approached this body also, seeking a second opinion (and possibly greater speed and objectivity). Initial recommendations were for 4-4-0 and 0-6-0 designs; later three more classes were outlined including an Atlantic with 6ft 6in driving wheels.

This was to be the BESA (British Engineering Standards Association) Atlantic; 117 were eventually built in the UK. Five Indian railways adopted them more or less in their original form. The Bengal-Nagpur Railway, which was a thorn of individualism in the side of the standardisers, insisted on a 4-cylinder de Glehn compound version. The BESA Atlantics were sound, basic machines and they lasted for some forty years, a few (including the world's longest-running Atlantic) even longer. But the Atlantic class was the smallest of the BESA categories. There were 916 of the 2-8-0s and 812 of the 4-6-0s out of a BESA total of just under 6,000, evidence that the Atlantic was on the wane by the time they were being delivered, mostly 1907-1909. It is doubtful that an Atlantic was a sensible proposition for Indian railway operation; even standardisers can multiply entities unnecessarily.

The second major standardisation of Atlantics took place in the USA when the 4-4-2 arrangement was chosen as one of the 'Harriman standard' locomotives. Railways can sometimes benefit when sharp-minded outsiders assume control and ask difficult questions of a world where custom and practice may have reigned for too long. The financier, Edward Harriman (1848-1909)[2] was one such. He assumed control of some major railroads in the late nineteenth century: the Union Pacific, Southern Pacific, Illinois Central, and Chicago & Alton, *inter alia*. Like the fictional being from another world who poses awkward but obvious questions of our peculiar terrestrial arrangements, Harriman asked, for example, why there were boxcars whose tare weight equalled that of their load; why there were not more powerful locomotives hauling larger, more economic trains, and so on.

Harriman tried to reduce the plethora of locomotive and carriage types on his 'Associated Lines' by standardisation. This included eight locomotive types with sub-classes (two kinds of 4-4-2, 4-6-0, 4-6-2, 2-8-8-2, 2-8-0, 2-8-2, 2-6-0, and 0-6-0) for which plans were drawn up by Baldwin in 1903. Atlantics came in two forms: simple, and compound; 48tons and 51tons respectively. The largest batch of Atlantics built to the 'common standard' went to the SP, fifty-six locomotives; the UP had a further twenty, the Oregon Short Line seven, and the Chicago & Alton five – give or take a few in that procurement and ownership were complex matters. The Harriman Atlantics were instantly recognisable from their distinctive 'chicken coop' cabs, and other, minor features familiar to locomotive cognoscenti. The basic Atlantic design had 6ft 9in driving wheels, a grate area of 50sq.ft and 200lb sq.in boiler pressure: strong engines.

Clear road ahead: *unidentified 'Harriman standard' 4-4-2 with Vanderbilt tender, hauling the* Overland Limited *past new signals on the freshly-constructed Lane Cut-off, Nebraska; another Harriman-inspired improvement, Union Pacific, 1908.* Photo: Collection of Howard W. Ameling.

In addition to the major and intended forms of standardisation there were some modest *de facto* ones. These included the distribution of the prestigious SACM de Glehn 4-cylinder Atlantic; very similar models were produced for eight railways: Est, 2; Paris-Orleans, 14; Midi, 34; Etat, 9 in France; KPEV in Prussia, 79; Egypt, 10; GWR, 3; and Pennsylvania, 1. The Baldwin 3ft 6in gauge Atlantics sent to Japan in 1897 were replicated by a further half-dozen near-identical versions for the Cape Government Railways and the design was dusted off and modernised for five engines sent to the Federal de l'Est railway in Brazil, 1913.

Sometimes a basic design was repeated, with modifications. The GNR large Atlantics were mirrored in the LB&SCR Atlantics – quite above board in that the designer of the Brighton model, D. Earle Marsh was a former GNR engineer who had been closely involved in the creation of Ivatt's various Atlantics. Other Atlantic families included the 'American categories', mainly the Henszey model (Baldwin); the Brooks, Schenectady, and Pennsylvania types.

The standardisation of locomotives and much else is, however, a problematic concept.[3] Perceived one way, some 99% of all steam locomotives were simply variants on the basic, standard 'Stephenson cycle'. An individualist like Oliver Bulleid spoke of 'the tyranny of standardisation.' When he learned that BR, with its 400 inherited classes of locomotive was to have a dozen new, standard types he remarked drily that the outcome would be 412 classes, highlighting the standardiser's dilemma: what to do with existing stock, much of it far from life-expired. There is social resistance to standardisation: the process is acceptable 'if it is my model that is chosen as the new standard; not if it is your model' – and so on. The virtues and vices of standardisation are as much economic and social as technical and raise as many questions as they solve.

Atlantic Economics

How far standardised Atlantics saved their operators capital or current expenditure is quite another matter. Hard economic facts about Atlantics are relatively few when compared to the deluge of technical data available. The imbalance arises partly from the relative inaccessibility of specific financial details, although enough is on record to suggest that there are lines here worth pursuing.

The 'going rate' for a 2-cylinder simple Atlantic in the classic era was about £3,500-£4,500; a £1 of 1913 having the purchasing power of about £5 in 1970. The LB&SCR Atlantics of 1905 were supplied by Kitsons for £3,950 each, less £45 for delivery in grey primer paint instead of Stroudley's 'improved engine green.' The NER Atlantics varied from £3,876 for a class V in 1905 to £3,967 for the slightly improved V/09 four years later, or £3,485 for a 3-cylinder class Z of 1910.

One frequently-stated snag of the compound engine was its higher initial cost; the class 4CC 4-cylinder Smith Atlantics of the NER cost £4,661 in 1905, that is about £800 more than a contemporary class V. Costing was a highly complex business partly because the share of general costs to be borne by an individual locomotive was necessarily a notional figure. The GWR *North Star*, No.40 of 1905 cost the GWR company £3,218 22s 10d of which the wages bill was £1,515 2s 8d, after which materials and a notional share of 'factory charges' had to be added.

The inflation of the Great War raised costs steeply, although few Atlantics were built in the UK after 1914. The North British 4-4-2s had cost £4,525 in 1905; two identical engines ordered in 1920 then cost £15,450 apiece.

The last of the American Atlantics, the Milwaukee Road *Hiawathas* were costed together with a consist of six new cars; in 1935 this package came to $279,847 which seems a great bargain even by the standards of the time. However, extensive track relaying was required in order to run these high-speed trains so the total cost of 're-Atlanticising' the road was considerably higher than merely purchasing four locomotive-and-train sets.

The rapid upsurge in business resulting from the *Hiawathas* persuaded the Milwaukee Road to extend the experiment, again successfully. But the precise cost-effectiveness of Atlantics is virtually impossible to measure. We know the mileages of some of them: 1.2 million miles for one of the original ACL 4-4-2s; 1.4 million miles for the longest-running of the NBR Atlantics, and so on. But not all of these were revenue-earning miles, which were in any case often 'notional'. Nor do precise figures exist concerning actual revenue earned by Atlantic-hauled trains. Given that many of these were prestige trains, with a relatively high proportion of premium fares, it would be a sensible guess that Atlantics were good earners in their youth; it was said in the 1920s that one first-class fare on a London-Newcastle express paid for the locomotive coal, although this is folklore, not accountancy. The use of superannuated Atlantics on fish, excursion or fast freight trains would do their economic record no harm, nor would the comparative absence of empty or

Old Soldiers: *fading away at Doncaster plant; two Ivatt large Atlantics LNER 3274 and 3285 (Doncaster, 1904), in June 1950 with their famed steam-raising powers doing duty as a combined stationary boiler, pipage leading away from steam domes. They worked in this capacity 1946-1952, still paying their way; a good return on an initial outlay of £3,365 each.* Photo: L.R. Peters.

stock trains run by Atlantics. But most of the necessary data for forming judgements about this kind of cost-effectiveness were either not collected (even virtually impossible to collect without an army of clerical staff) – or they have gone with the snows of yesterday.

Notes to Chapter 13

1. Czechoslovak Class 264: the first digit meant 2 powered axles; the next digit had 3 added and was then multiplied by 10, so:6+3x10 = 90 (maximum speed in km/h) and then the last digit 4 had 10 added to give the maximum axle load in tons, 14. In Poland the former Austrian Atlantics became class Pf 12, meaning: *Pospiean* (express); f – a 4-4-2 (or 2-4-4), and 12 – part of the series 11-19, awarded to former Austrian stock. In the USA, the Wheeling and Lake Erie awarded numbers based on 10% of starting tractive effort; hence Atlantics became 23XX.

2. Maury Klein, *The Life and Legend of E.H. Harriman*, 2000.

3. For an analysis of locomotive standardisation, see M. Rutherford: 'Locomotive Standardisation and Standard Locomotives' *Back Track*, Vol 15, Nos 1 and 2, 2001.

Chapter 14
The Atlantic in the Americas

The USA

The Atlantic was developed to its greatest extent in the USA. American Atlantics were bar-framed; most were powered by two cylinders, driving the rear coupled wheels.

American Atlantics can be put into nine main categories[1]: *Camelback* Atlantics (anthracite burners with wide Wootten fireboxes); *early Baldwin* Atlantics (lowish boiler pressure, short wheelbase, narrow cylindrical boiler, modest firebox, some of it still over drivers); *later Baldwin* Atlantics (higher boiler pressure; extended and broad wagon-top boiler; firebox well behind drivers); *Brooks* Atlantics (the 'Chautauquas') with piston valves and radial, inside-bearing rear axles; *Schenectady* Atlantics with outside bearing rear axles; *early* or *light Pennsylvania* Atlantics, often with Belpaire fireboxes; the later *E6s* Atlantics, like no others; the last-phase Milwaukee Road *Hiawatha* Atlantics; and various *rebuilt and improved* Atlantics. There were other builders of Atlantics including Manchester; and Richmond with its generously large trailing wheels and muzzle-straight stacks. Most Atlantics were built by the big three, reducing to two after the Alco merger of 1901. A few railroads built or rebuilt their own Atlantics: the Pennsylvania, Erie, SP, AT&SF, and others.

Sixty seven American railroads ordered new Atlantics and many were subsequently acquired second-hand from their original owners so a blow-by-blow list would be vast, and probably lose the wood for the trees; for a summary of the main picture see Appendix 4. The main Atlantic users and a few typical ones selected by size can brush-stroke the broad picture. For practical purposes a 'large' user means about eighty or more Atlantics; 'medium' – twenty-five to eighty and 'small' – fewer than twenty-five.

The Large Users

The *Pennsylvania* was the leading Atlantic operator and developer by a wide margin. Originally stung into action by the Philadelphia & Reading's Atlantic City expresses, the Pennsylvania found the Atlantics to its liking and used them widely, mainly on its Lines East. The first were untypical of what was to follow: class E1, three Camelback 4-4-2s with Wootten fireboxes (68sq.ft grate areas). They had 6ft 8in driving wheels, the norm for Pennsylvania Atlantics. Good, strong track enabled these drivers to carry 44.6 tons, the first four-coupled locomotives to do so. Shortly afterwards the Pennsylvania built a more orthodox, bituminous coal-burning, rear-cab machine, class E2 with a 55.5sq.ft grate. This evolved into the E3, distinguished by its Belpaire firebox, rare in the USA but a Pennsylvania standard. The E2 and E3 classes became the basic express passenger locomotives of the PRR until the coming of the Pacifics and the E6s Atlantics; about 460 were constructed in four main batches, 1901-1910. Most were similar but there were variations and sub-classes, mainly types of fireboxes, valves and valve gears, but no major deviations apart from some experiments like the SACM de Glehn Atlantic displayed at the World's Fair, and nineteen Schenectady engines in three classes, E21-E23 taken over with the *Terre Haute & Indianapolis*.

As trains became heavier, procurement policies diverged. Lines West moved gradually towards Pacifics, Lines East developed the Atlantic to a higher power, first with the transitional E5 (one dozen built 1910-1913), then with the record-breaking E6s 'in effect a middle-weight Pacific with only two sets of drivers'[2]. The Pennsylvania Pacifics were worthy successors to the Atlantics, which had shouldered express passenger tasks for nearly a decade. Even the Pacifics had to be double-headed in due course.

The *New York Central*, effectively a system of associated railroads, ran a total of 313 Atlantics. The *New York Central & Hudson River* had most of them, 213 in fourteen sub-classes, mainly built by Schenectady 1901-07. The NYC also flirted briefly with balanced compound Atlantics, but only acquired three of them. Of the associated NYC subsidiaries the *CCC&StL*, 'Big Four' had sixty in two classes and two very early 4-4-2s converted to eight-wheelers (class 76a, c1893); the *Lake Shore & Michigan Southern*, ten; the *Boston & Albany*, six; *St Lawrence & Adirondack*, three; the *Maine Central*, forty; the *Canada Southern*, ten; and the *Toledo, Canada Southern & Detroit* and *Pittsburgh & Lake Erie* two and five respectively. Virtually all the NYC Atlantics were from Schenectady; it was not a Baldwin line.

Most NYC&HR Atlantics were compact machines with 50sq.ft grates, and 6ft 7in driving wheels. The NYC abandoned its Atlantics as mainline power very swiftly, relegating them to secondary work. The system had well over 300 Pacifics by 1910, fifty on the Big Four.

The *Atchison Topeka & Santa Fe* had 183 Atlantics. They came in waves rather than batches, reflecting the twists and turns of technical development; the Santa Fe was a grand experimenter with compounding, and more besides. The` pattern was set by its first 4-4-2, the second Strong prototype and by most criteria the third 4-4-2 to be built anywhere. This was No.738, Schenectady 1889. However, it was soon converted to a 4-4-0 and spent most of its life in the shallows, on passenger trains between Topeka and St Joseph, 1892-1925.

The Santa Fe Atlantic era really started with ten 2-cylinder simples by Dickson, class 454 of 1899. They were unsuccessful and converted to 4-6-0s, 1904-1907. The four locomotives of class 256 (Baldwin 1903) were balanced compounds, found satisfactory and replicated (most mainly by Baldwin, 1904-1910) with a further 168 in six sub-classes. Mechanical unorthodoxy appeared in many ways on the Santa Fe; its early Atlantics had drive to the front coupled axle, unusual in American practice, as was running a fleet of 4-cylinder locomotives with cranked axles. Some had 'traction increasers' to transfer weight to the drivers on starting. The 1480 class or 'Bull Moose' variety sported Jacobs-Shupert corrugated steel fireboxes, reheaters as well as superheaters and inverted Walschaerts valve gear, the apogee of the Santa Fe school of originality. Many of the Santa Fe 4-4-2s were converted to 2-cylinder simples later in life; the Bull Mooses lasted until 1953 in this plainer guise.

The *Chicago & North Western* ran ninety-one Atlantics of nearly identical design constructed by Schenectady 1900-1908 and all designated class D. These were the original Schenectady wide-firebox coal burners; outside the Palatinate railways, the first such Atlantic to be built, and more advanced in design. Their grates were just over 46sq.ft; the second batch of 1908 slightly more. There were some minor differences within class D. Until 1903 they had four-bar crossheads, thereafter the alligator version; all had Stephenson inside valve gears with piston valves except the class of '08 which were fitted with Walschaerts valve gear, the last ten having rotary valves. All these engines worked on mainline expresses until about 1910, slipping into secondary work on mainlines until the mid-1920s when about half were put on to commuter work around Chicago. The last were withdrawn in 1954. The elegantly spare appearance of this class, enhanced by high-stepping 6ft 8in drivers remained to the end an authentic touch of 'early Atlantic' style enduring into the space age.

The *Southern Pacific* had eighty-five Atlantics in four classes. Its Atlantic history was distinguished in unusual ways: its class A-3 of fifty-one engines were 2-cylinder simples built by Baldwin and Alco (Brooks and Schenectady works, 1903-1908) according to the Harriman standard specifications, instantly recognisable by their plain but generously-proportioned cabs. A slightly larger version, A-5 went to the SP subsidiaries in Mexico, returning to the USA after 1912. The original SP Atlantics were Vauclain compounds (class A-1, sixteen by Baldwin, 1902). A further thirteen were delivered the next year, with smaller driving wheels. They had also all-steel Vanderbilt boilers with their large, cylindrical fireboxes that suffered restricted grate areas and a tendency to wear thin quickly; they were not repeated. Most SP Atlantics worked in relatively easy country bounded by Oakland, Sacramento, Redding and Bakersfield. Although some lasted nearly forty years many had short lives; the A-1 and A-2 classes were scrapped after twelve to twenty-three years work. Four of the A-3s were rebuilt in 1927 as class A-6, provided with steam boosters for the reliable handling of prestige passenger duties; they lasted until 1948-1952. The most curious Atlantic conversion of all metamorphosed seven of the A-3 engines into 0-8-0 shunting engines.

The Middle-Range Users

Some middle-rangers were large railroads which tried out a few Atlantics and went no further; others, like the Rock Island, offered as much variety as any line in the world. On the *Milwaukee Road* and the *Baltimore & Ohio*, modest-sized fleets were living microcosms of Atlantic evolution.

The *Illinois Central* served reasonably-graded territory which might seem promising for 4-4-2s, but after early Atlantic experiments it invested in Pacifics from 1905. A Baldwin 4-4-2 was evaluated in 1901 and it encouraged the IC to try a larger scheme: twenty-five Atlantics of one class from Rogers 1903-1904, in two batches. But their mainline express life was short; they were soon at work on stopping passenger trains. The Depression killed off much of this traffic, particularly on branch lines and most IC 4-4-2s were scrapped 1939-1941. In an interesting twist, eleven were rebuilt as 'freight Atlantics' exchanging their 6ft 8in drivers for 5ft 3.5in ones, at the same time having boiler pressure raised from 185lbs sq in to 225lbs sq in. This increased their tractive effort from 24,271lbs to nearly 40,000lbs. The reconfigured Atlantics, of low-slung and potent appearance were true Atlantics at heart and slipped as seriously as ever on their new duties working the Mississippi branch lines; they were soon retired.

The *Chicago, Rock Island & Pacific* had thirty Atlantics, starting in 1902 with seven Brooks Chautauquas (Road class A24 – for the mysteries of Rock Island classification schemes, see Chapter 13). That year the Rock Island leased the *Burlington, Cedar Rapids & Northern* thereby acquiring three more Chautauquas (Brooks, 1900) with the Player adaptation of the Belpaire fireboxes. More Atlantics were purchased in small lots: ten from Schenectady in 1905; and eight Baldwin balanced compounds in 1905-1906.

The use of the Player-Belpaire firebox was not the only coincidental touch between the Rock Island and Britain's GWR; it acquired two great rarities, 4-cylinder simple Atlantics from Schenectady in 1909. These twins (Road class W28) had all four 17x26 in cylinders driving the front coupled axle; they looked well and ran exceedingly smoothly. When tested against 2-cylinder simples between Chicago and Rock Island they demonstrated a fuel saving of 18.4%, but their mechanical complication was not to American railroading tastes and they remained unique, lasting until 1937. The Baldwin compounds were rebuilt as modern simples with super-heaters and Walschaerts valve gears in 1920. Some of the Rock Island's purchases had to be postponed because of financial problems; for example, the 4-cylinder engines came after a two year moratorium on passenger power brought about by the great financial panic of 1907. The 'Rock of Ages' adopted Pacifics early; fifty from Brooks in 1903 which soon became its favoured passenger power instead of the neatly-proportioned and unusual 4-4-2s.

Another railroad which acquired a miscellany of Atlantics by taking control of other lines was the *Baltimore & Ohio* whose 4-4-2s were sorted into twelve classes and sub-classes within A to A-10. Its original Atlantics were six Vauclain compounds from Baldwin, 1900 (class A), soon rebuilt as 2-cylinder simples (class A-1, 1904). They were typical early Baldwins with a short wheelbase, 6ft 9ins between rear driver and trailing axle centres. The A-2 class (twenty locomotives, Schenectady 1903) demonstrated the 'march of technology' with a longer wheelbase, 11ft 8in between driver and trailing axle centres which made room for a much larger firebox and grate set well back, South German fashion (grate area 55.2sq.ft compared to the A-1 42.2sq.ft). The A-3

Methuselah; from the days of McKinley to Harry S. Truman: *the long-lived Milwaukee Road No.3010 of class A1; 1899-1947 (Baldwin); original simplicity of line obscured behind improvements: outside piston valves and gear; twin air pumps; to-and-fro air cooling pipes required by Federal law; turbo-dynamo and electric lighting, also a vertiginous walkway of Russian proportions. Kansas City, Mo, 1938.* Photo: J.R. Quinn.

class was a Baldwin version of the same, (twenty-six locomotives, 1910) and with a slightly longer wheelbase still.

From the *Chicago & Alton* (bought by the B&O in 1929) came three remaining Atlantics from its original ten. One of these had been the lone Harriman standard Atlantic, exhibited at the St Louis World's Fair in 1904 and sold to the *Texas & New Orleans* in 1906. From the *Buffalo, Rochester & Pittsburgh* (bought 1932) the B&O inherited ten Atlantics in four classes, the residue of a former fleet of fifteen in five classes; most were scrapped within four years. The *Buffalo & Susquehanna*, also bought in 1932 brought three more Atlantics, Brooks products of 1903-1904 one of which lasted until 1947.

The *Chicago, Milwaukee, St Paul & Pacific* was a bold technological experimenter. Its long Atlantic tradition commenced with two 4-4-2s bought from Baldwin in 1896 in order to accelerate the Chicago-Milwaukee run. Their success inspired further purchases until, by 1900, this original class A totalled thirteen with a few later additions. Milwaukee Road individuality expressed itself again in the larger locomotives of class A-2, eventually of thirty-five engines with plain, non-flanged tyres on the front drivers. There were also some compounding experiments: a Vauclain in 1898, two balanced compounds in 1907 and a dozen Vauclain compound versions of the A-2, built 1908-1909. Only one Atlantic came by corporate take-over, a robust Baldwin product of 1909 for the *Idaho & Washington Northern*, acquired in 1916 and later superheated; a rare survivor of the great Atlantic purges of the 1920s, it lasted until November, 1952. After the purges, when it seemed the Milwaukee Road had left Atlanticism well behind, it acquired the class A *Hiawathas*, the four largest and fastest Atlantics of all time and further examples of Milwaukee Road technical audacity. Alas for all that, the line was technically bankrupt within a month of launching the *Hiawathas*; it recovered for a while although by the century's end it was but a fond memory, like its fabled Atlantics.

The *Philadelphia & Reading*[3] was part of a corporate empire which owned one third of the USA's anthracite fields. Its wide-firebox anthracite or culm-burning Atlantics came in seven classes comprising fifty-eight locomotives, virtually all Camelbacks, some of striking appearance. The earliest were the Atlantic City flyers, Vauclain compounds in two classes, P1 and P3, 1896-1900. Thereafter 2-cylinder simples prevailed although class P-6 of 1909 contained two great rarities, 3-cylinder simples which were much favoured by their crews, but which were replaced when the dreaded crank axles started to wear. Even so, they flew: 'fitted with a Swiss speed indicator of undoubted accuracy' one of them touched 97mph. When rostered on special expresses the P5s were occasionally accorded two firemen, the quicker to shovel anthracite into the incomparable horsepower-generator; claims for a P5 attaining 100mph are not unreasonable. Long after their flying days the P&R Atlantics were at work on locals; Bert Pennypacker[4] remembered:

> *The Reading-Harrisburg all-stops local proved to be a real thriller ride with fast, surging starts, sharply barking exhausts and screaming whistle blasts, then heavy breaking from short, galloping sprints.* [He expressed amazement at] *the engineering know-how that permitted king-sized trailing truck wheels to support the huge Wootten firebox…94.5sq.ft of hand-fired grate area!*

The *Chicago, Burlington & Quincy* had a long Atlantic record. Having recently won the US Mail contract from Chicago to Omaha it invested in a 2-4-2 *Columbia* in 1895 for some fast running[5]. Assuming rightly that a 4-4-2 would give a steadier ride the 'Q' bought a range of

Vauclain compound Atlantics from Baldwin (eleven, 1899-1902) and then 2-cylinder simples (twenty-five from Rogers, 1903) used mainly on secondary service and subsidiary lines. There was a reversion to compounding in 1904-1905 with twenty Baldwin balanced compounds. In later years a few of these P-3-Cs became single-expansion locomotives with 5ft 9in drivers for mixed traffic work, along the lines of the Illinois Central experiment. The CB&Q locomotive chronicler Richard Campbell thought this 'an amazingly elegant way to haul a few freight cars and a single passenger accommodation from small town to small town.'

The Lesser Atlantic Users

The railroads with few Atlantics could be extensive systems like the Northern Pacific or small 'pikes' which present us with a puzzle: why did they invest in Atlantics at all when good, all-purpose 4-6-0s with up to 50% more adhesion would have sufficed?

The mighty *Northern Pacific* acquired three Atlantics with the *St Paul & Duluth* (Baldwin, 1899). They hauled the crack *Lake Superior Limited*, but as it grew in weight they faltered. The NP consequently bought three new Atlantics (Baldwin, 1909) suitably arranged with fat boilers towering over 6ft drivers, an Atlantic for more undulating lines than the high-steppers of the East. The *Great Northern* had a very similar clutch of Atlantics to the NP, ten by Baldwin, 1906 also with 6ft drivers and Belpaire fireboxes. The *Norfolk & Western* and the *Southern Railway* had small and partly-experimental sets of seven and ten Atlantics respectively: neither was particularly successful because of limited scope and poor riding qualities. The N&W machines were another Atlantic paradox. By raising their adhesion factor to 3.92 the N&W reduced their wheelslipping tendencies, but they turned out to be rough riders, hard on the track. After a spell on the *Cannon Ball* express (Richmond-Norfolk via Petersburg) they moved to quieter duties.

Other large railroads with few Atlantics included the *New York, New Haven & Hartford* (twelve locomotives, Schenectady, 1907) and the *Chesapeake & Ohio*, twenty locomotives in two batches, 1902-1907, and a one-off by Pittsburgh in 1916, an advanced machine with a superheater and Walschaerts valve gear.

Another group of late Atlantics, the last of the classic form to be built in the USA were two for the *Pittsburgh & Shawmut* in 1920, close copies of some LS&MS machines of 1907. Many of the lesser Atlantic stocks were held by railroads with few miles and items of rolling stock, like the *Gulf & Ship Island* (five locomotives, 1904-1907); *Idaho & Washington Northern,* one (see CMSt&P above); *Interstate*, one by Baldwin, 1916; *Evansville & Terre Haute*, two by Brooks, 1903.

Ironically, the *Atlantic Coast Line* after which the type was named was no great fan of the Atlantic. It bought the five 'original' Atlantics from Baldwin in 1894, adding one more in 1895. This latter locomotive was sent to work on the *Wilmington & Weldon*, a component of ACL. The ACL also purchased some 2-4-2s for comparative tests. Since the 4-4-2 was found superior, four more were ordered 1897-1900. But the ACL soon found its 'Copperhead' (copper-capped stack) 4-6-0s superior to the 4-4-2s in many respects, especially in adhesion. The 4-4-2s went on to secondary services where they lasted until 1934.

Canadian Pacific: *No.209 at Ottawa, shortly after completion in the CPR shops, 1899, one of Canada's half-dozen Atlantics; the Belpaire firebox had a 31.7sq.ft grate. With its seven-foot drivers, the largest ever on CPR, a normal-sized human is dwarfed by technology.* Photo: Harold K. Vollrath.

Canada

There was a brief, exciting Atlantic interlude on the Canadian railways, the child of competition sparked by the *Canada Atlantic* which connected Ottawa with Coteau on the St Lawrence River, thence to Montreal and the US frontier. By 1899 it was carrying a million tons of freight per annum, efficiently managed by the American E.J. Chamberlin, who turned the heat on its chief rival, the *Canadian Pacific* by ordering two Vauclain compound Atlantics from Baldwin for Ottawa-Montreal express work; they had 6ft 5in drivers. The CPR responded swiftly by building three Vauclain compound Atlantics in the Spring of 1899, designed by its Mechanical Engineer, A.W. Horsey and built at its own works. In order to cover the 113 miles in 140 minutes with the four-car *Metropolitan Limited* they were given 7ft coupled wheels. The CA response was as quick; Chamberlin ordered another Vauclain compound Atlantic from Baldwin, also built for great speed with 7ft 0.25in drivers, an all-time Canadian record. But in 1904 the CA was purchased by the *Grand Trunk Railway* which was not an Atlantic line so the class developed no further. The CPR used its Atlantics on prestige duties including the Royal Train, but found the Atlantic generally unsuited to Canadian conditions. One was converted to a 2-cylinder simple in 1908; all players in the short-lived drama were summarily withdrawn, starting with the CPR Atlantics in 1917.

Mexico

The Southern Pacific had two subsidiaries in northern Mexico, the *FC Sonora* (Sonora Railway), and the *Cananea, Rio Yaqui & Pacific*, by 1912 absorbed in the *Sud Pacifico de México*. For a short time these lines used SP Harriman standard Atlantics; the CRY&P had seven and

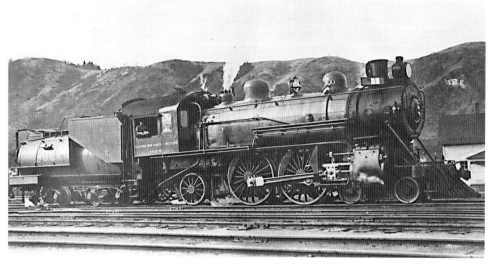

Mexican Atlantic: *a Harriman standard 4-4-2 (Alco, Brooks 1908) on the Cananea, Rio Yaqui & Pacific (FC Cananea, Rio Yaqui y Pacífico), an SP subsidiary in Mexico, with 'Common Standard' features including chicken-coop cab, Vanderbilt tender, round-topped boiler and 6ft 9in driving wheels; Empaline, Mexico, June 1910 – the year the Mexican Revolution got under way.* Photo: Harold K. Vollrath.

the FC Sonora had four. Building was shared between Alco, Brooks (1908) and Baldwin (1911) close to 'Common Standard' specifications: 6ft 10ins drivers, 20x28in cylinders, grate areas of 49sq.ft, boiler pressures 210lb sq.in, and a resulting tractive effort of 24,680lbs. After the SP's Mexican reorganisation most of the Atlantics returned North of the border.

Another Mexican Atlantic ran on the *FC Unidos de Yucatán* (United Railways of Yucatan), a Baldwin 4-4-2 of 1904 with 5ft 8in drivers, and a tractive effort of 17,500lbs. This wood-burning Atlantic, originally given a stovepipe chimney, was later supplied with a balloon-type spark arrester and spent much of its life hauling passenger trains between Mérida and Progreso, a growing coastal resort benefitting from the sisal boom. This was a modest journey of some thirty miles, hardly justification for a fully-fledged 4-4-2 – but the railway compli-mented its clientele with the *dernier cri*, the highly fashionable Atlantic. It was withdrawn in 1958 and partially dismantled. Plans for its preservation have hovered about since.

Brazil

The geography of Brazil did not render it very promising Atlantic territory, but the *Federal de l'Est* (Federal Eastern) network, government-owned but leased to a French company, ran five small Atlantics on its metre-gauge lines radiating from into Bahía and Minas Gerais. They were built by Baldwin in 1913, updated versions of the Nippon Tetsudo/Cape Government type of 1897 with smaller driving wheels, outside Walschaerts valve gears and various imped-imenta for local usage; a large canopy cab overlapping a long tender roof to provide shade and a large rear headlight on the tender for reverse working.[6]

142

Argentina

Argentina is the 'Atlantic land that never was', blessed with rolling pampas, an excellent railway network, much of it British owned and *au fait* with world developments. During the Atlantic era the Argentine Republic had a high standard of living, measured on a per capita basis, although the extremes of wealth were marked. And yet the sophisticated metropolis of Buenos Aires saw few 4-4-2s. The *Buenos Ayres & Pacific*, a 5ft 6in gauge line of 2,500 miles owned fourteen Atlantics; they came from NBL, 1905-1907 and had a passing resemblance to the Indian standard Atlantics although their dimensions were entirely different except for their rather mean grate areas, 29.8sq.ft. There were small differences in the axleloadings and tender sizes between the first eight and the remainder, which had greater loading and smaller tenders, possibly evidence of the familiar problems with adhesion; more seriously they were unsteady riders and their trailing wheel bearings ran hot. One of these locomotives was exhibited at the Buenos Aires Exposition, 1910 but the Atlantic never caught on 'down Argentine way', a land of competent 4-4-0s, ten-wheelers and Pacifics, to which the Atlantics were quickly converted in 1914.

The 4ft 8.5in gauge *Argentine North-Eastern* and the associated *Entre Rios* ordered ten successful 4-4-2+2-4-4 'double Atlantics' 1927-1930, one of them at least gravitated to Paraguay on loan. The metre-gauge *Córdoba Central* of 1,218 miles, radiating North-Westwards from Buenos Aires ran five Atlantics (NBL, 1907). These were long, low and lean machines with outside frames, radial trailing axles and huge tenders well-supplied with railings for containing firewood; emphatically not run-of-the-mill engines.

REFERENCE No. L.205.   GAUGE OF RAILWAY, 3 ft. 3⅜ in

CORDOBA CENTRAL RAILWAY

TYPE 4.4.2.—PASSENGER LOCOMOTIVE

ENGINE.

CYLINDERS— Diameter, 17 in.,	Stroke, 24 in.	
WHEELS—Coupled, Diameter,	4 ft. 9 in.	
Front, Diameter,	2 ft. 7 in.	
Hind, Diameter,	2 ft. 10 in.	
WHEEL-BASE— Rigid, 5 ft. 3 in.,	Total, 24 ft. 4 in.	
Engine and Tender,	47 ft. 7 in.	
WORKING PRESSURE,	200 lbs. per sq. in.	
HEATING SURFACE—Tubes,	981 sq. ft.	
Firebox,	97 ,,	
Total,	1,078 ,,	

FIREGRATE AREA,	23·7 sq. ft.
BOILER FEED,	2 Injectors.
TRACTIVE FORCE at 75% of Boiler Pressure,	18,252 lbs.
WEIGHT—In Working Order,	50 tons 0 cwts.
On Coupled Wheels,	26 tons 0 cwts.

TENDER.

TANK CAPACITY,	3,300 gallons.
FUEL SPACE,	360 cub. ft.
WEIGHT, Full,	42 tons 13 cwts.

Metre-gauge Atlantic: *run by the Córdoba Central in Argentina, (NBL, 1907) with radial trailing axle and large tender for wood fuel.* Photo: Christopher Walker.

Notes to Chapter 14

1. W. Reuter and Claus Bock, *op cit*, which employs six main categories.

2. George H. Drury, *Guide to North American Steam Locomotives*, 1993.

3. During the Atlantic era the P&R was a subsidiary of the *Reading Company* which owned the *Central RR of New Jersey* (another operator of Camelback Atlantics) from 1901 and was, in turn, controlled by the *B&O*. In 1923 some subsidiaries, including the P&R lost their identity in a merger whereby all were subsumed in the Reading Co.

4. Bert Pennypacker, *Eastern Steam Pictorial*, 1966. The 3-cylinder machines were unusual in another way: they had outside Walschaerts valve gear, but Joy valve gear on the middle cylinder.

5. Paul T. Warner, 'The Strong Locomotives', *Bulletin* 92 of the Railway & Locomotive Historical Society.

6. Were they equipped for burning coffee surplus during the depression like some other Brazilian loco-motives? It would be interesting to know; the singular aroma would have added to the Atlantics' many other sensuous attractions.

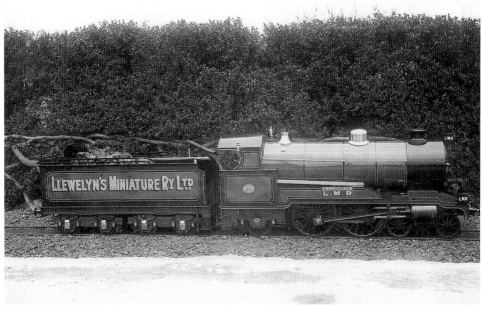

Llewelyn's Atlantic: *a 4-4-2 temporarily named* G.V. Llewelyn *on what became the Southport Miniature Railway, now Lakeside Miniature Railway, 15in gauge. The number 1914 may also be temporary; LMR nomenclature was apt to be cavalier. Probably the Greenly-designed* Prince Edward of Wales *(Bassett-Lowke, 1912; class 20, 'improved Little Giant' type) – in impeccable condition, advertising the identity of the line's new moving spirit.* Photo Campbell McCutcheon.

Chapter 15
The British Atlantics

Britain ranked third in Atlantic ownership (310 locomotives) but it could offer a greater range of Atlantic types than any other system outside the USA, although some of the sub-species came in very small batches. British Atlantics were plate-framed (a generalisation mindful of some minor framing complications on the GWR); the majority had outside cylinders with inside valve gears and drive to the rear coupled axle. The two major exceptions were the NER 3-cylinder simples which drove on the front coupled axle, and the Lancashire & Yorkshire fleet of inside-cylinder 4-4-2s. Only two classes, Ivatt's large Atlantics on the GNR and the nearly identical LB&SCR 4-4-2s had wide fireboxes which took full advantage of the Atlantic arrangement. By world standards the British Atlantics were reasonably long-lived, many exceeding forty years.

Great Northern Railway

The GNR was Britain's premier Atlantic railway with 116 locomotives. Its successor, the LNER had 241 Atlantics, 78% of the national total. The GN stock comprised two main classes with seven varieties. H.A. Ivatt was the guiding hand behind them, his first Atlantic class, the GNR 'small Atlantics' known as 'Klondykes'[1] (GNR class C1, LNER class C2)

Klondyke: *one of the original GNR small Atlantics in later life, not clean but its delicate form made correspondingly clearer; LNER No.3259 of class C2 not strained by a four-coach train, c.1935. Built Doncaster, 1903, ended up as a stationary boiler at Doncaster Plant, 1943-1946.*

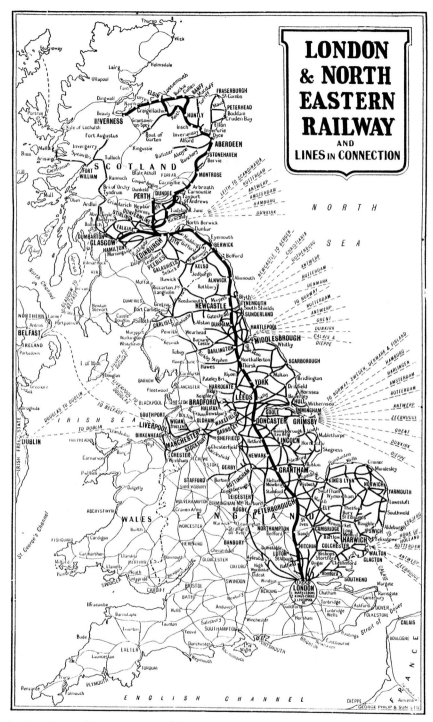

The Racing Grounds: *a 1925 map of the LNER, Britain's largest operator of Atlantics which still dominated the East Coast Route (London-York-Newcastle upon Tyne-Edinburgh-Aberdeen) as well as taking a good share of the former GCR Manchester-Leicester-London expresses.*

appeared in 1898 with the still-extant No.990. A neat locomotive, rather diminutive by later standards, it was regarded as huge in its day. A further twenty-one Klondykes were built by the GNR at Doncaster 1898-1903. A single 4-cylinder simple version was tried out in 1902 (No.271) with all four cylinders in line driving the front coupled axle. The idea was not a great success; the locomotive was rebuilt in 1911 with two inside cylinders.

The Klondykes had narrow fireboxes, a grate area of 24.5sq.ft and 6ft 8in driving wheels. At first they ran on saturated steam, but No.988 was fitted with a Schmidt superheater in 1908, the first GNR locomotive to be so treated; the rest followed over many years, the last was converted in 1924. Their general reputation was summarised by Cecil J. Allen as 'curiously variable engines, as far as performance goes.' It remains an open question whether their occasional 'sluggishness' perceived by contemporaries was the outcome of cautious driving, deficiencies of steam distribution or, most likely, Ivatt's conservative combination of a good steam-raising boiler feeding modest 18.75 x 24in cylinders.

Ivatt was similarly cautious with his more famous 'large Atlantics', the wide-firebox class C1 (so classified by both the GNR and LNER). These were famous steam-raisers with grate areas of 31sq.ft. They also had 6ft 8ins driving wheels placed close together, and still the modest 18.75 x 24 in cylinders. The centre line of the boiler was 8ft 8.5in above rail level which imparted a massive, dominant appearance to the engine, at least to British eyes. They were constructed in two batches, eighty-one between 1902 and 1908, and ten in 1910; the latter received superheaters when new, the rest had them installed in due course with generally startling results.

H.A. Ivatt may have traded sparkling performance for ease and economy of maintenance. In addition to their small cylinders they had low boiler pressures, as with the class of 1910: 150lb sq.in. His successor, H.N. Gresley transformed these good engines into near-brilliant ones with a succession of ever more potent superheaters and raised boiler pressures. The great years of the Ivatt Atlantics came therefore in their middle age, the era when Cecil J. Allen and others recorded one amazing performance after another on the East Coast expresses. 'It was not until Gresley had fitted them with 32-element superheaters that they reached the zenith of their powers, and in fact achieved their world-wide reputation' (Martin Evans, *Atlantic Era*). The highest recorded speed of a GNR large Atlantic, 93mph by No.4456 on the Leeds-London *Queen of Scots* and one of the highest loads, seventeen coaches, 585 tons gross (Grantham-York; the legendary run recorded by Allen in 1936) both belong to this period.

R.A.H. Weight, who knew these improved Atlantics well, wrote of their performance in the 1930s: 'it was just *joie de vivre*: delight at speeding along with those grand engines, which were not thrashed to achieve such superlative performance...' (*Great Northern Locomotives 1847-1947*, 1947).

There was also a clutch of GNR 4-cylinder compound Atlantics, participants in an inconclusive feasibility study. How far this was Ivatt's idea, or the result of company director agitation is a moot point. Ivatt's two designs suffered from undersized cylinders, one, No.292 (Doncaster 1905) from inappropriate hp:lp ratios also. The third compound Atlantic, No.1300 was from Vulcan Foundry, loosely based on the de Glehn system with outside hp cylinders set well back. Cylinder dimensions were more generous than in Ivatt's examples. Each of the experimental Atlantics could be worked as a simple, although only Ivatt's designs really allowed for continuous working in single expansion; Nos 1300 and 1421 were later converted to 2-cylinder simples.

Great Northern (UK): *LNER No. 4419 (GNR Doncaster, 1906) at speed on East Coast Route; this engine was fitted with a booster (1923-1935); its steam pipes are clearly discernible beside splashers and firebox. Here a surfeit of water at trough's end gives the leading coach the Niagara treatment; GN somersault signal, as much an emblem of the road as the Ivatt Atlantic.* Photo: R.K. Blencowe.

The one fully modernised GNR Atlantic appeared as late as 1936 with Gresley's remodelling of No.3279, an already much-modified large Atlantic which had been rebuilt as a 4-cylinder simple in 1914. It was now reconverted to a 2-cylinder Atlantic and given well-configured steam passages, outside Walschaerts valve gear, and long-travel valves. But this 'improved Atlantic', the apogee of the Ivatt type, technically the most advanced British 4-4-2, remained a one-off development unable to stem the rising tide of Pacifics which in most respects were superior machines as modern express engines.

London, Brighton & South Coast Railway

The LB&SCR was Britain's lightest user of Atlantics. They came in two virtually identical batches, five from Kitson (class H1, 1905-1906) and six built at its Brighton works, class H2 of 1911-1912. They were closely modelled on the GNR large Atlantics. The connecting link was Douglas Earle Marsh, Locomotive Superintendent of the LB&SCR and formerly Ivatt's right-hand man as Chief Assistant Mechanical Engineer at Doncaster. Before that he had trained and worked on the GWR at Swindon, wherein may lie his major contribution to Atlantic development. The GWR broad gauge 4-2-2 express locomotives, well known to the young Marsh, had massive fireboxes. Two converging streams of evidence suggest that he may have been the originator of the GNR large Atlantic firebox. First, E.L. Ahrons who knew much of what went on in locomotive engineering circles had reason to think it so and, secondly, later scholarship has unearthed the Doncaster Chief Draughtsman's notebook which stated that the new boiler for No.251 (the first large Atlantic) was a 'Boiler with BG firebox.' Might that refer to 'broad gauge'?[2] Whatever the truth, Marsh had a good claim to ask for the loan of the Doncaster drawings; his relationship with Ivatt was excellent and he had played a strong part in the design and construction of the GNR Atlantics.

Marsh's motive for adopting the GNR design was its easy readiness at a time of an acute shortage of express locomotives on the LB&SCR. His Atlantics answered this need very capably; they were Doncaster Atlantics raised to a higher power with boiler pressure increased to 200lb sq.in, and a piston stroke lengthened by two inches. This arrangement gave them a tractive effort of 19,029lbs compared with the GNR large Atlantics' 17,580lbs. There were other refinements: a screw reversing gear which permitted finer-tuning of valve events than the Doncaster 'pole' could offer; and superior suspension (Timmis helical springs on bogie and driving wheels) which gave a smoother ride than the GNR 4-4-2s. They had one weakness, a curious propensity to stop on dead-centre making their restarting a difficult operation; no one got to the root of this problem which had, perforce, to be lived with. They were popular with their drivers, were good steamers, and had commodious cabs since they had longer frames than their meanly-cabbed Doncaster cousins. They balked only at the steep 1 in 64 gradient out of London Victoria; the enduring Atlantic problem of 'strong lungs, slippery feet.'

The H1 class were built as saturated-steam locomotives. They received superheaters when they were some twenty years old; the H2 class (originally designated H1/S, i.e. superheated H1) were built with superheaters, and a slightly reduced boiler pressure. Whatever managers decreed, the railwaymen had their folkways which were hard to penetrate. Drivers of H1 Atlantics ran on 'full throttle' with regulators wide open, adjusting the screw reverse carefully as track configuration, train loads and gradients demanded. But H2 drivers had regulators partly closed and preferred long cut-offs. Marsh's successor L.B. Billinton complained about these Atlantic driving habits in May 1912, but he could do little more than record the fact and regret that the superheated engines offered less fuel economy than was intended. Like the 'simple versus compounding' controversy, the 'regulator versus cut off' argument ran and ran, unresolved into the very twilight of steam traction.

Lancashire & Yorkshire Railway

The Atlantic days were an age when 'that which Manchester said today, London thought tomorrow.' Here ran the 'Lanky', the L&YR whose forty unique Atlantics were like no others on Earth. They were built at Horwich, Lancashire, to the designs of the L&Y locomotive chief, John Aspinall and the Chief Draughtsman, Zachariah Tetlow. There were two batches of twenty each, in 1899 and 1902. Although they narrowly missed being the first British Atlantics they were more sophisticated than Ivatt's Klondykes by a long chalk.

Aspinall's Atlantics, the '1400 class' have not generally been recognised for the extraordinary machines they were, perhaps because the opinion-formers of the South had too little acquaintance with them. Their qualities were apparent in many ways: their huge, 7ft 3in driving wheels were the largest on any Atlantic; their inside cylinders placed them in the tiny minority of 4-4-2s so arranged. Atlantic No.737 of the 1899 batch was fitted with a low-degree superheater; apart from earlier experiments, the first British locomotive to receive superheat. Five other L&Y Atlantics received these early 'steam driers' also – none too successful, but decidedly a move in the right direction.

Some innovations presented difficulties. A few of the 1400s had outside admission piston valves, but these developed problems and were later removed in favour of slide valves. Their steam reversers were none too reliable and had to be replaced by screw reversers. The inside bearing trailing axle contributed to rough riding and gave way to a better outside bearing version; Adams bogies replaced the earlier swing-link variety and also gave a better ride. Like American locomotives, the 1400s had cab doors leading out on to the running plates.

When constructed, the 1400s had the largest boilers in Britain, pitched high to clear the massive driving wheels. Altogether they were of arresting appearance. Cecil J. Allen recalled their

> *graceful gait...with side-rods peeping coyly once per revolution from under the voluminous splashers, and the radius rods of the Joy's valve-gear performing a rhythmic dance as they appeared over the main frames, an aspect of effortless ease was engendered by the low muffled sound of the exhaust...*[3]

They were relatively light engines (58.75 tons) and with only 35 tons available for adhesion they were difficult to start under load, even for an Atlantic. But when under way with their fairly light trains they went like the wind, for example on the Liverpool-Manchester 'forty minute flyers'; the Fleetwood boat trains, and the Southport 'Club Train' with its special, luxurious carriage.

The 1400 'Highfliers' received a further lease of life on express duties when their 4-6-0 successors ran into difficulties. They were all inherited by the LMS in 1923 but faded from the scene fairly quickly; a few lasted until 1933.

Great Western Railway

The GWR Atlantics were also unusual, but in other ways. They were central to Churchward's search for a minimum set of standard locomotive types. His enquiries drew on and tested the best practice available, notably from the world-leaders in France and the USA.

There were three types of GWR Atlantic, each a stage in the careful evaluation. First were three de Glehn type 4-4-2s purchased from SACM, Belfort. No.102, *La France* was a typical Nord Atlantic, Nos. 103 and 104 (later *President* and *Alliance*) were based on the enlarged P-O version. The 'Frenchmen' were excellent machines, swift, steady and economical. They were also powerful: 'A steady pull on the drawbar... of 2 tons at 70mph on a 6ft 6in wheel takes, if I may use a colloquialism, a great deal of getting... The GWR has two or three engines running today which will do this, and *La France* is one of them' (Churchward, 1904).[4] But did this power arise from their compounding or from a high boiler pressure? To investigate the problem Churchward organised a 4-cylinder simple Atlantic, No.40 (later *North Star*) with a boiler pressure of 225lb sq.in, slightly less than *La France* and her sisters but high by British standards. The performance of *North Star* equated well with the Frenchmen and although the locomotive remained unique it became the basis of the famous and long-lived 4-cylinder simple design of Swindon 4-6-0s, and their derivatives.

Churchward pursued the question of wheel arrangement with equal care. In 1904 he converted a newly designed 2-cylinder 4-6-0, No.171, *Albion* (Swindon, 1903) into a 4-4-2 by removing the rear coupled wheels and substituting 4ft 1.5in diameter trailing wheels with outside bearings. Thirteen more such Atlantics were built in 1905 as well as six of the 4-6-0 version. The GWR 2-cylinder Atlantics had identical boilers to their 4-6-0 sisters[5] with grate areas of 27.22sq.ft in all cases. For a time *Albion* was run against *La France*; all of the 4-4-2 version of the 'Saint' 4-6-0s as they came to be called, ran against their ten-wheeler sisters in a series of comparative tests.

The greater sure-footedness of the latter was more important in operational terms; accordingly, books were closed on the great evaluation and the Atlantics were converted into 4-6-0s April 1912-January 1913; *North Star* lasted as a 4-4-2 for barely three years. The GWR Atlantics were amongst the shortest-lived of the type but cannot be classed as failures since their main and successful purpose was experimental.

The provisional nature of the GWR Atlantics was evident in the slightly 'bolt-on' appearance of the trailing axle boxes; the main set of 2-cylinder engines had supplementary outside frames for the trailing wheels, masking horn gaps which had been left in the main frames for trailing coupled wheels 'as and when' required. The GWR 4-4-2s also embodied some successful French and American devices, for example the 'de Glehn bogie' as Churchward described it, and long-travel valves. The new conical boiler with Belpaire firebox was derived from a Brooks design evident in modified form on some early Chautauqua 4-4-2s on the Burlington, Cedar Rapids & Northern (1900). Churchward's questionable insistence on putting valve gears inside the frames was something he did not, however, learn from either French or

Great Western: *2-cylinder simple Atlantic No.186,* Robin Hood *of the 'Scott' class (GWR, Swindon, 1905), readily convertible to a 4-6-0 type against which it was tested as part of G.J. Churchward's long comparative evaluation; converted to 4-6-0 in 1912.*

American practice. In spite of this inaccessible arrangement, and some other Swindon quirks, the Churchward Atlantics were technically superior to their British rivals, part of a rapid evolution which put GWR locomotive practice ten to twenty years ahead of the rest.

Great Central Railway

Although the GCR also carried out a '4-4-2 or 4-6-0?' comparative trial, it did not command the resources of the GWR. The outcome was less clear and the Great Central 4-4-2s remained in their original form. The Locomotive Superintendent, J.G. Robinson once described as 'one of the most successful designers of the British hit-or-miss school'[6] was more successful with his 4-4-2s than his 4-6-0s. The GCR Atlantics were competent machines and, in the eyes of many commentators, without peers for elegant form.

They came in two main classes, the standard 2-cylinder variety and four 3-cylinder compounds. The first two Atlantics, Nos 192 and 194 were built by Beyer, Peacock in 1904, typical products of the British Atlantic school. More followed: five from Beyer, Peacock 1904; twelve by North British Locomotive, 1905; and eight from the GCR works at Gorton, 1906. Originally built as saturated steam locomotives they received superheaters when undergoing major overhauls from 1912 onwards.

The standard GCR 4-4-2s, generically class 8B, differed in minor ways. Because the first two were conceived as possible 4-6-0 conversions they had unusually shallow fireboxes for Atlantics. They were, however, never converted and the rest of the class were given deeper fireboxes. The first seven and last eight locomotives had boiler pressures of 180lb sq.in; the NBL set were pressed to 200lb sq.in; grate areas differed slightly around a standard of 26sq.ft, rather low for an Atlantic but able to cope with the undemanding tasks set for these 'Jersey Lilies' as they became known. The London extension for which they were chiefly intended had its difficult stretches, but many of the trains they hauled were short and light; four or five coach expresses were common. Later, many of them were shedded at Leicester after which they were dispersed to secondary services before their withdrawal in the late 1940s.

One of the GCR standard Atlantics was converted to 3-cylinder simple propulsion (No.1090, 1908) although it reverted to being a straightforward 2-cylinder *Zwillingslokomotive*, as the Germans have it, in 1922. Robinson's reasons for this conversion were never made clear but given the more even torque and smooth working of 3-cylinder machines, very probably he was responding to a major weakness of the 8B's, their heavy hammer-blow. Also, No.1090 was given Walschaerts valve gear, lighter than the Stephenson system used on the standard 8B, another way of reducing the imbalances set up by reciprocating motion.

The GCR already had experience of 3-cylinder Atlantics with its four Smith compounds (Gorton works, 1905-1906). These were class 8D, with divided drive (outside cylinders driving the rear coupled axle; inside cylinder the front coupled axle). They saved about 2 – 2.5lbs per mile although this advantage was lost when the 8Bs received superheating. The reasons for constructing the compounds may have included comparisons with simples or even the testing of prototypes for a new class. They were not replicated, however. Any economies they offered were offset by higher initial and maintenance costs, possibly also by a culture inimical to compounding. Their allocation and fate mirrored that of the 8B class, broadly from prestige London flyers to Cleethorpes locals.

North Eastern Railway

The mighty NER, virtual railway monopolist of industrial North East England, adopted the Atlantics cautiously at first; from 1906-1910 it ran only a dozen of them. Thereafter it went into higher gear and had seventy-two to bequeath to the LNER in 1923. They came in three main forms; the 'old standard' class V, an orthodox British 2-cylinder model; the 'new standard' 3-cylinder simple class Z, and a brace of fine 4-cylinder compounds, class 4CC.

The original NER Atlantic, class V, may have been influenced by a recent visit to the USA of the Locomotive Superintendent, Wilson Worsdell – himself a graduate of Altoona and like Churchward a close student of American engineering. The Pennsylvania 'Flyers' to Atlantic City had apparently impressed him. Ten Atlantics were constructed at the NER Gateshead works, 1903-1904, following on the heels of a successful 4-4-0 (class R) and a disappointing set of 4-6-0 classes, S and S1. Although given more generous cylinders than Ivatt's large Atlantics (20 x 28 in) their grate area was on the small side, 27sq.ft. In traffic they proved 'not disappointing', but none too brilliant either. They were heavy on fuel, largely because their inadequate valves required a late cut-off for fast running; they 'punched their way along by wasteful force than by flowing finesse.'[7] Rough and tough they may have been, but they proved by the mysterious workings of fate to be extraordinarily safe. The worst to befall class V in all their years of storming between York and Edinburgh was a bump suffered by No.649 when it collided with an 0-6-0 near Belford.

Ten modified locomotives (referred to as V1 or V/09) were built by the NER at Darlington, 1910 with slightly smaller cylinders and heavier frames. The 'Gateshead Infants', as the first series were nicknamed might have been more successful if the NER Chief Draughtsman, the gifted W.M. Smith, had not been absent with illness at the time of their conception. By the time he returned to duty his critical comments came too late for action. Worsdell, a creative delegator of duties allowed Smith to design his own Atlantic. The outcome was an intellectual masterpiece, a 4-cylinder Smith compound which has ever since attracted 'thinking locomotivists', rather like the de Glehn compounds and for similar reasons. Their higher initial and maintenance costs (they cost £800 more per locomotive than class V Atlantics) and the requirement to train enginemen to operate their sophisticated compounding arrangements tend to get played down in the under-standable admiration accorded to them. They were also good-looking with fine propor-tions, 7ft 1.25in driving wheels and a slim boiler with Belpaire firebox; at 29sq.ft the grate area was higher than that of class V.

There were only two of these class 4CC Atlantics, (Gateshead works, 1906). Walter Smith died a few months after they appeared. They ran like a dream on the East Coast expresses and became the NER showpiece engines *par excellence*, doing turns on Royal Trains. They walked the comparative tests (September, 1906) against the class V Atlantics, as well as the class R 4-4-0 and class S1 4-6-0. Although they were lighter on fuel than the class V the margin of advantage was not great. The NER locomotive committee was persuaded to approve the building of ten more of them in 1907, but no more were constructed. There is a well-circulated story that Smith's executors demanded too high a royalty for his patents, but it rests on a narrow evidential basis and in cases like this it is often difficult to disentangle who was manipulating whom.[8]

A Connoisseur's Engine: *LNER No.730 of class C8 (NER, Gateshead, 1906 – NER same number, but class 4CC) W.M. Smith's 4-cylinder compound Atlantic near Darlington in 1930, of finely drawn appearance, but tough. Belpaire firebox, Ramsbottom safety valves, Schmidt superheater and able to work compound, semi-compound or simple. On the costly side, but that is the way with quality.*

Instead the NER built the ten improved class V Atlantics, and later the exceptional 3-cylinder Atlantics designed by Worsdell's successor, Vincent Raven and Chief Draughtsman, George Heppell. Ten saturated and ten superheated examples were built by NBL in 1911 (classes Z and Z1 respectively, later simply Z). The NER built the rest at Darlington, ten in 1914, ten 1915-1917, and one in 1918.

Although they were not the last British Atlantics to be built, the Z class was the last new design and in many ways the 'apex of the British Atlantics', at least, of the classic era, embodying many lessons of the past decade. Their technically advanced 3-cylinder drive gave an even torque and they rode evenly and smoothly.[9] They were more frugal than the class Vs, 45.6lb of coal per mile contrasted with 56.1lb per mile, and an average of 73,000 miles between repairs compared with 58,000 miles. Until the coming of the LNER Pacifics in the 1920s, they dominated express working on that part of the East Coast route from York to Edinburgh; the evening Glasgow-Leeds dining car express was their particular *forte* with timings (1923) of forty-three minutes for the 44.1 miles from Darlington to York.

The outline of the class Z Atlantics was discernibly post-Victorian, even neo-Georgian with neat, clean lines. Their famously rapid, triple-beat exhaust was known to divisions of railwayists in Yorkshire, Northumbria and the Lothians. Drivers had a high opinion of them; Norman McKillop, a highly experienced driver and locomotive expert, and a North British man no less, wrote of them: 'The superb Z Atlantic [was] a locomotive that in riding, speed and brake power, was unequalled in its hey-day.'[10]

Another Atlantic City: *LNER class C7 No.2207 (former NER class Z, Darlington, 1917) leaves York on a Scarborough-Liverpool express c.1930; York Minster in the distance. York is a true 'Atlantopolis', 4-4-2s from the GNR, NER and L&YR all met here; two carefully restored and preserved GN Atlantics repose in York's National Railway Museum together with many records of Atlantic history: one way or another Atlantics have been coming and going here for over a century, and spanning three.* Photo: Collection of Ian G.T. Duncan.

North British Railway

The first fourteen NBR Atlantics were delivered in 1906; the last two appeared in 1920 and were therefore the last British Atlantics to be built, outside the sphere of miniature railways. In the meantime a second batch of six had been delivered in 1910. Their designer, W.P. Reid had good experience of running locomotives having been, *inter alia*, a shed foreman. He preferred straightforward engines which would get their business done reliably. The Scottish school of locomotive engineering was well able to oblige, famed the world over for constructing sturdy locomotives able to work hard. Such were the 'NB Atlantics', classes H and I.[11]

They had a rough birth and infancy. The long-suffering Reid was under pressure to design quickly a new set of prestige express engines, in time for the summer season of 1906. Urging came both from the NBR board and the General Manager, W.F. Jackson, a touchy interventionist given to deluging his subordinates with memoranda. Certain similarities between Reid's design and the GCR Atlantics (their wheel spacings were identical) have given rise to a theory that the NBR Atlantics were derivative, but there is no hard evidence that Reid borrowed anything except general concepts. The NBR Atlantic boilers, for example, were broader and pitched higher than the GCR ones; cylinders were larger as were grate areas, by 2.5sq.ft. The NBR Atlantics were impressively massive, so much so that the company's chief engineer James Bell waxed cautious, and then hostile, about their deployment.

So great was the rush to get them into service that the first NBR Atlantic appeared at Waverley station in workshop grey paint. Shortly after they entered traffic a great row broke out

North British: *NBR 4-4-2s on the Waverley route; at Hawick in 1907 with two new NBR Atlantics; Nos.879* Abbotsford *and 880* Tweeddale *(both NBL, August 1906); textile mills in the mists beyond.*

when Bell recommended that they be withdrawn from the Carlisle-Edinburgh 'Waverley Route ' because they had allegedly damaged the track. First Ivatt then Raven were summoned up from England to report on the supposed deficiencies of the 4-4-2s. After much heat had been generated the crisis fizzled out. Once crews got used to these engines, very large ones by contemporary British standards, they performed well with expresses from Edinburgh to Glasgow, Carlisle, Dundee and Aberdeen, and in later years to Newcastle upon Tyne.

If the NBR Atlantics had a defect it was their initially voracious appetite for coal, later curtailed when superheaters were installed. Fuel consumption was not helped by Reid's installation of a reverse lever with eight notches either side of centre, not a device for the fine-tuning of cut-offs.[12] Also, the NBR generally used coal of lower calorific value than the northern English lines. Later improvements brought coal consumption down, and No.878 performed well in comparative tests against NER and GNR Atlantics in 1923. The fuel-gobbling reputation endured, however, perhaps an example of the injustices perpetrated by cultural inertia. Even so, Norman McKillop, who knew them well, wrote of the 'bogie-to-trailing-wheel crashing pitch' and his attempts to fire No.876, *Waverley* against its 'diabolical jigging, heaving turmoil.'[13]

The Scottish Atlantics, like the English ones, had a strong local following. There was a vigorous campaign in 1937 to save the last NBR Atlantic, No.9875 *Midlothian*. By the time officialdom woke up to public clamour, much of it conducted in the columns of *The Scotsman*, *Midlothian* was largely dismantled. The LNER chairman William Whitelaw ordered that it be preserved and Gresley took the necessary steps unaware that the locomotive was already in pieces, which says a good deal about the information flows within large corporations. Much of *Midlothian's* detritus was tracked down and reassembled; its boiler had gravitated to Stratford, London for example. In June 1938 No.9875 reborn was in steam once more, destined eventually for museum preservation. But war came a year later and she went for scrap, a rare if not unique example of a twice-junked Atlantic. A great loss, but not the worst exacted by the war.

Notes to Chapter 15

1. For the slight controversy about 'Klondyke' spelling, see Appendix 5.

2. See Charles Fryer, *The Locomotives of D. Earle Marsh*, 1994; the history sleuth was Michael Rutherford.

3. Cecil J. Allen, *British Atlantic Locomotives*, 1976.

4. In discussion arising from the paper 'Compound Locomotives in France' presented by E. Sauvage, April 1904.

5. The pattern is complex, involving long and short cone boilers on different locomotives at different times, but the generalisation holds good: see RCTS, *Locomotives of the Great Western Railway, Pt 8, Modern Passenger Classes*, 1953.

6. J.N. Westwood, *Locomotive Designers in the Age of Steam*, 1977.

7. W.A. Tuplin, *North Eastern Steam*, 1970.

8. Philip Atkins, 'The Four-Cylinder Compound Atlantics of the NorthEastern Railway', *Back Track*, Vol 11, No.8, Aug 1997.

9. Class Z were sufficiently novel to rate a mention in André Chapelon's *La Locomotive à Vapeur*: 'for the first time the three cylinders were produced in a single casting...' Chapelon also notes they were the first 3-cylinder simple express locomotives 'in recent times', but see reference to P&R 3-cylinder Camelback Atlantics, Chapter 14.

10. Norman McKillop, *Enginemen Elite*, 1958.

11. Typically complex locomotive classification: class H were originally the saturated version but later they became class I, at which point the superheated version became the new class H.

12. Originally some NB Atlantics had steam reversing gear (Nos.868-81) but this proved unreliable and occasionally a safety hazard; it was replaced by hand-worked levers.

13. N. McKillop, *op cit*.

Chapter 16
The Atlantic in Three Continents

France

The first French Atlantic, *Paris-Orleans* No.580 of 1899 was a one year-old 2-4-2 built by the Ivry works, now converted into a 2-cylinder simple 4-4-2 to improve its stability at speed. The experiment was a success and the remaining seven of the 1899 batch of 2-4-2s were converted to 2-cylinder compound Atlantics in 1909.

The conversion was the idea of Emile Polonceau. His successor, Emile Solacroup also 'Atlanticised' some older 2-4-2s. A dozen were altered into 2-cylinder compounds, 1906-1910. These were already veterans of conversion having started life as 2-4-0s constructed 1864-1872, converted to 2-4-2s by 1890. One of them, 203c had been exhibited at the Paris Exposition, 1867. Another set of three, built as 2-4-2s by SACM, 1878 were altered into Atlantics in 1910.[1]

The P-O conversions looked archaic with their small boilers, some with outside Gooch valve gear working large, slanting slide valves. The conversion reduced their tractive effort partly because boiler pressure was lowered, but they were an economical, logical improvement typical of a long-enduring policy in French steam engineering.

The rest of P-O Atlantic policy was straightforward: eight enlarged Nord-type 4-4-2s built by SACM in 1902, and a further six in 1906. They differed from the Nord Atlantics by having larger boilers and cylinders; No.3001 made technical news in 1903 by touching 1,890hp on its trials. The conversion tradition nearly changed them into 4-6-0s in 1925 but the plan was dropped when electrification was adopted instead, a move which also started the cull of the 2-4-2 conversions.

The *Nord* de Glehn-du Bousquet Atlantics were the classic French 4-4-2s. Tests carried out by the Nord's engineer of traction, M. Barbier concluded that the limits of the 4-4-0 had been reached and that enhanced performance could only come from the enlargement of the boiler and steam passages. The next step was two Atlantics (SACM, 1900), 16% more powerful than their 4-4-0 predecessors and the basis for a series production of a further thirty-three Atlantics 1902-1904; eighteen by SACM, ten by Cail, five by Fives-Lille. These locomotives differed slightly from the prototypes, with longer bogies and boiler tubes, and brought the Nord near to its 'big three' goal: 300 km in three hours on a 300-tonne train.

The Nord Atlantics were adopted by the *Midi* and the *Est*; the Midi had thirty (SACM 1902-1907) and the Est tried two by way of an evaluation (SACM, 1902). However, Est engineers concluded that their 4-6-0 design gave better adhesion and was superior; apart, therefore, from ten ex-Prussian de Glehn 4-4-2s acquired as war reparations, the Est had no more interest in Atlantics. The Est experiment was a significant and early rejection of the Atlantic, comparable with those of the Atlantic Coast Line or Britain's GWR.

During the locomotive shortage at the turn of the century, the *Etat* purchased ten 2-cylinder simple Atlantics from the USA (Baldwin, 1900). In 1905 it purchased ten P-O type Atlantics from Cail and after the Great War it received ten ex-Baden 4-cylinder compound 4-4-2s (Maffei, 1902). The *Paris-Lyon-Méditerranée* also purchased ten Baldwin Atlantics in 1900-1901, their 7ft driving wheels were the largest to run on the PLM. The home-grown PLM Atlantics, designed by Charles Baudry for parts of the Paris-Marseilles main line, were a 4-4-2 version of the line's successful 2601 class of 4-6-0. Nine were rebuilt in the late 1930s, seven by the PLM, two by the SNCF and some were given futuristic streamlining. French railways thus acquired Atlantics from many sources: converted 2-4-2s; enlarged 4-4-0s; modified 4-6-0s; war reparations and American imports. Although the 'de Glehn' 4-4-2 was an all-time classic, it was far from being the whole story of the notable French Atlantic tradition.

Germany

Some of the component states of the former German Empire had their own railway systems, and therefore their own Atlantic policies and designs. But a few states, Mecklenburg, Württemburg and Oldenburg chose not to run Atlantics. The earliest German Atlantics appeared on the *Palatinate* railways. They were the world's first coal-burning wide-firebox Atlantics, conceived by W Staby in 1897 and built the following year (class P3[1]). They had inside cylinders and a complex form of framing to support a large, low-slung boiler. The class of thirteen locomotives (1897-1904) was well able to meet its specification of hauling 220-ton trains on the level at 56mph.

The later Palatinate Atlantics (class P4, eleven locomotives) were more conventionally 'South German' in style, products of Maffei with combined plate and bar frames, based on the *Baden* Atlantics (class IId[1], 1902, twelve locomotives). These represented a leap forward

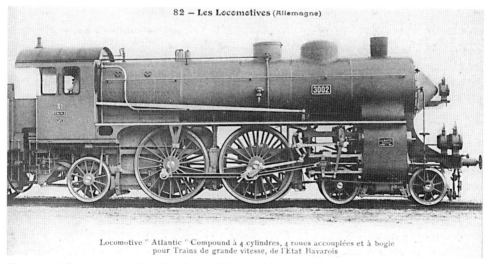

82 — Les Locomotives (Allemagne)

Locomotive " Atlantic " Compound à 4 cylindres, 4 roues accouplées et à bogie pour Trains de grande vitesse, de l'Etat Bavarois

Bavarian Atlantic: *a variation of the South German 4-4-2, Royal Bavarian State Railways No.3002 class S2/5 (Maffei, 1903), a 4-cylinder compound with bar frames, rear axle not set so far back as the Palatinate or Baden versions.* Photo: F. Fleury.

The South German model: *one of the excellent Baden class IId², No.739 (Maffei, 1902) with clean lines jarred by an outsize flower-pot chimney; well set-back trailing axle allowing a generous firebox, grate area 41.4sq ft (3.87m²).* Photo: Szaklap.

in the Atlantic concept with the characteristic German feature of having a trailing axle set well back to permit a generous firebox, grate and well-aired ashpan. Also, they were 4-cylinder compounds on the Maffei principle (low pressure cylinders outboard), all cylinders drove the front driving axle. At the time of their production they were the heaviest and most powerful Atlantics anywhere: 75.7 tons and able to produce 1,850 hp in the cylinders.

In *Bavaria* the locomotive shortage and a desire to investigate recent American trends first-hand produced a brace of Baldwin 4-cylinder Vauclain compound Atlantics, class S2/5. They were followed by more conventional Maffei compounds, ten constructed 1903-1904, also classified S2/5. The state railways of *Saxony* ran two classes of Atlantic, fifteen of the compound class XV (1900-1903), and eighteen of the superheated class XH1(1909-1913) all of them built locally by Hartmann of Chemnitz.

The *Prussian* 4-4-2s tends to exemplify the 'German Atlantic' largely because so many of them were built. They were classified S7 and S9 and covered a range of forms. Both classes had light axle loadings (13 tons and 16 tons respectively) and a consequent proneness to slippage unless given kid-glove treatment on starting. The earlier S7 class of 238 locomotives came in four types, the largest of which was a batch of 159 built by Hanomag, 1902-1906. These were 4-cylinder von Borries compounds. The remaining seventy-nine locomotives of class S7 were 4-cylinder compounds on the de Glehn system, built by EMG at Grafenstaden, and by Henschel. The last set of S7s, fifty-seven locomotives built 1905-1907 had enlarged, wide fireboxes, their grate areas being 32.2sq.ft (3.01m³) compared with the 28.7sq.ft (2.67-2.72m³) of the earlier class members, in an attempt to improve their steaming capacity.

The best-known Prussian 4-4-2s were the ninety-nine members of the heavier Atlantic class S9 (Hanomag, 1908-1911), one of the great missed opportunities of the Atlantic era. After the statutory gentle start they could work up to a steady 62.5mph (100 km/h) on 500-ton trains across the North German Plain. But like the S7s they used saturated steam, in spite of Germany being the homeland of Dr Schmidt, inventor of the improved superheater which was rapidly colonising the locomotive world at the time. The reason for this failure to turn a good locomotive into an excellent one seems to have been the decision of the controversial Robert Garbe, head of procurement on the Prussian State Railways.[2] Because the under-performing Atlantics became unpopular with their operators they were released as war reparations, and soon; the residue was scrapped in the first of the great Atlantic 'liquidations'.

Scandinavia

Sweden had two sets of Atlantics. Both deserved success, if intellectual boldness and good workmanship were sufficient conditions for that state. The Swedish State Railways (SJ) class A Atlantics of 1906 were remarkable machines, representing an imaginative synthesis of American, British and German ideas with some novel Swedish notions. Expensive imported coal caused them to be the first Atlantics to receive effective superheaters, and generous-sized ones they were, with 353sq.ft heating surface against 1,432sq.ft of the boiler. Their striking

Furthest North: *The original class A of the SJ in Sweden, No.1000 (Nydqvist & Holm, 1906) reposes on a roundhouse turntable set amidst Northern conifers; an advanced, eclectic design combining British, American, German and Swedish concepts, also a pioneer in large-scale, effective superheating. Striking, fast and powerful, if slippery - later sold to the East Coast Railway and converted to a 4-6-0.* Photo: collection of Ian G.T. Duncan.

appearance resulted from a combination of American-type bar frames, British inside-cylinder drive, and an outside frame bogie. Further noteworthy features included an inside Walschaerts valve gear, a windcutter V-front cab, steam and sand domes merged into a single turret in the manner of the Pennsylvania class E2 – and the famous planished steel boiler cladding.

All was set fair, but the bad fairy of folk-legend must have been present at the naming for the good qualities of these intelligently-conceived Atlantics could be vitiated by bouts of 'Atlanticitis'; the 6ft 2in driving wheels were prone to slip. Although this class A of twenty-six locomotives, built variously by Nydquist & Holm, and Motala 1907-1909 often gave remarkable service, they may not have lived up to live up to their theoretical promise. Five were sold to the *Ostkustbanan* in 1926-1927 and converted into good-looking 4-6-0s; the SJ converted three more. The remaining eighteen were withdrawn in 1937, but one was preserved for posterity at the SJ Museum, Gävle.

The two Atlantics of the *Malmö-Ystad* Railway were also imaginatively conceived but their performance was dire. Strongly based on German designs, these two von Borries 4-cylinder compounds were delivered by Hanomag in 1907-1908. Seven years later they went for scrap. Their experienced designer, Dan Olsson added various refinements to an underlying Prussian S7 format, notably a Lentz valve gear and Pielock superheater. But the twins steamed badly; their boilers may have been too long and fireboxes too small. Their grate area, for example was 22.4sq.ft (2.10m^2) compared to the improved Hanomag S7, 32.2sq.ft (3.01m^2). So long as Olsson was in office he kept them going but they were disposed of (to Motala) after his death in 1910, in part-exchange for two 2-6-2 tank engines.

Flying Dane: *one of the legendary class P Atlantics of the DSB in Denmark, heading an express in July, 1949.* Photo: Ian G.T. Duncan.

A short distance away over the Kattegat in *Denmark* ran one of the Atlantic family's greatest success stories, the Danish State Railways (DSB) class P 4-4-2s (nineteen from Hanomag, 1907-1909; fourteen from Berliner (Schwartzkopff), 1910). The two sub-sets were virtually identical: 4-cylinder balanced compounds with divided drive. The Schwartzkopff batch, designated P2 had slightly larger cylinders and higher boiler pressure. They were the last Atlantics to run in Europe; many ran into the late 1950s and No.909 lasted until 1963.

Why the longevity? First, they were well-designed, by O.F.A. Busse and two talented assistants, Dorph and Olsen. Busse resisted superheating but Dorph installed it, when his old chief retired in 1910. Secondly, these well-built and maintained engines benefited from the Danish railway speed limit of 100km/h (62.5mph). Most tasks they were called upon were well within their capabilities; in locomotive engineering as in life, it is better to be over-engined. These tasks were mainly expresses from Copenhagen to Korsør; Nyborg-Ålborg and Fredricia-Esbjerg, ideal Atlantic territory with an unemphatic terrain and steady traffic between a few major centres of population. Their long life ensured that they were among the few Atlantics to be replaced by diesel-electric trains; seven of them were converted to 4-6-2s, and two were preserved.

The Low Countries

The *Netherlands* and *Belgium*, like Denmark, provided good Atlantic territory, generally low-lying terrain, fairly densely settled. The record here, however, was mixed. The Netherlands State Railways were quick off the mark in the 'springtime of the Atlantics'; their chief designer S.E. Haagsma worked with Beyer, Peacock in Manchester to produce five large, inside-cylinder Atlantics in 1900, later classified PO[2]. These outside framed Atlantics had big driving wheels, 7ft (2,134mm) in diameter, inside Stephenson valve gear and Belpaire fireboxes. They were intended for the Flushing boat and mail trains but their riding proved unacceptably rough at high speeds. They punished the track and were soon relegated to slower work, even to freight trains. Superheaters were added in 1911 enabling them to work out useful lives, but not in true Atlantic style. The unsteadiness of the Dutch 4-4-2s has given rise to various theories: that they were essentially 'stretched' 4-4-0s and ought to have been conceived afresh; that the track was 'spongy' and prone to amplify unsteadiness; that their weight distribution was uneven.

The Belgian Atlantics were few but successful and in their last phase, spectacular. The first set for the Belgian State Railways were a dozen de Glehn-type compounds designated class 6 (Cockerill, 1905-1908) which worked on saturated steam for all their lives, about forty-five years, mainly on the Brussels-Antwerp expresses. They were not continued; the State Railways opted instead for 4-6-0s and 4-6-2s. But Belgium produced the last flourish of the Atlantics with six streamlined super-Atlantics of 1939, the unusual inside-cylinder flyers, whose careers were distorted and curtailed by the outbreak of war. They were a fitting *finis* to the Atlantic saga, stylish and fast and from the Belgian stable which, although no great user of Atlantics, had a long record of innovatory locomotive engineering.

Gölsdorf compound: *Austrian* Südbahn *Atlantic No.221, virtually identical to the Austrian State Railways class 108 model, both designed by Karl Gölsdorf. Seen here hooraying past Vienna-Atzgersdorf on a Semmering express. To rear of boiler top two* Südbahn *acoustic specialities, the courteous* Schalldämpferkragen *(safety-valve 'noise muffler column') and the* Schallteller, *an inverted saucer-shaped disc to deflect whistle sounds around the engine and not waste energy alarming birds, balloonists, etc.*

Austria-Hungary

Although the railway systems of Austria and Hungary were separate, their locomotive design policies had some similarities. The Austrian and Hungarian Atlantics for example had light axle-loadings, drive to the front axle, and a penchant for 4-cylinder compounding. The first and longest-lived Atlantics in Austria were the outside-framed world pioneers of the *Kaiser Ferdinands Nordbahn* (KFNB) designed by W. Rayl, mainly for the Vienna (Nord) – Cracow express trains. There were eventually fifty-seven of these class IId locomotives, built by Wiener Neustadt in two batches 1895-1908. Their fireboxes were situated partly between the rear coupled wheels, 4-4-0 style, and partly over the trailing axle in 'true' Atlantic form. This, and their front axle drive, gave a slightly foreshortened appearance to their broadside wheel profiles. They joined the stock of the Austrian State Railways (kkStB) in 1908 when the KFNB was taken over. Two lasted long enough to become part of the German DR after the *Anschluss* of 1938.

The eight *Austrian North-Western* (ÖNWB) Atlantics of 1901 were also extended 4-4-0s with most of the firebox between the coupled wheels. Four were completed with normal chimneys for the Vienna-Znaim (Znojmo) route, but the other four which worked towards Tetschen (Decín) burned soft, brown coal and were equipped with large spark-arresters. These 4-cylinder compounds had soon to be downgraded to lighter tasks as trains increased in weight. They joined the Austrian state railways stock in 1909; all eventually went to the Czechoslovak state railways.

The best-known Austrian Atlantics were Karl Gölsdorf's class 108, twenty-five elegant 4-cylinder compounds for the state railways, constructed 1901-1910 by Floridsdorf, Wiener Neustadt and First-Bohemian.[3] There was some British influence at work in the design of these engines; Gölsdorf had just returned from a working vacation in the UK much impressed by the clean lines of British locomotives which he adapted for Austria. Also British metallurgists had developed the special grades of steel from which tough and reliable crank axles could be made. The 108 class worked mainly on the Vienna-Gmünd-Prague and Vienna-Cracow expresses. A near-identical batch of eleven Atlantics was constructed for the Austrian Southern Railway, the *Südbahn*, 1903-1908. After 1918 many of the Austrian Atlantics went to other jurisdictions, most to Poland and Czechoslovakia; some of the 108s ended up rushing the nightly newspaper trains out of Prague. One lasted until 1948.

The state railways of Hungary, (MÁV) experimented with two Atlantics early in the twentieth century, a 2-cylinder compound later converted to a superheated simple, and a straightforward 2-cylinder simple (classes Il and Im of 1900-1901). Most Hungarian Atlantics were class In, later class 203; twenty-four locomotives which were constructed in its own workshops 1906-1908. These striking engines had Vanderbilt tenders, *spitzer* smokebox doors and the unmistakable combination of formal elegance and 'in your face' functionalism which characterised Magyar locomotives. Their work was mainly on Budapest-Vienna trains, as far as the frontier at Marchegg. They ran on saturated steam although one was rebuilt in 1943 as a superheated 2-cylinder simple, the fastest of them all.

Poland

Before 1918 a large portion of partitioned *Poland* lay in the Russian Empire. Unlike the main 5ft gauge Russian railways with their distinctive locomotive school, the Warsaw-Vienna railway, the most 'Western' of the empire's railways, was of standard gauge. It ran eighteen Atlantics built in two batches by Wiener Neustadt (eleven in 1898; seven in 1900). Their design followed closely that of the Atlantics of the KFNB whose main line was joined by the WVR main line from Warsaw and Czestochowa at the frontier near Granica. The reborn state of Poland inherited these locomotives which lasted until the 1930s.[4]

Cape to Cairo

In *Egypt* the State Railways (ESR) Atlantics came in three phases. The first started with some evaluation projects masterminded by F.H. Trevithick, Locomotive Superintendent. One of these was a Brooks convertible 4-4-2, transformable into a 4-6-0 with slightly smaller driving wheels, a conversion experiment which antedated the better-known work of Churchward and Robinson in the UK. Trevithick was cautious on the subject of Atlantics, although a set of ten de Glehn 4-4-2s was purchased by the 'International Commission of the Egyptian Public Debt' from Cail in 1905. In spite of the favourable terrain for Atlantics, Trevithick preferred the pulling-power of 4-6-0s.

Under his successor, R.G. Peckitt the third Atlantic phase established the ESR as a major Atlantic operator. Peckitt's brood came in three clutches, 1913-1926, distinct but very similar.

Equatorial Atlantic: *a neat 3ft 6in gauge Sudan Government Railways 4-4-2 (Robert Stephenson, 1910) of class 110, Well designed (to the requirements of SGR's C.G. Hodgson) and maintained. Photographed by Cyril Williams, Locomotive Running Superintendent, Atbara and later GM; his expertise included descaling Atlantic boilers with oils from local Eucalyptus trees.* Photo: courtesy Mr & Mrs D. Carswell.

The first five came from Berliner (Schwartzkopff) in 1913, class 735. After the war Baldwin delivered another twenty (later, class 740; 1920-1921) and in 1925-1926 the remaining fifty-five came from three other builders, originally designated class 760, later and better known as class 26. The use of many manufacturers reflected the International Commission's policy of 'shopping around', inherited by the ESR. A small number of the class 26 were named after pharaohs, khedives and other rulers; they ran a wide range of trains on most trunk routes, Cairo-Alexandria, to Port Said and El Qantara, and to Upper Egypt and Luxor.

The Egyptian Atlantics, rather like the Danish ones benefited from easy gradients, and speed limits well within their capabilities. Late in the day two of them were converted to 4-6-0s and given higher boiler pressures. The experiment was not a great success, resulting in cracked frames and undue stresses on the over-long rear coupling rods.[5]

The *Sudan* Railways had four 3ft 6in gauge Atlantics based at Atbara. To the district locomotive superintendent in the 1920s, Cyril Williams[6] they were 'my joy...beautiful locomotives capable of high performance with a light load in an emergency' but 'they were eventually scrapped in a period of austerity', ousted by Prairies, Pacifics and Mikados.

The *Mozambique* (CFM) Atlantics, four locomotives by Henschel, 1923 were to become the world's last working Atlantics, ceasing operations in 1978. Although many locomotives in Southern Africa were built with mixed traffic in mind, the CFM Atlantics (3ft 6in gauge) spent most of their lives on the light passenger work for which they were designed. They were well able to shift 250-ton trains at 45mph even in old age. The *Cape Government Railways* Atlantics in South Africa (also 3ft 6in gauge) were amongst the world's first 4-4-2s (six locomotives, Baldwin 1897), CGR 4th class. They were popular locomotives, great steam-generators, free-running and relatively cheap to maintain. Their bar-frame design so impressed the CGR Chief Locomotive Superintendent, H.M. Beatty that they were embodied in new designs for the CGR thereafter.

India

There were slightly under 120 Atlantics in India, originally disposed thus: *Great Indian Peninsula,* forty; *Bengal-Nagpur,* fifteen; *North-Western,* nine; *Eastern Bengal,* seven; and *East Indian,* forty-six. All were built 1907-1910 according to a standard specification. They were moved from railway to railway by imperial fiat. The largest such migration was of the forty GIPR Atlantics to the NWR in 1932-1935, after the electrification of the GIPR main line from Bombay to Poona displaced about a dozen steam locomotives classes. A more modest transference was of four new de Glehn Atlantics ordered for the EBR but sent instead to the NWR in 1910.

The GIPR Atlantics were adopted by its Locomotive Superintendent, Mr Sarjant for their ability to burn low-grade coal, and the location of main lines along river-valleys with gentle gradients. The Bengal-Nagpur de Glehn version was similarly used on the flat coast route from Calcutta along the shores of the Bay of Bengal. The Indian Atlantics were an untypical minority but because of the prestigious duties upon which they were often used, they were well-known. East Pakistan (Bangladesh) received four; Pakistan eighteen after the 1948 partition.

The Orient

In China the *Shanghai-Nanking* Railway main line was well suited to locomotives of limited adhesion; its administrators had already invested in some fast, free-running 4-2-2 locomotives in 1910, very late in the day to adopt a 'single'. The SNR ordered four super-heated Atlantics from NBL in 1914, its class-E, massive machines with 7ft driving wheels. The state-owned *Taokow-Chinghua* Railway purchased a solitary Atlantic in 1912, a neat machine from Kerr, Stuart designed by the TCR Locomotive Superintendent, Donald Fraser. It used saturated steam, but this was produced in generous quantities by a boiler which included a disproportionately large grate of 35sq.ft.

Five Atlantics ran on the 3ft 6in gauge *Manila Railway* in the Philippines (NBL, 1909), neat locomotives with continuous splashers and outside Walschaerts valve gear. They had the longest and slimmest of the narrow-gauge Atlantic fireboxes (grate area 16.3sq.ft). Their generous tender cabs and elaborate rear suspension linkage suggest that they were designed with a considerable amount of reverse running in mind. In 1897 the *Nippon Tetsudo* in Japan bought the twenty-four original Baldwin narrow-gauge Atlantics (class 6600) to contend with low-grade coal from the Joban field, hence the attraction of the large Atlantic firebox. But even the well-draughted grate area of 30sq.ft may not have been sufficient to extract full combustion from this fuel; four were rebuilt with combustion chambers at the Ohmiya works, 1901-1905, the earliest application of this development in Japan. The NT was nationalised in 1907; its Atlantics seem not to have been as popular as their South African cousins although they lasted slightly longer; scrapping started in 1925.

Australia

The few Atlantics which ran in *Australia* were unlike the rest, the marsupials of the 4-4-2 family. The 2ft gauge Atlantic built by Borsig in 1907 for the *Stannary Hills Mining & Tramway Co* (later on the *Irvinebank Tramway*) ran in rugged country near Mareeba, Queensland. The choice of an Atlantic might seem odd for such a line, but given its light axle loading, good steaming capacity and ability to hold the curves on difficult track it was logical. Weighing 14 tonnes and with 6 x 12in cylinders this was the smallest Atlantic in the world, outside the sphere of miniature railways and it outlasted the tramway, helping to dismantle it in the early 1940s. This tough survivor was purchased the Cattle Creek Mill, Finch Hatton, and hauled sugar cane for twenty years. It was converted to a 4-4-2T yet remained a pukka Atlantic with firebox to the rear of the driving wheels . Kind fate protected it long enough for it to be acquired by the Australian Narrow Gauge Railway Museum Society in whose care it remains, a unique Atlantic from the golden age.

The *Western Australian Government Railways* (3ft 6in gauge) converted some of its R class 4-4-0s (Dübs, 1897-1899) into Atlantics from 1909, designating them Ra. These were originally express engines now surplus to requirements, but with too great an axleload for secondary, branch-line working, some of it on 45lbs rails. By adding a trailing wheel, and easing out the axleload, fourteen of the R class received a new lease of life as mixed traffic 4-4-2 locomotives. After the last R class were scrapped, the Ra Atlantics reverted to the R classification. In the 1930s the remaining eight worked on a range of duties between Perth and Northam, or banking between Midland and Chidlow, an unusual task for a 4-4-2. The last of them was withdrawn in 1953, reconverted to a 4-4-0 and preserved. In 2000 it adorned the Centrepoint shopping centre, Great Eastern Highway, Midland.[7]

World's smallest: *the Borsig Atlantic (1907) built for the Stannary Hills Mines & Tramway, Queensland, Australia, later used by Irvinebank Tramway. The smallest 4-4-2 for normal commercial use, fortunately still extant and named* Robbie Burns. Photo: David Mewes, via Ken McHugh.

The southernmost Atlantics might not be considered Atlantics at all by hard-line purists, but the Garratt class M 'double Atlantics' in Tasmania were members of the clan even if unorthodox ones. They were undoubtedly 4-4-2s and they had large fireboxes behind the driving wheels. The *Tasmanian Government Railways* (3ft 6in gauge) purchased two Garratts from Beyer, Peacock in 1912 for working passenger traffic on the main line from Hobart to Launceston. They had 5ft driving wheels and were in the small elite of 4-4-2s with 4-cylinder simple drive, eight cylinders for each locomotive array. Their speed was remarkable and for a period they held the world record for articulated loco-motives, 53mph. The last of the pair was eventually scrapped in 1953.

In the first flush of their youth, however, they were one of the mechanical wonders of the world. The *Launceston Examiner*, 30 November 1912, reported a test run on one of the new Garratts, attended by W.R. Deeble, the TGR mechanical engineer and Mr York, a superheater expert from 'Dr Schmidt's Company.' A local critic of railway expenditure, Mr Norman Cameron, MP for Wilmot, did the decent thing and volunteered for fireman's duty, thereby at a stroke joining the elite of Atlantic firemen and becoming unusually useful for a politician. After a hard spell at the shovel, well coated in coal dust he was asked by the *Examiner's* reporter what he thought of the double Atlantic. 'Magnificent' responded the erstwhile critic, 'simply magnificent.' Another Atlantic triumph.

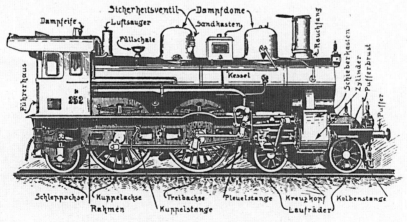

European pioneer: *KFNB Austrian Atlantic of Rayl's design (1894) used to 'name the parts' from Alexander Niklitchek,* Das Buch von der Eisenbahn, *1923.*

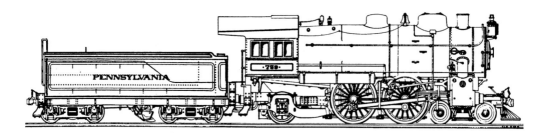

Pennsylvania E6s, 1914.

Notes to Chapter 16

1. One, 319c lived long enough to bear the modernised numbering 221.319 in the PO-Midi scheme, eventually being scrapped in 1937, Dr John Davies, *Chemins de Fer du Midi and Chemins de Fer de Paris à Orleans, Locomotive List 1840-1938.*

2. A good engineer, but going through a difficult phase. Garbe was responsible in large part for the Prussian P8 class 4-6-0, a world locomotive classic of which some 3,850 were eventually built.

3. First-Bohemian: *První Ceskomoravská* (Czech); *Erste Böhmische-Mährische Maschienenfabrik* (German); the 108s were First-Bohemian's initial foray into the construction of large locomotives. See Paul Catchpole, *The Steam Locomotives of Czechoslovakia*, 1995, and A.E. Durrant, *The Steam Locomotives of Eastern Europe*, 1966 and 1972.

4. See A.D. de Pater and F.M. Page, *Russian Locomotives*, Vol I, 1987 and reference to: Dost, *Die Warschau-Wiener Eisenbahn*; also B Schmeiser, *Lokomotivlisten Wiener Neustadt*, 1992.

5. O.S. Nock (*Railways at the Zenith of Steam 1920-1940*, 1970) states that the conversion of a number of Atlantics was 'a great success.' But this is not borne out by Hugh Hughes (*Middle East Railways*, 1981) nor by an note in the *Railway Magazine* (October 1936), nor by the collective wisdom of some 'old Egypt hands' privately communicated; one such conversion may have been re-converted to an Atlantic.

6. C.R. Williams, CBE later General Manager of the SGR; see his *Wheels & Paddles in the Sudan, 1923-1946*, 1986.

7. Leon Oberg, *Locomotives of Australia*, 1975. One of the R class in 4-4-0 days took part in a famous and exciting race against time to rush rescue equipment in order to save a trapped miner at Bonnievale, Coolgardie, 1907; fortunately with success, see Patsy Adam Smith, *Romance of Australia's Railways*, 1974.

Chapter 17
The Atlantic in History

The Past is a Foreign Country

Does the history of the Atlantic really matter in any case? Of course it does: any item which can illuminate the development and logic of technology should be welcomed by a world which faces great challenges from that quarter, but is culturally poorly-equipped to objectify and analyse them. The setting, ups, downs, successes, failures and unintended consequences within the Atlantic saga are grist to the historical mills.

Historical analysis rests on three bearing points: artefacts, memory and secondary-sources.[1] The *artefacts* include – designs, drawings, photographs, records of the stop-watchers like Rous-Marten and Cecil J. Allen, the proceedings of professional bodies, papers and correspondence in the *Railway Gazette*, *La Vie du Rail* and so on, as well as preserved Atlantics. *Memory*, although valuable, has but a brief life; even though many people still remembered the long Atlantic twilight, by the early twenty-first century virtually all players and observers of the 'classic' Atlantic era have passed away. Interpreting these memories and artefacts results in *secondary-source* history, a ceaselessly renegotiated chronicle of which this work is a part. The history of the Atlantics has been well-served in these three respects.

There are about twenty-two preserved Atlantics around the world and they include the British pioneer, GNR No.990, *Henry Oakley*, the Stannary Hills locomotive, a Nord de Glehn-du Bousquet 4-4-2, a Swedish class A, a Pennsylvania E6s, and even an E2 of 1902; two class P Atlantics of the Danish State Railways and the last of the Indian BESA standard Atlantics. Because the Atlantic purges came early, and historical consciousness in this field came late, people can no longer gaze upon other classics: a Prussian S9, a Gölsdorf compound Atlantic or one of the Milwaukee Road *Hiawathas*.

Fortunately, enough Atlantics remain to demonstrate their size, scale and elegant proportions. These survivors bear out Henry Ford's intention to 'show the past as it really was' when he started to collect the gadgetry which has shaped human history quite as much as the kings and queens, about whose history he made a notorious and invariably decontextualised pronouncement.[2] There is an addition to these riches bequeathed by the past. In the UK, a volunteer group has set about constructing a full-scale Brighton Atlantic around a miraculous survivor, the boiler of an Ivatt large Atlantic, thereby re-learning the long-lost art of constructing Atlantics, last put into practice in Belgium, 1939.

There is copious archival material relating to Atlantics. Official drawings, minutes, reports and records exist in their thousands, and photographs in their tens of thousands ranging from official builders' photographs (pin-sharp if lacking in animation), commercial postcards and private snaps. Some Atlantic photographers were famous pioneers of the craft: H. Gordon Tidey, F. Moore, F.E. Mackay, H.C. Casserley and O. Winston Link.

Memory: This book has drawn on many people's memories. Hence its story is coloured by 'old hands' of the Egyptian, Sudanese, and Indian railways, as well as former spotters who spied Ivatt Atlantics climbing out of London, or performing evolutions about York; engineers who took note of the sights and sounds of Nord 4-4-2s or who recalled Camelbacks hauling excursion trains. Your author's credentials are more modest, but include tenderless Ivatt Atlantics, cold and awaiting scrap; a filthy Brighton Atlantic moving smartly in reverse prior to hitching-up with a South Coast stopping train, a BESA 4-4-2 slumbering in a siding near Saharanpur; and, most vivid of all, an Egyptian Atlantic shimmering along beside the Suez Canal, immaculate as its rake of cream-white carriages. The only sounds it emitted were a slight swishing and the soft clatter of its motion. The dynamics of its Walschaerts valve gear were mesmeric to one who had largely known only inside-motion engines. The pyramids, the Nile irrigation schemes and the great canal had been seen in short measure, but the impeccable Atlantic was as fine a piece of technology as any.

The Historiography of the Atlantic

The long 'history of Atlantic history' is instructive. At first, Atlantics were written about by and for people who lived with them, as professional engineers and operators, or the interested laity. Their work came in many forms ranging from reports of engineers' meetings where, for example, F.H. Trevithick, or A.W. Gibbs presented papers or commented upon those of others, to popular presentations such as Frederick Talbot's description of the Atlantic City flyers in *Railway Wonders of the World*. Atlantic 'history' only emerged as the Atlantic dynasty had passed, leaving records, traces, memories – but not actual 4-4-2s in steam, going about their daily tasks.

Historical commentary on the 'Atlantic project' emerged in the 1950s and was well under way twenty or so years later when the last Atlantics had gone. Since they had been a major part of the past railway scene, and an important transitional locomotive form, they frequently received mention in the growing body of railway history. Thus Eric Mason's *The Lancashire & Yorkshire Railway in the Twentieth Century* (1954) had an entire chapter devoted to 'Aspinall's '1400' class 4-4-2 Tender Engines.' O.S. Nock's *British Locomotives of the Twentieth Century, Vol 1 1900-1930* (1983) had a chapter entitled 'The Atlantics'. The Railway Correspondence and Travel Society's chronicle of all locomotives owned by the LNER contained a detailed and scholarly volume on its Atlantics alone: part 3A of *Locomotives of the LNER*.

There were also books devoted entirely to Atlantics; in the UK, for example, Martin Evans' *The Atlantic Era* (1961) and Cecil J. Allen's *British Atlantic Locomotives* (1976). Individual classes were recorded in: Ken Hoole's *The North-Eastern Atlantics* (1965); O.S. Nock's *Great Northern 4-4-2 'Atlantics'* (1984); in Sweden, Ulf Diehl's *SJ ånglok litt A*, (1971), which described the standard Swedish 4-4-2s; and in the USA, Frederick Westing's definitive *Apex of the Atlantics* (1963), the saga of the Pennsylvania E6s class, put in its American context. Some classes have been better served than others. The GNR Atlantics in Britain were also the subject of a learned monograph by Ron Scott: *G.N. Large Atlantics*, No.30 in the 'Loco Profile' series (1972). In late 2000 they were put in further retrospect by two articles in the *Railway Magazine* by Keith Farr, 'Atlantic Swells'; there were many others, some duly noted in this text. In the USA, locomotive histories of particular railroads have often devoted a chapter or article to Atlantics: 'The Atlantics 4-4-2 class A' in John Tigges' *Milwaukee Road Steam Power* (1994), or 'Rock Island Steam Power – Atlantics and Pacifics' by Richard P. Campbell in *Rock Island Digest* (1983).

The *Hiawathas* have received more historical treatment than most other Atlantics. Another 'Loco Profile', No.26 by Brian Reed was entitled *The Hiawathas*, and in the USA two books have been devoted to the class; Jim Scribbins' *The Hiawatha Story*, and Charles H. Bilty, *The Story of the Hiawatha*. Bilty played a large part in designing these locomotives; like Cecil J. Allen or O.S. Nock, he had first-hand knowledge of Atlantics and was a 'transitional historian' who has one foot in the world of the Atlantics, another in the post-Atlantic world.

The most complete chronicle of the Atlantic dynasty appeared in 1982, with Wilhelm Reuter and Claus Bock's *Eleganz auf Schienen*, suitably subtitled *Die Enzyklopädie der Atlantic*. It was a sumptuously produced work on art paper bearing hundreds of photographs, numerous tables and analyses – a criterion of excellence for locomotive historians, although being in German, not always accessible to the English-speaking world in which most Atlantics once ran.

With this wealth of sources we can now enjoy a more objective picture of the coming and going of the Atlantic than was possible in its own day. Whether this picture is congruent with the truth, or even rings true, depends in large part on the standpoint of the audience or reader.

Santa Fe: *Four-cylinder compound Atlantic No. 1443 of the 1400 class built by Baldwin, 1905-1907 with 6ft 7in drivers; spidery, but elegant.* Photo: Howard W. Ameling.

Atlantic Perspectives

Atlantic history, like other branches of railway history, has shared some important assumptions. In the main it has been a chronicle of gradual improvement, each stage (including the Atlantic itself) giving way to something better.

However, there are other perspectives on history than that seen from the post-Enlightenment liberal standpoint. In the post-modern era what might a 'green' or ecological historian have to say about an Atlantic, burning two tons of irreplaceable coal each hour, spewing unburnt carbon, char and residue about the environment? And what of the fuel and raw material that went into its making? A feminist historian might question how come the Atlantics were designed, built, operated by (and largely recalled by) men. Marxists might tell us that Atlantics were 'capital', and that the people who designed, built and operated them did not generally share commensurately in the wealth their efforts had created. Other historians might perceive Atlantics as tools of imperialist penetration; and yet others might emphasise moral progress, or a lack of it, as the defining feature of the human record: where do Atlantics fit into that? In history's house there are many mansions, and Atlantics appear differently in each of them.

Was the Atlantic a success, or a failure? How wise were those Russians who framed the proverb: *success is due to a temporary misunderstanding.* Histories, like the rise and fall of the Atlantic, put the point in sharp focus. The Atlantic contained the seeds of its own destruction, a quality most obviously seen in its early success which generated traffic that it could not then handle. It represented a major step forward in locomotive technology, but then it literally let its chances slip because of its generally poor adhesion. So there is the quality of tragedy in the Atlantic story; all the more obvious because it was compressed into so short a period.

The Atlantic story is poignant in another way; it was the admired product of a time and a society which have slipped inexorably away. It may not have been an epoch of such ordered content as our selective memories suggest, but it was the last era before the deluge of war, violence and commotion which clouded the remainder of the twentieth century. The Atlantic enjoys the magic of association with a particular period, to Gustav Reder it was the essential example of 'the *Belle Epoque* of locomotive construction.'[3]

There is also a third way in which the Atlantics affect our sentiments; their wheel-slippage, rolling gait, and furious progress were indications of a mettlesome temperament, of a challenge thrown down to mere mortals by strong forces that threaten to run out of control. Handling a thoroughbred at full stretch presents the kind of challenge that many people like to face by way of proving their worth. The designers, drivers and firemen of these touchy machines played with Promethean fire and were consequently no mean people in our eyes

Into the twilight

We begin our *envoi* with the assistance of J.P. Pearson on his seventy-sixth and last journey, July–November, 1913 (*Railways and Scenery*, Vol III, 1932).

Pearson and his companions were traversing Canada and the Northern USA, 27 September, 1913. A few days before they had been resting in the Canadian Pacific Hotel, Vancouver, admiring a 'superb boudoir' and the 'blue writing room' and hearing musical selections from

The Arcadians. Now Pearson was returning eastward on the Great Northern taking careful note of its 2-8-8-2 'beyond Troy' and the 'picturesque display of brown rock, pines, birches and light green water' near milepost 1362; vintage Pearson.

At Havre, Montana his train was handed over to an Atlantic, No.1700. He did not note the details but we can soon run its basic data to earth: class K-1, Baldwin 1906, driving wheels suitably sized at 6ft for tough work out West. His train consisted of four twelve-wheeled cars, three eight-wheeled and a further twelve-wheeler, a sleeping car ex-Butte and Helena added at Havre.

The Atlantic soldiered on with this load, pausing to meet the westbound *Oriental Limited*, half an hour behind schedule 'but, of course, after the fashion of American trains, [it] might easily recover this.' Evening set in as they put Havre behind them and Pearson gave full rein to his observational powers. As the GN Atlantic pounded away ahead they traversed the valley of the Milk River:

> *a most glorious evening... a fine pink flush rose in the sky...just before we came to Chinook ... the whole of the western sky soon became suffused most richly, first with pink and then changing with salmon... I do not think I have ever seen so deep a red-orange tint as that of this evening.*

Moving along briskly behind a well-found Atlantic, past the ink-black pines etched against an icing-pink sky, about year before the Great War ended the old order for good or ill, is as suitable a time and place as any to start taking leave of the Atlantics.

Finis

There were about 3,500 Atlantics and most lasted thirty or fewer years; in academic argot 'the Atlantic project had a short trajectory.' At one level, therefore, the Atlantic story is straightforward. The 4-4-2 was a rational, technological development which gave way to superior designs drawing on the Atlantic's own strengths whilst trying to avoid its flaws. It was used at first chiefly in the USA, then in Northern and Eastern Europe on fast passenger trains, but later on secondary duties. The gains and losses from the era of routine high-speed travel ushered in by the early Atlantics present a complex, problematic picture with which we have barely grappled; we have no 'felicific calculus' whereby to equate or measure them.

The history of technology is much enriched by stories like those of the Atlantic which throw beams of light on fundamental questions like the sources and broadcasting of invention, the mechanics of technical evolution, the social effects of mechanical ingenuity.

The Atlantics were ultimately an enigma, many things to many people. To their chief chronicler, Wilhelm Reuter, they were essentially 'elegance on rails.' The scientist and industrialist Peter Allen thought the Atlantic 'the best-looking type ever conceived.'[4] Marjorie Bulleid, *née* Ivatt remembered the 'ghost-like' No.990. Norman McKillop who knew the North British Atlantics first-hand remarked: 'you didn't drive or fire the Atlantics, you fought them.' And once, when Cecil J. Allen went to the front of an Atlantic-hauled train to congratulate the crew on their remarkable performance, the driver whacked the cab side affectionately and grinned: 'grand engines, these.' Taking these observations together we have the alpha and omega of the Atlantic story: technical virtuosity, temperament, and indefinable style, rare qualities in combination. Hence, the well-beloved engine.

In the Borders: *NBR Atlantic in LNER days No.9905* Buccleuch *(Robert Stephenson, 1911) now of class C11 at Carlisle Citadel on an Edinburgh train, via the Waverley route, 1931.*

Notes to Chapter 17

1. The three-point theory was a contention of David Lowenthal, *The Past is a Foreign Country*, 1985; the phrase comes originally from L.P. Hartley, 'The past is a foreign country, they do things differently there.' (*The Go-Between*).

2. Most people recall 'History is bunk' – but Ford was provoked into saying this when riled by a lawyer who poked fun at his lack of orthodox historical knowledge. His words about recounting the past 'as it really was' echo precisely those of a founder of modern historiography, Leopold von Ranke.

3. Gustav Reder, *The World of Steam Locomotives*, 1974.

4. Peter Allen, *On the Old Lines*, 1957.

Bibliography

I Atlantic-Specific Works

C.J. Allen: *British Atlantic Locomotives,* 1968.

Charles H. Bilty, *The Story of the Hiawatha.*

D.L. Bradley, *The Locomotives of the London, Brighton & South Coast Railway, Part 3,* RCTS, 1979.

Ulf Diehl, *S J ånglok litt A*, 1971.

Martin Evans, *Atlantic Era, The British Atlantic Locomotive,*1961.

M. Harris (ed) *GNR Ivatt Atlantics*, Locomotives Illustrated No.14.

M. Harris (ed), *The Larger Brighton Locomotives*, Locomotives Illustrated No.37.

K. Hoole, *The North-Eastern Atlantics*, 1965.

C. Leigh (ed) *Reid NBR Atlantics and 4-4-2Ts*, Locomotives Illustrated No.62, 1988.

O.S. Nock, *Great Northern 4-4-2 'Atlantics'*, 1984.

RCTS *The Locomotives of the Great Western Railway Part 8, Modern Passenger Classes*, 1953.

RCTS, *Locomotives of the LNER, Part 3A, Tender Engines – Classes C1 to C11*, 1979.

Brian Reed, *The Hiawathas*, Locomotive Profile No.26.

W. Reuter and Claus Bock, *Eleganz auf Schienen, Die Enzyklopädie der Atlantic*, 1982.

Jim Scribbins, *The Hiawatha Story.*

Ron Scott, *GN Large Atlantics*, Locomotive Profile No.30, 1972.

John Thomas, *The North British Atlantics*, 1972.

Frederick Westing, *Apex of the Atlantics*, 1963.

Yeadon's Register of LNER Locomotives, Vol 13, Classes C1, C2, C3 and C5 Atlantics.

II Amongst other sources consulted

E.L. Ahrons, *The British Steam Locomotive* 1825–1925, 1925.

P. Atkins, *Dropping the Fire*, 1999.

W. Bay, *Locomotives of Danish State Railways.*

Seth Bramson, *Speedway to Sunshine: The Story of the Florida East Coast Railway*, 1984.

K. Brenner, *Verzeichnis der deutschen Lokomotiven, 1923-1965*, 1970.

Alfred W. Bruce, *The Steam Locomotive in America*, 1952.

Paul Catchpole, *The Steam Locomotives of Czechoslovakia*, 1995.

André Chapelon, *La Locomotive à Vapeur*, 1938, 1952, and English translation by George Carpenter, 2000.

George H. Drury (comp) *Guide to North American Steam Locomotives* 1993 and 1999.

C. Hamilton Ellis, *Model Railways 1838–1939.*

K. Gölsdorf, *Lokomotivbau in Alt-Österreich*, 1978.

Alfred Horn, *Die Kaiser-Ferdinands-Nordbahn*, 1971.

Alfred Horn, *Die Österreichische Nordwestbahn*, 1967.

Hugh Hughes, *Indian Locomotives Part 1, Broad Gauge 1851-1940*, 1990.

J. Jahn, *Die Dampflokomotive in entwicklungsgeschichtliche Darstellung ihres Gesamtaufbaues*, 1924.

RCTS, *The Standard Gauge Locomotives of the Egyptian State Railways and Palestine Railways 1942-45*, 1946.

Gustav Reder, *The World of Steam Locomotives*.

J.T. van Riemsdijk, *Compound Locomotives*, 1994.

M. Rutherford *Great Western 4-6-0s At Work*, 1982, 1985.

E. Sauvage, *Les Locomotives au Debut du XXe Siècle*.

E. Sauvage and André Chapelon, *La Machine Locomotive*, 1947.

Lloyd Stagner, *Rock Island Motive Power, 1933-1955*, 1980.

J. Tigges, *Milwaukee Road Steam Power*, 1994.

J. Westwood, *Locomotive Designers in the Age of Steam*, 1977.

Cyril R. Williams, *Wheels & Paddles in the Sudan, 1923-1946*, 1986.

III Also consulted

John Davies, *Locomotive* Lists for French railways, viz.: Alsace-Lorraine, 1999; Est; Etat, 1997; Midi & P-O, 1992 and later; Nord, 1997; PLM, 1996.

Relevant numbers, of which there are many, of *Back Track*; *Bulletin* of the Railway & Locomotive Historical Society*, The Engineer, Engineering, Glasers Annalen*; *The Locomotive*; *Locomotive, Carriage & Wagon Review*; *La Vie du Rail*; *Locomotive Cyclopaedia*; *Locomotive Dictionary*; *Railway Engineer, Railway Gazette* (UK and USA); *Railway Magazine*; *Trains*; *Journal* of the Stephenson Locomotive Society; *Journal* and *Proceedings* of the Insitution of Locomotive Engineers; and of the Institution of Mechanical Engineers.

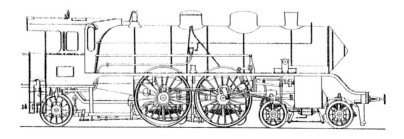

Palatinate Railways Atlantic, c.1904.

Appendix 1
World-Class Atlantics, Leading data

State	Railway	Class	Date	Cylinders inches	Driving wheels	Grate area sq.ft	boiler pressure lbs sq.in
USA	ACL	I	1894	24x19	6ft-0in	26.1	180
Austria	KFNB	IId	1894	23x18.5	6ft 5in	31	185
Japan	NT	6600}					
South Africa	CGR	4th}	1897	22x16	4ft 8in	31	165
USA	C&NW	D	1900	26x20	6ft 9in	46.3	200
Austria	kkStB	108	1901	26.7+13.7x23	7ft 0.25in	37.7	213
France	Nord	2640	1902	25.1+15.3x22	6ft 10in	29.5	228
France	Paris-Orleans	3000	1903	25.1+14.1x23.6	6ft 6.5in	33.17	228
Germany	Palatinate	P4	1905	25+14.1x23	6ft 7in	40.6	213
UK	GNR	C1	1902	20x24	6ft 7.5in	31	150/170
USA	PRR	E3d	1906	26x22	6ft 8in	55.5	205
Sweden	SJ	A	1906	23x19.6	6ft 2in	27.8	171
Hungary	MÁV	In/203	1906	26+14.7X26	6ft 10.5in	30.1	185
India	Various[1]	BESA	1907	26x19.5	6ft 6in	32	180
Denmark	DSB	P	1907	23.5+14.25x22.5	6ft 6in	34.2	213
Germany	Prussia	S9	1908	23+15x22.8	6ft 6in	42.8	200
UK	NER	Z1	1911	26x16.5 [3]	6ft 10in	27	175
USA	PRR	E6s	1914	26x23.5	6ft 8in	55.13	205
Egypt	ESR	26	1920	27.9x20	6ft 6in	31	165
USA	CMStP&P	A	1935	28x19	7ft 0in	69	300
Belgium	SNCB/NMBS	12	1939	28.3x18.8	6ft 10.75in	39.8	256

Notes

* *Date* when series production started

1. *BESA* 'notional standards' – production models differed in details.

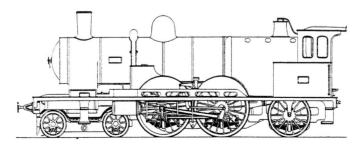

Paris-Orleans *version of de Glehn compound Atlantic.*

Appendix 2
British Atlantics
Some Comparative Data

Railway	Class	Year	Cylinders inches	Driving wheels ft in	grate area sq.ft	boiler press lb sq.in	tractive effort lbs
GNR	C2	1899	20x24	6ft 7.5in	26.8	160	15,400
GNR	C1	1902	20x24	6ft 7.5in	31	150	15,400
						170	17,450
GWR	2-cyl	1905	18x30	6ft 8.5in	27	225	23,090
GWR	4-cyl	1906	14.25x26	6ft 8.5in	27	225	25,090
GCR	8B (C4)	1903	21x26	6ft 9in	26.3	200	21,660
GCR	8D, 8E (C5)	1905	19+21x26 3	6ft 9in	26.3	200	13,231
L&YR	1400 (2P)	1899	19x26	7ft 3in	26.05	180	16,505
LB&SCR	H1	1905	18.5x26	6ft 7.5in	31	200	20,060
NBR	H (C10)	1906	21x28	6ft 9in	28.5	180	23,325
NER	V (C7)	1903	20x28	6ft 10in	27	175	20,317
NER	Z1 (C9)	1911	16.5x26 3	6ft 10in	27	175	19,260
NER	4CC (C8)	1906	14.25+22x26	7ft 1.25in	29	200	19,387

Notes

Tractive effort: at 85% boiler pressure

Year: in which first of class were delivered.

Classification: GNR: the more familiar LNER classification is used; the 2P classification given to the L&Y machines by the LMS in later years was a power classification, not that of a separate class.

GWR: for de Glehn-du Bousquet type see Appendix I; dimensions very similar.

Lancashire & Yorkshire class 1400 Atlantic, 1899.

Appendix 3
The Evolution of the American Atlantic: Some Comparative Data

Railroad	Class	Date	Grate area sq.ft	Weight on drivers tons	Tractive effort lbs
ACL	I	1894	26.1	32.5	18,400
P&R	P–1	1896	76	34.8	14,400
C&NW	D	1900	46.3	36.5	22,000
CCC&StL	I–61/3	1902	51.36	44.6	23,510
UP	A–2	1903	49.5	46.8	27,500
B&O	A–3	1910	55.19	51.7	27,409
PRR	E6s	1914	55.3	60.7	31,275
CMStP&P	A	1935	69	64.4	30,700

Home-made: *Erie No.531 of class E-1; originally a Baldwin Vauclain compound of 1901, Jersey City, March 1917 after extensive rebuilding at the Erie's Susquehanna shops as a 2-cylinder simple with slide valves, air reservoir slewed longitudinally along top of massive Wootten firebox (grate area: 63.6 sq ft). Short on elegance, but brimful with character.* Photo: Harold K. Vollrath.

Appendix 4

The Atlantic in the USA: American Railroads which ran Atlantics

Ann Arbor
Atlantic Coast Line
Atlantic City
Atchison, Topeka & Santa Fe
Baltimore & Ohio
Boston & Albany
Boston & Maine
Buffalo & Susquehanna
Buffalo, Rochester & Pittsburgh
Burlington, Cedar Rapids & Northern
Canada Southern
Central RR of New Jersey
Chesapeake & Ohio
Chicago & Alton
Chicago & Eastern Illinois
Concord & Montreal
Chicago & North Western
Chicago, Burlington & Quincy
Chicago, Indianapolis & Louisville (Monon)
Chicago, Minneapolis & Omaha
Chicago, Minneapolis & Sault Ste Marie (Soo)
Chicago, Milwaukee & Puget Sound
Chicago, Milwaukee & St Paul
Chicago, Milwaukee, St Paul & Pacific
Chicago, Rock Island & Pacific
Cleveland, Cincinnati, Chicago & St Louis
  (Big Four)
Erie
Evansville & Terre Haut
Fernwood, Columbia & Gulf
Florida East Coast
Georgia
Great Northern
Gulf & Ship Island
Gulf, Mobile & Northern
Idaho & Washington Northern
Illinois Central
Interstate
Lake Shore & Michigan Southern
Lehigh Valley
Long Island

Maine Central
Michigan Central
Missouri, Kansas &Texas
Missouri Pacific
Monongahela
Newburgh, Dutchess & Connecticut
New York, Chicago & St Louis
New York Central & Hudson River
New York, New Haven & Hartford
New York, Philadelphia & Norfolk
Norfolk & Western
Northern Pacific
Oregon Short Line
Oregon, Washington RR & Navigation
Pennsylvania
Pennsylvania-Reading Seashore Line
Pere Marquette
Philadelphia & Reading
Pittsburgh & Lake Erie
Pittsburgh & Shawmut
St Lawrence & Adirondack
St Louis Southwestern
St Paul & Duluth
San Pedro, Los Angeles & Salt Lake
Soo
Southern
Spokane, Portland & Seattle
Sullivan County
Terre Haute & Indianapolis (Vandalia)
Texas & New Orleans
Texas & Pacific
Toledo, Canada Southern & Detroit
Toledo, St Louis & Western
Union Pacific
Vermont Valley
Wabash
Wabash-Pittsburgh Terminal
Wisconsin Central
Washington & Plymouth
Wheeling & Lake Erie

The names listed here were placed on Atlantics. There may appear to be some double-counting of railroads because some lines were different facets of single corporate entities; for example the components of the CMStP&P, the 'Milwaukee Road' have been listed separately on the grounds that the three identities in question (CM&PS, CM&StP; CMStP&P) were marked on separate locomotives.

Evolution in Minnesota: (above) *St Paul & Duluth No.81, a true Baldwin 'early Atlantic' of 1899 designed for the wooden 4-coach consists of the* Lake Superior Limited *(Gladstone, Michigan, 1900).* (Below) *one of the three Northern Pacific class N-1 replacements for the heavier trains of same service (Baldwin, 1909) in its later, superheated form standing at St Paul, Minn 1935.* Photos: Harold K. Vollrath.

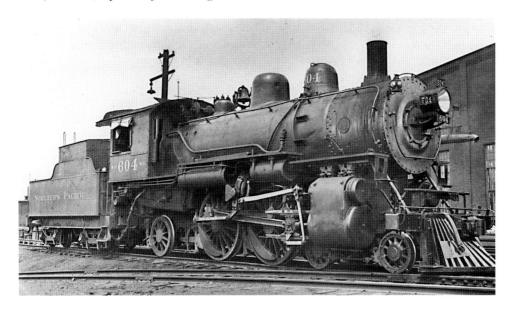

Appendix 5
Atlantic Nicknames

AT&SF: *Bull Moose* (class 1480 only)

DSB *Great Ps*; *Big Ps*

GCR: *Jersey Lilies* [1]

GNR (small Atlantics) *Klondykes* [2]

GWR: *Frenchmen* (but only of de Glehn compounds)

L&YR: *Highflyers*; *Highfliers* (sometimes as two words); *Zulu Chiefs*

NBR: *Whippets*, sometimes *Mankillers* (but this was used of other classes heavy on coal consumption)

NER: *Gateshead Infants* (mainly class V)

PRR: *French Aristocrat* (but only of the solitary de Glehn import), pronounced as American, with accent on second syllable. *Big E* (of class E6s).

General: In the USA Baldwin Atlantics with extended wagon-top fireboxes were 'Wrinklebellies' on more than one road, a term possibly extended to other classes; used especially on the SP, and T&NO.

1. Widely believed to refer to the 'Jersey Lily', Lily Langtry, a famed beauty who was reputedly the mistress of Edward VII, well-proportioned like a GCR Atlantic. But alternative folklore has suggested that the name was also derived from an ironic title accorded to a female pub-singer and tavern *habituée* of Gorton, the area of Manchester where the GCR Atlantics were built. Most people would have been ignorant of the latter, and would have appreciated the logic of the former.

2. *Sic*, the correct spelling of the place is Klondike, a transliteration in any case. Railwaymen always spelt it 'Klondyke', a useful distinction. O.S. Nock thought the railway usage erroneous, but socially-constructed versions like this are subtle; not, therefore, as straightforward a matter as it appears.

An interesting metaphor: to Reuter and Bock the Milwaukee Road Hiawathas were the 'Queens' (*Königinnen*) of the Atlantics, their streamlining was the dress or apparel of a Queen (*Kleid der Königin*); similarly to Hal Hughes, the 4-4-2 he fired on the Northern Railway in India was 'The Queen of Locomotives.' A title of respect and affection of this kind, spanning continents, raises interesting questions.

The Gateshead Infant: *LNER class C6 (NER vlass V) No.532 (Gateshead, 1903); the earlier 2-cylinder simple NER 4-2-2 with heavy splashers; the first of the 'Gateshead Infants', looking slightly battered here; superheated 1915, used in bridge stress tests, 1920s; withdrawn 1943.* Photo: Colling Turner.

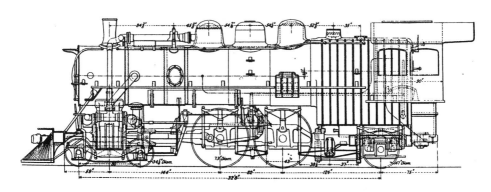

Santa Fe 'Bull Moose' Atlantic, Baldwin 1910.

Glossary

Some initials, acronyms and colloquialisms used in text

Alco	American Locomotive Company
ANGRMS	Australian Narrow Gauge Museum Society
AT&SF	Atchison, Topeka & Santa Fe
BESA	British Engineering Standards Association
Big Four	CCC&StL; Cleveland, Cincinnati, Chicago & St Louis
Brighton Line	LB&SCR, London, Brighton & South Coast Railway
C de F	Chemin(s) de Fer
CSD	Cekoslovenské Státní Dráhy, Czechoslovak State Railways
EMG	Elsässische Maschinenbau-Gesellschaft
Hanomag	Hannoverische Maschinenbau
KFNB	Kaiser Ferdinands-Nordbahn
kkStB	kaiserlich-königlich österreichische Staatsbahnen, Austrian State Railways
KPEV	Königlich Preußische Eisenbahn Verwaltung, Prussian State Railways
MÁV	Magyar (Király) államvasutak ,Hungarian (Royal) State Railways
NMBS	Nationale Maatschappij van de Belgische Spoorwegen, Belgian State Railways
ÖNWB	Österreichische Nordwestbahn, Austrian North-Western Railway
Ostkustbanan	East Coast Railway (Sweden)
Pfalzbahn (PfalzB)	Palatinate Railways of the Royal Bavarian State Railways
PKP	Polskie Koleje Pantstwowe, Polish State Railways
'Q'	Chicago, Burlington & Quincy
Rock Island	CRI&P; Chicago, Rock Island & Pacific
SACM	Société Alsacienne de Constructions Mécaniques
SJ	Statens Järnvägar (Sweden)
SNCB	Société Nationale des Chemins de Fer Belges, Belgian State Railways
SS	Staatspoorwegen (Netherlands)

Atlantics as 'Leisure & Tourism': *A new role for retired and preserved East Coast workhorses, GNR No.990 – the original Klondyke – and large Atlantic No.251 on an excursion at Peterborough North, 1953, closely studied by swarms of young males in mid-twentieth century leisure attire.* Photo: A.V. Fincham, Andrew C. Ingram.

Opening of the Ostkustbanan (East Coast Railway), Sweden, 31 October, 1927. Double headed Royal Train at Sandsvall station, with former SJ class A inside-cylinder Atlantics. Photo: Rolf Sten and Stig Nyberg.

Index

General

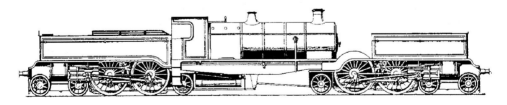

Proposed double Atlantic express engine with Swindonian touches; H. Woodgate-Dearberg, 1916.

Countries and Jurisdictions

Toy Atlantic: *a free interpretation in Gauge 1 of the GWR de Glehn compound* La France *by Märklin, c.1906.*

Eclectic Atlantic: *Bengal-Nagpur No. 399 of class K (NBL, 1907) at Howrah, 1922. A refined machine; 4-cylinder de Glehn compound with Walschaerts valve gear and many accoutrements: headlight, lifting jacks, cowcatcher and chime whistle.* Photo: Kelland Collection, BRC.